Finding Your Way Around: Web Directories

tear here

Sites That Can Help You Find Resources

Inter-Links: http://alpha.acast.nova.edu/help/about.html

Directory of Service Types: http://info.cern.ch/hypertext/DataSources/ByAccess.html

Telnet Browsers List: http://info.cern.ch/hypertext/WWW/FAQ/Bootstrap.html

ArchiePlex: http://web.nexor.co.uk/archie.html

Internet Resources—Meta-Index:
http://www.ncsa.uiuc.edu/SDG/Software/Mosaic/MetaIndex.html

Internet Services List: http://slacvx.slac.stanford.edu:80/misc/internet-services.html

Web Sites That List Directories

The World Wide Web Initiative: http://info.cern.ch/hypertext/WWW/TheProject.html

The Mosaic Communications Internet Directory:
http://home.mcom.com/home/internet-directory.html

ANANSE—Internet Resource Locators: http://ananse.irv.uit.no/law/nav/find.html

List of Robots: http://web.nexor.co.uk/mak/doc/robots/active.html

Commercial and Business Lists

Open Market's Commercial Sites Index: http://www.directory.net/

Interesting Business Sites on the Web: http://www.rpi.edu/~okeefe/business.html

Sell-it On the WWW: http://xmission.com/~wwwads/index.html

The Business Page Yahoo: http://akebono.stanford.edu/yahoo/Business/Corporations/

The Internet Business Directory: http://ibd.ar.com/

CommerceNet: http://www.commerce.net/

MecklerWeb: http://www.mecklerweb.com/

Most Excellent Site of All

Macmillan Computer Publishing: http://www.mcp.com

At the Macmillan Computer Publishing site, you can get free sample chapters from hundreds of computer books, download most of the free or shareware software I talk about in this book, and lots more. Check it out!

Cool Sites to Explore

Yahoo: http://akebono.stanford.edu/yahoo/

The World Wide Web Worm (WWWW):
http://www.cs.colorado.edu/home/mcbryan/WWWW.html

Web Crawler: http://www.biotech.washington.edu/WebCrawler/Home.html

The WebCrawler Top 25: http://www.biotech.washington.edu/WebCrawler/Top25.html

The JumpStation: http://www.stir.ac.uk/jsbin/js

Wandex: http://www.mit.edu:8001/afs/sipb/user/mkgray/ht/compre.bydomain.html

The Spider's Web: http://gagme.wwa.com/~boba/spider.html

Zorba (Formerly Nomad): http://www.rns.com/cgi-bin/nomad

RBSE's URL Database: http://rbse.jsc.nasa.gov/eichmann/urlsearch.html

Best of the Web '94: http://wings.buffalo.edu/contest/

The Web of Wonder: http://www.digimark.net/wow/index.html

ALIWEB: http://web.nexor.co.uk/aliweb/doc/search.html

The Mother-of-all BBS:
http://www.cs.colorado.edu/homes/mcbryan/public_html/bb/summary.html

NCSA's What's New on the Web:
http://www.ncsa.uiuc.edu/SDG/Software/Mosaic/Docs/whats-new.html

NCSA's Starting Points:
http://www.ncsa.uiuc.edu/SDG/Software/Mosaic/StartingPoints/NetworkStartingPoints.html

The WWW Virtual Library: http://info.cern.ch/hypertext/DataSources/bySubject/Overview.html

The CUI W3 Catalog: http://cui_www.unige.ch/w3catalog

Lycos: http://fuzine.mt.cs.cmu.edu/mlm/lycos-home.html

Virtual Libraries: http://info.cern.ch/hypertext/DataSources/bySubject/Virtual_libra

EINet Galaxy: http://galaxy.einet.net/

The Harvest WWW Home Pages Broker:
http://www.town.hall.org/brokers/www-home-pages/query.html

W3 Servers: http://info.cern.ch/hypertext/DataSources/WWW/Geographical.html

W3 Servers—By Area: http://info.cern.ch/hypertext/DataSources/WWW/Servers.html

GNN NetNews: http://nearnet.gnn.com/news/index.html

Multimedia Information Sources: http://cui_www.unige.ch/OSG/MultimediaInfo/index.html

Web Exhibits: http://155.187.10.12/fun/exhibits.html

U.S. Government Web: http://sunsite.unc.edu/govdocs.html

Irena, Australia's Beauty: http://coombs.anu.edu.au/bin/irena.cgi/WWWVL-Aboriginal.html

URouLette: http://kuhttp.cc.ukans.edu/cwis/organizations/kucia/uroulette/uroulette.html

Yahoo's Random Link: http://akebono.stanford.edu/~jerry/bin/myimagemap/hothead/Art?31,9

**alpha
books**

The COMPLETE IDIOT'S GUIDE TO World Wide Web

by Peter Kent

alpha books

A Division of Macmillan Computer Publishing
A Prentice Hall Macmillan Company
201 W. 103rd Street, Indianapolis, IN 46290 USA

Publisher
Marie Butler-Knight

Managing Editor
Elizabeth Keaffaber

Acquisitions Manager
Barry Pruett

Product Development Manager
Faithe Wempen

Production Editor
Kelly Oliver

Manuscript Editor
San Dee Phillips

Book Designer
Barbara Kordesh

Cover Designer
Scott Cook

Illustrator
Judd Winick

Indexer
Greg Eldred

Production Team
*Gary Adair, Angela Calvert, Dan Caparo, Brad Chinn, Kim Cofer,
Dave Eason, Jennifer Eberhardt, Rob Falco, David Garratt, Joe Millay,
Erika Millen, Beth Rago, Bobbi Satterfield, Karen Walsh, Robert Wolf*

*Special thanks to Scott Parker for ensuring
the technical accuracy of this book.*

Contents at a Glance

Contents

26 Webs'ploration 315

Preface

Dear Reader,

Welcome to *The Complete Idiot's Guide to World Wide Web*. At first glance, that title might appear self-explanatory—this is a book about the World Wide Web, that amazing Internet hypertext system. But at the time of writing, that title needed a little more explanation—this is *not* a book about Mosaic.

In many people's minds, the Web and Mosaic are synonymous. We've heard an awful lot about the Web and Mosaic in recent months, and the press seems a little confused about the relationship between these things. Some think that they are both the same; others believe that although the Web is distinct from Mosaic, the only way to use the Web is with Mosaic. Both beliefs are misconceptions. There are dozens of different Web browsers (about 18 that run in Windows alone) and Mosaic is by no means the best.

This book is about the Web itself. We'll look at various browsers—we'll even look at Mosaic in detail. But you'll learn about a lot of other ways to use the Web; you'll learn about other browsers and their strengths and weaknesses. By the time you've finished this book, you may even decide that, like me, you need more than one browser; one for office use, one for home use, one for fast jobs, one for graphics.

You'll learn plenty more, too. You'll learn about some interesting sites on the Web. This book isn't a directory, though. I'll give you a mere *taste* of what's available. I'll also tell you where to go on the Web to search for subjects of interest.

I'll even explain how you can publish your own Web documents, so you can work with your own home page (your Web starting point) or provide information for the world at large. Web publishing is surprisingly easy; you'll find enough information in this book to set up a simple Web site, with multiple documents and inline graphics.

So read on, and enjoy your journey in Webspace!

Peter Kent

Introduction

Just about everyone has heard of the World Wide Web—they may not know what it is, but the media hype is so strong that even old Aunt Edna has heard of it. (She thinks that it's some kind of criminal conspiracy.) If you know that it's part of the Internet, then you know more than most.

Few Internet users know how to use the Web though, and fewer still—some estimates put the amount at around 2% of all Internet users—have Mosaic, the most famous of all Web tools.

The Web is a great tool, and everything's going to change pretty soon. Moves are afoot that will bring really cool Web tools to millions of computer users (without them even realizing it, probably).

Welcome to The Complete Idiot's Guide to World Wide Web

There's a lot of confusion concerning the World Wide Web—all sorts of misconceptions and misunderstandings. (But hey, that's the nature of the Internet.)

I've spoken with many people who would like to know about the Web, who would like to *use* the Web, but who don't really know what it's all about. Some think the Web is the Internet, and the Internet is the Web. Some think the Web is just another name for Mosaic and that Mosaic is a giant hypertext system. Others know the Web and Mosaic are two different things, but think that the only way to use the Web is with Mosaic. Almost none realize that you can use *e-mail* to work on the Web!

Let's cut the confusion and lay it all out in easy-to-understand terms. You don't need to know the intricacies of the HyperText Transfer Protocol. You don't want to take a course in Internet GeekSpeak (though we'll include a little GeekSpeak here and there—just enough so you can understand a geek if you run into one), you just want answers to a few simple questions:

➤ What is the Web?

➤ What can it do for me?

➤ How do I get on the Web?

➤ How do I work on the Web?

I'm going to answer those questions, and I think that once you've learned about the Web, you'll enjoy it so much you'll want answers to a couple of questions you can't even imagine asking right now:

➤ How hard is it to put my *own* information on the Web?

➤ How do I go about doing it?

I'll answer the first question now: it's easy. As for the second question, you'll find the answers later in the book (starting at Chapter 21, to be precise).

It's a Weird, Weird World

The Web is a fantastic place. The difference between working on plain vanilla Internet with a plain vanilla terminal program and working on the Web with a fancy Web browser is like the difference listening to someone playing the spoons and listening to the Rolling Stones. (Oh, by the way, if you're a Stones fan, remember to visit their Web site; you can find the "address" in Chapter 26.) Sure, that tapping sound can be catchy, but it doesn't really *rock* you.

Imagine traveling through cyberspace in color—you have pictures, sounds, video. You can enter museums and see their exhibits and even in some cases, see exhibits that mere mortals walking through the show can't see.

Visit scientists at the South Pole; read a biweekly newsletter about life in the ice. Confess your sins and be given your penance, all online. See how to dissect a frog, check on the Dow Jones, and find out about conspiracies, both real and imagined. You'll find this and more weird and wonderful stuff on the Web (see Chapter 26).

Furthermore, with the right *browser*—a program that can take you on a trip around the Web—you can use all sorts of Internet resources, in many cases more easily than you can use the original tools. You can use Gopher and FTP through the Web. Believe me, using FTP with Mosaic is a lot easier than using plain old command-line FTP. You can even use finger and WAIS. (If Gopher, FTP, finger, and WAIS sound Greek to you, don't worry; you'll learn all about them soon enough.)

The Web's a lot of fun and, well, useful, too. (I don't want to talk too much about *work*, but some people really are being productive online.) We're going to see a lot more business done on the Web. And I don't mean just shopping (though there's plenty of that). How about, for instance, a company putting all its documentation on the Web so a customer can see the very latest information. (At least one large telecommunications company is doing just that.)

You Know Just a Little, Right?

I must admit, I've assumed a few things about your knowledge. I assume you know about your computer, whatever that happens to be, and I assume you have a basic knowledge of the Internet. I've covered it in simple terms in Chapter 1, just in case. But if you want more detailed information, you should read *The Complete Idiot's Guide to the Internet* (though even complete newcomers to the Internet may find that they can work their way through this book without any prior Internet knowledge).

How Do I Use This Book?

I've broken this book down into several Parts.

I'll start, in **Part 1**, with the basics: basics about the Internet, about the Web, and some information on the different ways you can work on the Web.

In **Part 2**, I'll go into detail about several Web *browsers* you can use right away—browsers that are probably already installed on your service provider's system.

In **Part 3**, I'll explain how to set up a TCP/IP connection on both Macs and PCs, and I'll discuss a couple of alternatives, such as SlipKnot and The Internet Adapter, that can give you graphical browsers on a dial-in terminal connection. We'll look at the *viewers* you'll need and the neat programs that will let you listen to sounds and view the graphics and video you'll find on the Web.

In **Part 4**, we'll take a quick look at alternatives—the different browsers and how they stack up. We'll also take a close look at Mosaic, as it's the browser that all others are compared with.

Then in **Part 5** we'll get down to the nitty-gritty: how to run around the Web, how to carry out basic Web procedures, and also how to use other Internet tools through the Web, such as FTP and WAIS.

In **Part 6**, I'll show you how to set up your own Web site and how to publish your own data, whether for fun or profit. It's really quite easy.

Finally, in **Part 7**, I'll give you my own little Web directories. I'll tell you where to go to find Web sites that contain directories of thousands of other sites—some let you actually search, some simply list sites. I'll also give you a Web sampler—some interesting sites you may want to visit. I'll finish off with a short glossary of Web terms so you'll never be confused in Webspace.

I have used a couple of conventions in this book to make it easier to use. For example, when you need to type something, it will appear like this:

`Type this`

Just type what it says. It's as simple as that. If I don't know exactly what you'll have to type—because you have to supply some of the information—I'll put the unknown information in italics. For instance:

`Type this *filename*`

I don't know the filename, so you'll have to supply it.

Also, I've referred to the "Enter" key throughout the book. Your keyboard may have a "Return" key instead.

Sometimes, I'll need to show you longer examples of what you'll see on the Internet. They will appear in a special typeface, arranged to mimic what appears on your screen:

```
Some of the lines will be in actual English.
Some of the lines will seem to be in a mutant dialect of English.
```

Again, don't panic.

If you want to understand more about the subject you are learning, you'll find some background information in boxes. Because this information is in boxes, you can quickly skip over the information if you want to avoid the gory details. Here are the special icons and boxes used in this book that help you learn what you need:

 Skip this background fodder (technical twaddle) unless you're truly interested.

 These notes and tips show the easiest way to perform some task.

 There's help when things go wrong!

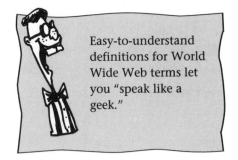 Easy-to-understand definitions for World Wide Web terms let you "speak like a geek."

Acknowledgments

Many thanks to Faithe Wempen and Barry Pruett at Alpha, who listened to my rantings; to Kelly Oliver and San Dee Phillips at Alpha, who cleaned up the book; to the gods of cyberspace for providing *just* enough cybertime to get the book done; and to my family members, who are still moaning that I work too much.

Trademarks

All terms mentioned in this book that are known to be or are suspected of being trademarks or service marks have been appropriately capitalized. Alpha Books cannot attest to the accuracy of this information. Use of a term in this book should not be regarded as affecting the validity of any trademark or service mark.

Part 1
What's It All About?

The Web, Mosaic, the Internet, browsers, HTML, HTTP, URLs, on and on. What is all this stuff? Like anything new, it can seem a little confusing at first, but it's really not that complicated, as you'll discover in this Part of the book.

I'll explain everything right from the start. I'll tell you about the Internet (okay, skip that chapter if you know all about the Internet already). I'll explain the basic concepts about the Web itself. I'll tell you how to figure out the sort of connection you need, and the sort of browser you can work with. And I'll show you the wide range of browsers that are available.

SKIP HAD SOME TROUBLE WITH WORLD WIDE WEB...

## Chapter 1

The Least You Need to Know

There's a lot of confusion about the World Wide Web. What is it? Is it Mosaic? Is Mosaic the Web? How do you use it? Why? For all the talk in the magazines and newspapers about the Web, you'd think that half the country's working on it. Don't worry—they're not. (Though the way the Web is growing, they may be soon!) So if you are unsure about how to get onto the Web, or what to do when you get there, you're not alone.

You've come to the right place. By the time you finish this book, you'll have a broad overview of the Web; you'll know about the different Web *browsers* (not just one); you'll know how to find a subject you are interested in and what to do when you get there. You'll even find out how to get your own information onto the Web; it's really not hard. First, though, let's have a look at a list of important things you should know about the Web.

1. The Web is *not* a computer network. The *Internet* is the actual network, the wires connecting thousands of computers together—computers all around the globe. The Web is a software system running on the Internet. First there are Web *documents*, computer files stored on computers all over the place. Then there are Web *servers*, special programs that know where these files are and can send them across the Internet. And there are Web *browsers*, programs that ask the servers to send the documents. When you use the Internet, you are reading documents displayed in a browser.

2. The way you connect to the Internet determines the type of browser that you can use. There are four types of Internet connections: permanent, dial-in direct, dial-in terminal, and e-mail (see Chapter 4). The first two are the best; with a permanent connection, though, you are at the mercy of the system administrator. With your own dial-in direct connection, you can set up and run whatever browser is available for your operating system.

3. If you don't have a permanent connection and can't get a dial-in direct connection, all is not lost. If you have Windows, you can run SlipKnot, a graphical Web browser (and a very good one, too) for terminal connections (see Chapter 15). Otherwise, you can use The Internet Adapter to "fool" your software into thinking it's running on a dial-in direct connection (see Chapter 11).

4. There are two Web browsers available to just about everyone, no matter what type of connection they have: Lynx and the Line Mode browser. They don't have neat pictures or sounds, but they work and they work fast.

5. If you only have an e-mail connection—from CompuServe, GEnie or America Online, for instance—you can still use the Web (though it won't be a lot of fun!). See Chapter 8.

6. If you read the popular press, you may have come away with the impression that Mosaic is the only browser around, or at least that it's the best. It's neither. There are dozens of different browsers, from the very basic to the "Wow, take a look at that!" variety. There are 18 for Microsoft Windows alone, maybe more by the time you read this. There are browsers for the Amiga, Macintosh, OS/2, DOS, UNIX, X Window, VMS, NeXTStep, VM/CMS... . You can even use the Web through an e-mail connection. I'll list all the different browsers available (Chapter 5), explain many of the differences (Chapters 13 through 16), and tell you where to find them (Chapter 27).

7. If you have Microsoft Windows, you're really in luck; we've bundled a beta version of InternetWorks, an excellent Web browser from BookLink (a division of America Online). This has loads of neat features that most other browsers don't have. It's fast, it lets you place Web documents into your other Windows programs, and it has a great directory of Internet sites. See Chapter 9 for installation instructions.

8. Mosaic is the best-known browser and comes in various "flavors": for Windows, the Macintosh, X Window, and VMS. It's the "father" of graphical browsers (okay, mother, if you wish), and the one that most users have worked with. As it's often regarded as a kind of "benchmark" for other browsers, we'll take a close look at it.

9. Working on the Web is, in most cases, quite easy. The basics come down to a few point-and-click procedures (see Chapter 17). To get the most from your browser, though, you need to know a little more, such as what the *cache* does, and why you need reload to stop it from doing what it does (Chapter 18); how to use history lists and hotlists (Chapter 18); and how to save information you find on the Web (there are actually eight different types of data you can save—see Chapter 19).

10. Your browser doesn't work only with the Web. It also lets you use other Internet tools, such as FTP, WAIS, Gopher, newsgroups, even finger.

11. Creating a home page on your hard disk is a good idea, and it's not too hard. Doing so lets you create links to places *you* want to go, not places that a software publisher thought you might like. You can even create several pages on your hard disk, one for music sites, one for art, one for conspiracy, one for humor... . I'll show you all the neat little "HTML tags" you need to know (see Chapter 21).

12. Creating your own Web page, so the world can be privy to your deepest thoughts and most creative impulses, is quite easy. If you already have an Internet account with a good service provider, you may be able to do so for *free*! If you don't, you can visit a site that will let you use some of their disk space to create your page, and ask nothing in return. (See Chapter 23.)

13. Creating Web documents is not difficult, but it can be tedious—typing all the funky little tags can get boring; each time you make a typo, you screw something up. There's help available, though. There are loads of programs that will help you write Web documents, and more are appearing all the time. Some are free; some will cost a couple hundred bucks. If you plan to get into Web publishing, you need to take a look. (See Chapter 24.)

14. The Web is massive. Without an index it would be very difficult to find what you want. Luckily, there's not just one index; there are dozens. These are Web directories that let you search for a keyword, or simply look through lists of subjects and pick a subject you are interested in (see Chapter 25). Spend some time at a few of these sites, and you'll be amazed at the range of information you can find.

## Chapter 2

The Inter-What?

In This Chapter

➤ What is a BBS, and what is the Internet?

➤ Why is the Internet so complicated?

➤ The common Internet tools, from Archie to WAIS

➤ What is the World Wide Web?

Let's start with a few basics. The World Wide Web is an Internet tool, so before we get into the Web, we'd better make sure you understand a little about the Internet.

If you know little or nothing about the Internet, you'll get an idea of what it's all about by reading this chapter, but also read *The Complete Idiot's Guide to the Internet*. It introduces the Internet to the new user in easy-to-understand terms (it got good reviews, too). In this chapter, we're going to skim over the Internet basics pretty quickly, but if you want more detail, read the book.

Let's Start with the Simple Stuff

Let's start right at the beginning—what is a *bulletin board system* (BBS) and what is a *computer network*? A BBS is a computer running special software that enables other computers to connect to it. (Actually, a BBS could be several computers connected together, but the principle is the same.) A computer user installs a *modem* in his computer, connects the modem to the phone line, uses *communications software* to dial the BBS, and voilá—he's "connected."

 The word modem is a contraction of "**mod**ulate-**dem**odulate." That's what the modem does with the digital signals from your computer when it converts them to and from the analog signals used by most telephone networks.

What can you do once connected to a BBS? Well, you can read messages left by other BBS users, reply to those messages (or leave your own), and copy files to and from the BBS. There may be other services available—perhaps you can play an "online" game with another BBS user (chess, for instance, or some kind of arcade game). You may be able to "chat" with another user, typing what you want to say and reading the other user's almost-instant response. You may be able to search a database, or view photographs or weather maps stored on the other computer.

There are thousands of BBSs spread around the world; all you need to start a BBS is a computer, a phone line, BBS software (which can be found quite cheaply), a modem, and the money to pay the electricity bill. You've probably heard the names of a number of the larger BBSs, such as CompuServe, PRODIGY, GEnie, America Online—even Penthouse Online. These services often don't use the term BBS; they may call themselves *online services*, or *information systems*, but the principle is the same. They are computers (or groups of computers) to which computer users can connect to communicate with others, find computer files, play games, do research, and so on.

But That's Not the Internet!

The Internet is not a BBS. The Internet is a *network* of networks. A computer network is a group of computers that have been connected together so they can communicate with each other. They can send messages to each other and can share information in the form of computer files. The Internet connects tens of thousands of these networks with more being added all the time. On those networks are millions of computers, computer terminals, and users—as many as 30 million users, according to some estimates (though these numbers are a little fuzzy and very hyped). The number is growing by around 1,000 computers *a day*.

There's nothing astounding about computer networks. I have a small one in my home connecting my work computer and my kids' "play" computer (which used to be my work computer until technology raced past). Many small companies have networks connecting two or three computers, or maybe thousands of them.

The Internet is a network of thousands of different networks; it's the world's largest group of connected computers. Some of the networks belong to government bodies, some to universities, some to businesses, some to local-community library systems, and some even belong to schools. Most are in the United States, but many are overseas, from Australia to Zimbabwe.

As remarkable as all this may seem, there's more, much more. What makes the Internet so special is the fact that many of the computers on the network are, in effect, BBSs. A purist would say that they are *not* BBSs, of course—they don't function *exactly* like BBSs, but they *are* like BBSs in the sense that people can get into these systems and *do stuff*. You can log in and run programs, copy files, search databases, and so on.

That means that when you connect to the Internet, you have the opportunity to connect to thousands of different systems. Those computers contain government archives, university databases, local-community computing resources, library catalogs, messages about any subject you can imagine, and millions of computer files containing photographs, documents, sound clips, video, and whatever else you can put into digital form.

To *log on* or *log in* to a computer system means you tell it who you are, and it decides if it wants to let you use its services. A log-on (or login) procedure usually entails providing some kind of account name and a secret password. In many cases, though, you can access information on computers connected to the Internet without even logging on.

The Internet is more like a data highway than a BBS. Dial up a system on the Internet or log on through an institution's terminal, and you're on the road. Then you have to navigate your way through the network to the city that has the data you need. When you dial up a service, such as CompuServe, you are connected to a big room with a lot of computers. When you access the Internet, you may find yourself in a government computer in Washington D.C.; a university's computer in Seattle, Washington; or a community computer system in Elyria, Ohio. You could also find yourself reading the *Gazeta Wyborcza* in Poland.

It's Like the Phone System...

Perhaps the best analogy that one could use to describe the Internet is that it's like a phone system. A phone system has many different "switches," owned by lots of different organizations, all connected together. When someone in Denver tries to call someone in New York, he doesn't need to know how the call gets through—which states and cities the call passes through. The telephone network handles it all for him. These private companies have decided amongst themselves the mechanics—the electronics—of the process, and it doesn't matter one whit to the average caller how it's done. The Internet works in much the same way. Just as there's no single telephone company, there's no single Internet company.

So What's the Catch?

The Internet's resources dwarf those of other online systems, but there's a catch. The Internet is relatively hard to use. Systems such as CompuServe, PRODIGY, and America Online make money each time someone uses their services, so it's a good idea for them to make their services easy to use. If it's too hard, people will log off and won't come back.

"Sorry, It's Not Our Problem"

Unfortunately, you may run into a case of "it's not our problem." While most *service providers* (organizations that can connect you to the Internet) claim to provide great technical support, many of them are small nonprofit organizations that have trouble keeping up with the demand. Because the Internet is such an amorphous creature, these organizations can always claim that your problem lies in another area.

For instance, if you are having trouble getting your Internet connection working, they can always point you in the direction of the manufacturer of your software. The Internet has grown so fast in the last year or two that some service providers are providing lousy service.

Complaints that it's hard to get a connection and that calls and messages for technical support go unanswered are becoming more common.

The Internet was originally intended to be a noncommercial system, so many service providers are nonprofit organizations. They are often understaffed and underfunded and don't have the incentive provided by the "profit motive." In recent years, the Internet has opened up to commercial service providers, and the result seems to be easier-to-use software and better service.

Why, then, is the Internet so difficult to use? Well, it's because of the way the Internet was born, the way it grew, and the way it is currently managed.

Who Owns the Internet?

BBSs are owned by someone. A company or individual buys a computer, puts it in a room somewhere, and then sells the general public time on the computer. (Or, in many cases, a company lets interested parties onto the BBS for free. Many computer companies have BBSs for their customers so they can contact technical support, find the latest program files for their systems, and so on.)

There are literally thousands of such BBSs, from the giants I named earlier down to the small systems owned and run by one person. Take a look at a local computer newspaper and you'll see dozens of BBSs listed, designed for use by everyone from *Star Trek* fans to computer-game nuts to swingers. In each case, though, *someone* owns the BBS, whether it's H & R Block (who owns CompuServe), or Fred down the street (who owns The Wizard's Secret Games BBS).

Nobody Owns the Internet...

The Internet's not like that. Nobody "owns" the Internet. Who owns the nation's, or the world's, telephone network? Nobody. Sure, each component is owned by somebody, but the network as a whole is not owned by anyone—it's a system that hangs together through mutual interest. The world's telephone companies get together and decide the best way the "network" should function. They decide which country gets which country code, how to bill for international calls, who pays for transoceanic cables, and the technical details of how one country's lines connect to another.

11

The Internet is very similar. It all began in the early '70s with various government computer networks, and it has grown since as different organizations realize the advantages of being connected. You can trace the origins back to ARPANET, a Department of Defense computer system that was intended to test methods of making computer networks survive military attack. By dispersing the network over a wide area and using a web of connections between the computers, a system could continue functioning even when portions of it were destroyed by redirecting communications through the surviving portions of the network. (This system works so well that it caused the Department of Defense plenty of frustration when Iraq used it during the Gulf War to keep its "command and control" computer system in operation.)

The NSF (National Science Foundation) gave the Internet a big boost when it realized that it could save money by creating several super-computer centers connected to a network so that researchers all over the place, such as in major universities, could connect to them. In the past decade, the Internet has grown tremendously; all sorts of organizations figured they would get in on the act, each one connecting its own network with its own particular configuration of hardware and software.

What's in It for ME?

Let's get down to the nitty-gritty. Why do people use the Internet? This is a book about the World Wide Web, so our primary focus is going to be there. However, you need to know about many important Internet tools because most of them can be accessed via the World Wide Web. Let's take a quick look.

E-Mail

The single most-used Internet tool is e-mail. It lets you send messages and, in some cases, computer files across the world. As I explained in *The Complete Idiot's Guide to the Internet*, it's possible to get free Internet accounts—providing international communications for nothing! E-mail isn't much good to you if none of your friends, family, or colleagues have e-mail access, but if you hang around with people who *do*, you'll be amazed at how useful it is. I write magazine articles and deliver them by e-mail, allowing me to do rush jobs. I communicate with corporate clients via e-mail, keep in touch with friends via e-mail, and send questions to my editor via e-mail. It really is a fantastic tool.

fred, whois, and Friends

The problem with e-mail is, where do you get the address of the person you want to send mail to? Actually, it's not *that* much of a problem, because you probably already know most of the people you want to e-mail, so they can give you the information.

Still, if you want to track down someone on the Internet, it's not always easy. There is no single Internet directory. Instead, there are tools such as *fred*, *whois*, *Netfind*, *KIS*, and various "White Pages" that you can use to find people. Even with these tools, though, you may still be out of luck.

Newsgroups

There are literally tens of thousands of newsgroups on the Internet. These are discussion groups—people send messages to the group and then wait for others to respond. You can get involved in these groups, posting your own messages and responses, or you can simply *lurk*, or "listen in" to what other people are saying.

You'll find newsgroups on just about any subject, and if you *can't* find what you are looking for you can start your own (I discuss this in *The Complete Idiot's Next Step with the Internet*).

You'll often hear the term Usenet used to describe newsgroups. This refers to the network that they originate in. You'll also hear the term LISTSERV used to refer to mailing lists, though not all mailing lists are LISTSERV lists. LISTSERV is the name of a mailing-list management program.

Mailing Lists

Mailing lists are like newsgroups, except that they use the e-mail system to swap messages. To view mailing-list messages, you have to subscribe to the list. Then, each time a message is sent to the list, a copy goes to you. You can respond by sending a message back to the list's address, and everyone else on the list will receive a copy of your e-mail message. There are thousands of mailing lists on all sorts of weird and wonderful stuff.

The finger?

You'll hear a rather strange term on the Internet now and again. You may see an e-mail message that says, "Finger me," or hear someone say, "I'll finger him," "I've been fingered," or some such oddity.

No, there's nothing crude or rude about this. The UNIX *finger* command lets you get information about someone if you know their e-mail address (and, sometimes, if you know only their last name and hostname). For instance, if you finger me (you simply type **finger pkent@lab-press.com** at the UNIX command line and press **Enter**), you'll see the contents of my *.plan* file—at the time of writing it contains information about the Macmillan Internet site, which was planned but not yet opened by the time my last book was published. (It will be running by the time you read this—see Chapter 27.) The finger command lets me easily distribute information to anyone interested. It's used on the Net to distribute information about earthquakes, weather, football teams, TV programs, and more.

Gopher, Veronica, and Jughead

A *gopher* is, as many of you know, someone who "goes fer" stuff. On the Internet, it's a menu system that makes it easy to navigate around the Internet, "going fer" all sorts of things. (The original Gopher comes from the University of Minnesota, which has as its mascot... a gopher, of course!)

Gopher is an easy system to use, and it has two important tools you'll hear about: Veronica (*Very Easy Rodent-Oriented Net-wide Index to Computerized Archives*) and Jughead (*Jonzy's Universal Gopher Hierarchy Excavation And Display*). These, apart from being characters from the *Archie* comic strip, are systems that let you search *gopherspace* for subjects that interest you. Veronica lets you search throughout the world, while Jughead is limited to a particular Gopher *server* (a single host computer).

FTP

FTP stands for *File Transfer Protocol*, and, if you'll excuse me for stating the obvious, it transfers files. What files? There are literally millions of computer files *publicly* available on the Internet, everything from an ASCII text version of the Gettysburg Address to an audio file of Homer Simpson shouting, "Shut up, boy!" You'll find documents containing information on a myriad of subjects, computer programs for any computer you can name (well, almost, let's not get pedantic), sounds, pictures, and whatever else you care to think of.

There are thousands of *public* FTP sites. That is, anyone can log on—usually by using the username *anonymous* (thus the term, *anonymous FTP*)—and download files.

Archie

Ah, Archie again. This is *not* an acronym. Take the word *archive*, remove the *v*, and what have you got? *Archie*. (Veronica and Jughead came later.)

Archie is a system that lets you search thousands of FTP sites for a file that interests you. For instance, let's say you've heard about a program called Wincode, a Windows program used to "uuencode" and "uudecode" a computer file into ASCII so you can send it in an e-mail message.

You simply search Archie for the word *wincode*. Archie will respond (after awhile; he can be a little slow, but he's been pretty busy recently) with a list of FTP sites containing files that may be the ones you want. Then you can use FTP to download them.

Telnet

Telnet is a system that lets you log onto another computer connected to the Internet and run some kind of program. You may be playing chess or GO, immersing yourself in a role-playing MUD game, or using a Gopher or World Wide Web server, for instance.

In order to telnet, you often need to know the correct login name, though not always. Some telnet sites are set up to let everyone in without making them log in first.

WAIS

WAIS means *Wide Area Information Server* and provides a way to search hundreds of databases. You may be looking for information on biology, archaeology, geography, physics, sociology—whatever you are looking for, there's a good chance you'll find something using WAIS.

The World Wide Web

And here we are, back where we need to be, the World Wide Web (also known as the *Web*, *WWW*, *W3*, and anything else computer geeks can think up). The Web is a giant hypertext system. What's hypertext?

A *geek* is someone who knows more about computers than people—and probably prefers them to people, too. It's often used derogatorily, but many geeks now wear the label proudly; you can visit some on the Web, at the **http://klinzhai.iuma.com/~falcon/geeks/geekhouse.html** Web page. (You'll learn how to use Web "addresses" like this later.)

Have you ever used a Windows Help file or an encyclopedia or book on a CD? Such systems contain documents (topics or chapters or whatever you want to call them) that contain links. The most common form of link is a *text link*. Click on a word and you jump to another document with related information. Links can be other things, though, such as pictures, menu options, or buttons.

The Web is special, of course. When you click on a link in a Web document, you may end up reading a document on the other side of the world or viewing a picture on the other side of the continent. The Web is huge; it is thousands of sites containing tens of thousands of documents and files.

The Web is often called *hypermedia*, and in a sense it is. Web documents contain not only text, but also graphics and sometimes even video. It may contain links to any kind of computer file, too: graphics and video in various formats, sounds, .ZIP archived files, anything. Links may point at other Internet resources, such as FTP and Gopher sites, WAIS servers, Archie, and finger. Almost anything that runs on the Internet can be accessed through the Web, as we'll see in Chapter 20.

That's It for Now

That's all the overview you get. If you need to know more about the Internet itself, I suggest you read *The Complete Idiot's Guide to the Internet*. If you want to know how to distribute information via the Internet and how to install fancy Windows software for the Internet, read *The Complete Idiot's Next Step with the Internet*. If you want to know more about the World Wide Web... read on!

The Least You Need to Know

➤ The Internet is a network of networks.

➤ Some of those networks contain systems that act like BBSs, so the Internet is a pathway to thousands of different sources of information.

➤ Nobody owns the Internet; it's a cooperative venture linking a multitude of companies, government bodies, universities and schools, and community computer networks.

➤ E-mail is the Internet's most popular feature, providing low-cost international communications.

➤ Newsgroups and mailing lists are discussion groups; you have your choice from thousands of different subjects.

➤ Other important tools include Gopher (a menu system), Veronica and Jughead (which search Gopher for you), FTP and Archie (which help you find files online), Telnet (a way to log onto other computers), and WAIS (a database-searching tool).

➤ The World Wide Web is a giant, international hypertext system.

## Chapter 3

Spinning the Web—How It All Fits Together

In This Chapter

➤ What HTML and HTTP do for you

➤ The two meanings of the term *home page*

➤ Using Web servers and Web clients (browsers)

➤ Understanding URLs

➤ Using browser features

Before we get into how to *use* the Web, it's probably a good idea to understand a few basics. What *is* the Web? How does it all fit together?

As you've already read (in Chapter 2), the Web is a hypertext system— documents linked together electronically. The Web lets you "navigate" between documents by clicking on links between those documents and lets you go directly to a document by providing your *browser* (your Web program) with the document's address.

So let's start at the beginning, with the basic building blocks of the Web.

HTML—Web Bricks

The primary building material on the Web is the *HTML* document. HTML means *HyperText Markup Language*. HTML documents are computer files containing ASCII text—just plain old text.

The text contains special codes; the codes are created using the normal ASCII-text characters, but they are codes nonetheless. They are not there for *you* to read, they are there for *browsers*.

A browser is a program that helps you read HTML documents. When your browser opens an HTML document, it looks closely at the codes. They tell the browser what to do with each part of the text— "These few words are a link to another document, this line is a heading, this is the document title," and so on.

When it has read the codes (this happens very quickly, by the way), the browser then displays the text on your computer screen. It strips out the codes; you don't see them, but it formats the text according to what the codes told it to do. (You can tell some browsers how to interpret the codes, too, as we'll see in a moment.)

You really don't need to know what these HTML codes are for the moment—or ever, unless you want to publish your own Web documents. You'll learn more about the codes in Chapter 21, but for now, take a quick look at the following figures. The first is a document displayed in the Netscape browser, after the browser has decided how to format the HTML document. The second is the same document displayed in Netscape's special "source" window, which shows you what the actual HTML document looks like, codes and all.

Where Is All This? The Web Server

So where, physically, are these documents stored? On computer systems throughout the world. How do you get to them? A Web *server* makes them available. This is a program that receives requests from your browser and transmits the Web documents back to you. What term should we use for the actual information stored on the computer? Each individual HTML file is known as a *document* or *page*. You'll also often hear the term *site*, to mean a collection of documents about a particular subject, stored on a particular computer.

Travels with Samantha, shown in Netscape (http://www-swiss.ai.mit.edu/ samantha/travels-with-samantha.html).

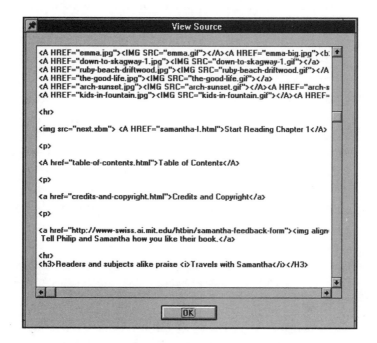

Not quite so pretty. The same document's HTML source file.

Smaller Bricks—Other Media

The Web is based on text, but there's plenty more out there, too. Just about any form of Internet tool or computer file can be linked to the Web. You'll find pictures, sounds, video, FTP sites, Gopher sites, WAIS database searches, finger links, and more. (See Chapters 19 and 20.)

You'll usually find that you start by reading a document, and then you jump from that document to something else. However, these days, *many* documents have *inline graphics*, which are pictures that are embedded into the documents and appear when you open the document. (You can find out how to embed a picture into an ASCII document in Chapter 22.)

Your HTML "Player"—Browsers

If you want to listen to a music CD, you need a CD player. If you want to listen to an LP, you need a record player. If you want to see a video, you need a videocassette player, and if you want to see an HTML file, you need a *browser*.

Browsers can be very simple, letting you view nothing but the text in Web documents, letting you move between documents, but little else. They also can be very sophisticated, letting you save information, play sounds and video, and create bookmarks so you can find your way back.

You Have a Say, Too

Some of the more sophisticated browsers also let *you* decide how to display HTML files. You don't get to view each file's HTML codes and decide what to do with them. Rather, you give the browser a set of rules. "When you see the code for Heading 1, use the 16-point Arial font; use a blue underline for all links; make body text 12-point Times New Roman," and so on. We'll look at how to modify browser "styles" later in this book.

HTML is an offshoot of other "markup languages," such as SGML (Standard Generalized Markup Language). These systems of codes have two benefits. They allow a document to be viewed on any type of computer—it's basic ASCII, after all. They also let the viewer determine how the browser will display each component of the document.

But How Does It Get The Data?

When you want to view a Web document, your browser has to transfer it from its site—in Albania, Albany, or Australia—back to your computer. How's that done?

The Internet has all sorts of *Transfer Protocols*, systems used for transferring different forms of data across the Internet. There's SMTP, the Simple Mail Transfer Protocol, used for sending e-mail. There's NNTP, Network News Transfer Protocol, used for transmitting newsgroup messages all over the place. And there's HTTP, HyperText Transfer Protocol.

HTTP is the system used by the Web to transfer data to and fro. That's really all you need to know, and the only reason I'm telling you is that you'll run across the term HTTP now and again. You don't really need to know how it works.

> Browsers are sometimes also known as Web *clients*. A Web *server* is a system that contains Web documents and lets people in to view those documents. A client is the program that is served by the server—the program that views the Web documents. The term *browser*, however, is more commonly used.

URLs—The Web Address

Everything on the Internet needs some kind of address; otherwise, how would you find anything? The Web's no different. Each resource on the Web has an address, a URL, *Uniform Resource Locator*. Here's one, for instance:

```
http://www.secapl.com/secapl/quoteserver/djia.html
```

The URL starts with **http**. This indicates the site is a normal HTTP (HyperText Transfer Protocol) site; you are going to an HTML document. Sometimes, the URL starts with something different. If it starts with ftp://, for example, it means you are on your way to an FTP site. As you'll see in Chapter 20, Web browsers can access other Internet systems, not just HTTP. (See Chapter 22 for more information about URL formats.)

> URLs are case sensitive. That is, you must type them in the correct case. For example, don't type **HTTP:// WWW.COM/** when it's actually **http://www.com/**.

You may hear or read something like "point your Web browser to...." This simply means use your browser's URL command to go directly to the document.

Next comes the address of the host computer, in this case, **www.secapl.com**. Following that is the address of the file directory containing the resource: **/secapl/quoteserver/**. Finally, you have the resource itself: **djia.html**. In this case, you can tell that it's an HTML document; the **.html** extension makes that clear. (If the document is on a DOS computer or was originally created on a DOS computer, it will be **.HTM** instead.)

Sometimes, the URL won't have a filename at the end. That's not necessarily a mistake. Web sites are set up with a default document, which is what you'll see if you don't specify a document name.

What Can You Do with It?

What are you going to do with a URL? Well, you can get almost anywhere on the Web by following links in documents, but you may spend several weeks trying to get where you want to go! The URL is a shortcut. Virtually every Web browser has some way that you can tell it to go to a particular URL. With Netscape and Mosaic, you can type the URL into a text box near the top of the window and press **Enter**. With Lynx (Chapter 6), you have to type **g *url*** and press **Enter**. If you are using the Line Mode browser (Chapter 7), "Web mail" (Chapter 8), or any other browser, there's a way to go directly to the document you want.

You'll find URLs all over the place, such as in *Newsweek*'s regular Cyberscope column, in various directories of resources on the Net, and throughout this book (in particular Chapters 25 and 26, which will give you all sorts of places to point your browser to).

Tools to Simplify Life

We've covered the basics of the Web, but before we move on, let's consider some of the ways that a browser itself can make life easier for you.

Of course, the browser needs the basics. It has to let you select links by pointing at the link and clicking on it; by moving a text highlight to it and pressing **Enter**; or by typing the number of the link and pressing **Enter**. The exact method varies. It also has to let you jump to a particular URL and move back to the previous document.

There are a few other niceties that some browsers have and some don't. It's nice to be able to save the document you are viewing. Some browsers let you send it to yourself as e-mail, some let you put it in a text file, and some let you copy it to the Windows Clipboard. Some do none of these.

Then how about downloading files? There are many files on the Web that are "pointed to" by links in text documents. A good browser lets you download these files.

There are some other features that can be built into a browser to make things easier. The following sections discuss some of the most important.

The Home Page

Here's an argument I'm not going to win—"What is a *home page*?" It's a greatly misused term, that's what it is! You'll often hear the term used to refer to a particular Web site's main page. "Hey, dude, check out the Rolling Stone's home page," you may hear someone say (it's not a home page, dude, but nonetheless it's at **http://www.stones.com/**). It would be more correct to call it the Rolling Stones *Web site* or *page* or *document.*

Home page is actually a browser term, not a Web site term. It's the page that appears when you first open your Web browser. A company can set up a document for all of its employees. When they start their browsers they see this home page, with all the links they'd normally need. A service provider can set up a home page so that when any subscriber starts a browser, it displays that page. And you can even create your own home page, with links to all the sites you commonly use (see Chapter 21).

The home page is a sort of starting point, and most browsers have a command or button that will take you directly back to the home page, wherever you happen to be on the Web. (If every document on the Web is a home page, what sense does having a Home Page button make? *Which* home page should it take you to?)

Anyway, I've pretty much lost this argument. Many HTML authors are creating what they are calling "home pages," so the term now has, in effect, two meanings.

Where Have I Been?—The History List

Some kind of history list is useful. This is simply a list of all the documents you've viewed in the current session. Ideally, it's a list of the document titles. Unfortunately some browsers simply list the URL, and it's not always easy to figure out what document a particular URL points to.

A history list lets you quickly select a document and return to that document. By the way, the list may not be called the *history list*. The Pipeline's Web browser uses the term *document trail*. The principle is the same, though.

Where Did I Go Yesterday?—Bookmarks

A bookmark system lets you save the URLs and (if it's well designed) the titles of documents you think you'll want to return to. It's easy to get lost on the Web. Spend an hour online, close your browser, and then try to repeat your path through the Web—impossible. Just remember poor old Hansel and Gretel trying to find their way through the woods. And you are traveling across the world!

Bookmarks, though, let you create a list of this useful stuff, and then go directly back to one of the sites. The level of sophistication varies. Some bookmark systems let you add just a few bookmarks to a list; then you can select from the list. Others let you create menus (Mosaic, for instance, provides a menu editor—see Chapter 14) and place bookmarks on the menus, or create folders so you can categorize menus.

Again, some browsers don't use the term *bookmark*. You may hear the term *favorite places*, and you'll often hear the term *hotlist*—it's the same thing.

Add Your Own Stuff

Mosaic and some other browsers let you add notes—*annotations*— to Web documents. Let's say you're at the document; you read a little and then you hear your boss coming down the corridor. Obviously, you should be doing something constructive, so you add a quick note to the document, reminding you which links you want to try next time you're at this Web page, and quickly jump to the home page and pretend that you're working.

Of course, you are not really adding the note to the document itself, though it looks that way. You are really adding it to a text file saved on your hard disk. The next time you return to the document the browser will automatically create a link from the document to the notes in your text file.

Not many browser have this; Mosaic and its "derivations" do, but I don't know of any others.

> Here's a rule of thumb. The simple text-based browsers are just that—very simple. They work, and work well, but they don't have all the fancy features. For that, you'll need to go graphical, and get one of the big freeware or commercial browsers.

All Sorts of Other Stuff

There are many ways that browsers can load up with features. The better browsers let you customize, of course; you can add or remove a toolbar, status bar, URL bar, and so on. They'll usually have a tool for searching documents. You may be able to open a document on your hard disk—so you can create your own HTML documents for particular uses. Some let you view the source HTML; you can see exactly what all the codes look like, which is very handy when you start creating your own HTML files.

There are all sorts of features. InternetWorks has a number of unusual features, such as the capability to use OLE to link Web documents to other Windows documents, for instance. I'll describe Mosaic (for both Windows and the Mac) in Chapters 13 and 14, and in Chapters 15 and 16 I'll cover other freeware and commercial browsers.

It Asked Me Something! Forms Support

The Web is not a one-way street, with your browser taking information from the server (the Web site). Sometimes, you may be able to give back the Web site information.

Usually this is so the Web site can do something for you, generally so it can search for something. You provide it with the text you want to look for and then it runs off and searches. Sometimes, other weird stuff may be going on. For instance, the Confession Booth ("Bringing the net to its knees since 1994"—**http://anther.learning.cs.cmu.edu/priest.html**) asks you for your sins and then tells you your penance. You can type responses, click on option buttons and check boxes, and finally click on a command button to send the information to the "priest."

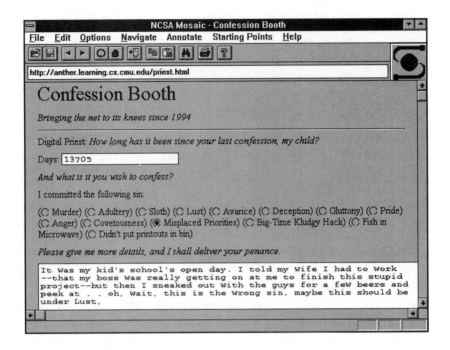

The Confession Booth provides a Web form—and a place to get those guilty feelings off your chest.

This is done using a form; Web browsers that can work with forms have *forms support*, or are *forms enabled*. Some browsers don't have true forms support, but many sites have two documents that do the same thing: one for forms-support browsers and one for those without. However, there's a limit to the type of "form" that can be faked, so there are some sites that simply require a forms-support browser. Without it, you can't do anything. (In this case, you'll have to find a real priest to confess to. You can, however, view the Scroll of Sin, a list of public confessions. A text-based browser is ideal for the Scroll, as it's a *very* large document.)

What Was That Again?

Now listen up. You need to know these terms so I don't have to keep repeating them. So here's a quick summary:

HTML   HyperText Markup Language; the "coding" system used to create a Web text document.

Web server   A program that provides information to a Web browser. The server manages the Web documents.

Web site   I generally use the term *Web site* to mean a group of related Web documents on one computer.

browser   A program that can read HTML documents and lets you navigate through the Web. Sometimes known as a Web *client*.

HTTP   HyperText Transfer Protocol; the system used to transfer Web data between the Web site and your browser.

URL   Uniform Resource Locator; a Web "address" used to tell a browser where to find a document or other resource on the Web.

home page   *Not* a Web site's main page. Rather, it's the first page that appears when the browser starts. (Okay, use the term to mean a Web site's main page if you want, see if I care!)

history list   A list of all the places you've been on the Web in the current session. Lets you jump directly back to a particular document.

bookmark or **hotlist entry**   A URL that has been saved in some kind of system from which you can quickly select it so you can jump back to a useful or interesting site.

forms   Some Web documents have text boxes, option buttons, check boxes, and command buttons, just like a dialog box. You can enter information and send it to the Web site, but many browsers can't use forms.

Before We Go...

One more thing before we go. How big is the Web? Well, to get a good idea, read the Web document at

```
http://www.mit.edu:8001/afs/sipb/user/mkgray/ht/wow-its-big.html
```

(You'll find out how to use this URL later in the book.) The author of this document claims that each day about 10 gigabytes of data crosses the Web; that's the equivalent of 10 million pages of text! And it's growing 1%... per day!

The Least You Need to Know

➤ HTML means *HyperText Markup Language*. It's the system used to create Web pages.

➤ HTTP means *HyperText Transfer Protocol*. It's the system used to transfer Web documents across the Internet.

➤ A URL (*Uniform Resource Locator*) is the "address" to a Web resource.

➤ Web *servers* administer groups of Web documents, or pages, and provide information to user's Web *browsers*.

➤ A *home page* is really the first page you see when you start your browser and the page that you return to when you use the browser's home-page command.

➤ Many HTML authors don't understand the previous item, so they call their documents "home pages."

## Chapter 4

First, the Tricky Bit: Internet Connections

In This Chapter

➤ The different types of Internet connections

➤ Why The Pipeline is a special case

➤ Matching browser types with connection types

To use the Web, you need a Web *browser*. This is a program that reads Web documents. It converts the codes of the HTML document (see Chapters 21-24) into something you can read more easily and provides various tools for navigating around the Web.

Almost every Internet user has a Web browser, though many don't realize it. With all the fuss about Mosaic, you'd think Mosaic was the only game in town. Mosaic's been mentioned in the press so much that many people who've never even been on the Internet have heard of it; many think that Mosaic is an *Internet* browser and have no idea what the Web is.

You've got plenty of choices, though. You can find free browsers and commercial browsers. There are browsers for UNIX, VMS, DOS, Windows, the Macintosh, and more.

How Do You Connect?

How you connect to the Internet will affect the sort of browser you can use. Let's quickly review the different sorts of connections.

Permanent

If you don't have to dial over the telephone lines to get to your Internet account, you have a *permanent connection*. Probably, you are connected through a network at your company, government department, or school. The big computer that your little computer (or computer terminal) is connected to has a connection to the Internet. This is the best type of connection. It's generally very fast, and you may be able to install a wide range of software.

That installation depends on a few more factors, though. If you are working on a "dumb" terminal—a computer *terminal* connected to the big computer, rather than a little *computer* connected to the big computer—you only can run software that will run on the big computer (the *host* computer). So if your terminal is connected to a UNIX mainframe, you won't be able to run Windows Internet software; you can only run UNIX programs.

If you do have a computer connected to a host, though, the situation still depends how the system administrator has set up your connection to the host. For instance, if you have a PC acting as a simple UNIX terminal, you won't be able to run Windows Internet software unless you can convince your system administrator to install the necessary TCP/IP software (which you'll learn more about in Chapter 11).

Dial-in Direct

A *dial-in direct account* provides a true Internet connection across a phone line. You'll hear the terms SLIP, CSLIP, and PPP to describe this type of account. You have to dial over the phone lines to connect to your service provider's computer, but once connected, your computer acts like it's a host computer on the Internet.

Permanent and dial-in direct connections are *TCP/IP* connections: *Transmission Control Protocol/Internet Protocol*. This is a special form of communications used on the Internet. SLIP (*Serial Line Internet Protocol*), CSLIP (*Compressed SLIP*), and PPP (*Point-to-Point Protocol*), are all forms of TCP/IP communication that work over phone lines.

Dial-in Terminal

A *dial-in terminal connection* lets you dial over the phone lines to connect to your service provider's computer. Once connected, your system operates like a terminal of that computer. This is a simple *serial* communications connection, not a TCP/IP connection. That's important, because most Web browsers are designed to use TCP/IP communications.

The Pipeline

I'm mentioning *The Pipeline* because it's a special case. The Pipeline is a service provider in New York (with national access through a data-communications network) that provides its Windows and Macintosh users with special software. The connection is not a TCP/IP connection, but it's not a simple "terminal" connection, either. It's a special system called "Pink SLIP" which acts, in some ways, like TCP/IP; most importantly, it lets the user do several things at once (download a file via FTP while exploring on the Web, for instance).

E-Mail Connection

You have an *e-mail connection* and you want to use the Web! Get real! (Well, maybe there is a way… .) Many systems have e-mail access to the Internet, but nothing more. For instance, a BBS may let you send e-mail across the Internet but not use any other Internet tools, such as telnet, FTP, Gopher, and so on. Some companies sell e-mail accounts that are not intended to do anything but provide you with e-mail service.

So, can you use the Web? Well, not directly. You can't run a Web browser, but there is a way to grab Web documents using e-mail. It's pretty clunky and limited in what it can do (well, what do you expect?), but if you want to know more about it, see Chapter 8.

So, What Connects Where?

Now that we have that out of the way, let's try to match Web browsers to account types.

Permanent

With a dumb terminal connected to a computer with a permanent connection, you can run any software that will run on that computer. Your system administrator may already have installed a Web browser for you. If not, or if you don't like the one provided, you may be able to install your own.

If you have a computer connected across a network that has a permanent connection, you can run any software that will run in the operating system you use on your computer, as long as that operating system has the necessary TCP/IP connection. (We'll talk a little more about this in Chapter 11.) If you are running a PC, for example, you may have DOS, Windows, or OS/2; however, only the operating system that has the necessary TCP/IP connection will work. So if you have a TCP/IP connection set up in DOS but not in Windows, you won't be able to run a Microsoft Windows Web browser. Talk to your system administrator.

Dial-in Direct

With a dial-in direct connection, your computer becomes a host on the Internet. In order to set up a dial-in direct connection, you'll need SLIP, CSLIP, or PPP software. Once connected, though, you can run any program designed for that operating system. If you are using Windows, you'll be able to use a Windows browser; if you are using a Macintosh, you can use a Macintosh browser.

Until recently, this type of account was very expensive—from $100 to $200 for a setup fee, for instance—but now setup fees are coming way down (generally $25 to $45, but some are as low as $10 to $15) and the hourly connect fees generally match those for dial-in terminal accounts. However, dial-in direct accounts are often difficult to set up.

Dial-in Terminal

Here's where it gets interesting. Most people who know a little about the Internet will tell you that with a dial-in terminal account you can only run a Web browser on your service provider's computer. So if you dial into a UNIX host—the most likely case—you will only be able to run a plain vanilla UNIX Web browser, because it has to run on the host computer, not on your computer.

There are *two* ways around this problem. The first is to use SlipKnot, a graphical Windows program that runs across just about any terminal connection. (See Chapter 15 for more information about SlipKnot.)

There's another way, one that lets you run any TCP/IP software on a terminal connection. A $25 product called The Internet Adapter (see Chapter 11 for more information) lets you fool your software into thinking it's running on a TCP/IP connection. So, for instance, if you have Microsoft Windows and you are using a dial-in terminal account, you can still use TCP/IP software (such as the Mosaic and Cello browsers) that is designed for permanent and dial-in direct accounts. You still have to set up the TCP/IP software on your computer though, and that is sometimes tricky; there is some setup work to do on your service provider's computer, too.

The big advantage to TIA, though, is that you don't have to buy a SLIP or PPP account in order to run all the different TCP/IP programs. SLIP and PPP accounts are not expensive these days, but in many cases, they are simply not available; if you have a Free-Net connection, for example, you almost certainly can't get a dial-in direct account. Many colleges don't provide dial-in direct accounts, either. So The Internet Adapter lets you run dial-in direct software when you simply can't get the dial-in direct account.

The Pipeline

The Pipeline has its own Web browser built into its software, and it's provided free to subscribers (see Chapter 16 for more information). If you want to use a different browser, you can still connect to The Pipeline using a dial-in direct or dial-in terminal connection. The Pipeline is very easy to install, and as it's being licensed to other service providers, it's turning up all over North America. (By the way, I'd better declare my conflict of interest. I'm writing The Pipeline user manual!)

E-mail

I *told* you, no browser! See Chapter 8 instead, or go out and buy a *real* Internet connection of some sort.

The Least You Need to Know

➤ With a dumb terminal on a permanent connection, you can run any browsers installed on the computer.

➤ With a computer on a permanent connection, you can run any software that runs on the operating system that you have connected to the network.

➤ With a computer on a dial-in direct account, you can run any browser that runs in the operating system you are using to connect.

➤ With a dial-in terminal account, you can run software on your service provider's system *or* use SlipKnot (a Windows browser), *or* use The Internet Adapter to "fool" your software into thinking it's on a dial-in direct connection.

➤ The Pipeline is a special case: a nonterminal, non-TCP/IP connection. It's a proprietary protocol called Pink SLIP.

Part 2
Basic Browsers

Virtually all Internet users have three Web tools available to them, even if they don't realize it. There's Lynx, a good text-based browser that anyone can download and install if it's not on your system already. There's the Line Mode browser, a very basic browser that runs on any service provider's computer, and there's Webmail, a system that lets you request Web documents via e-mail.

Before you skip this Part of the book for the neato graphical stuff later, wait just one moment! There are good reasons to use a text-based browser such as Lynx or the Line Mode browser. They may not have sound and pictures, but they are very fast. So at least give them a try.

## Chapter 5

Take One Browser...

In This Chapter

➤ Your FREE Windows Web browser!

➤ You want a browser? Believe me, we have browsers!

➤ Browsers for DOS, Windows, and the Macintosh

➤ Browsers for NeXT, Amiga, UNIX, VMS, and more

➤ Text-based browsers

It's time to get on the Web. But where are you going to start? Which browser are you going to use? There are literally dozens available—for all sorts of computer types. In Chapter 27 I'll explain where to find them, but first let's get an overview of your choices. This chapter lists most browsers you'll run into. (Not *all*, because new ones are popping up on the Internet like prairie dogs on my jogging route. It's hard to keep up. By the time you read this, there will probably be a few more.)

What Do You Have... Right Now?

You already may have a Web browser. If you have a dial-in terminal or permanent connection, you'll probably find that your service provider or system administrator has installed one. It's probably Lynx or the Line Mode browser, both of which are *text-based* browsers. They are fast and easy to use, and will give you a good introduction to the Web (we'll look at them in detail in Chapters 6 and 7). Ask your service provider or administrator what you already have.

A *text-based* or *text-mode* browser is one in which you see text and nothing else—no pictures. These tend to be very fast but difficult to use in some Web documents.

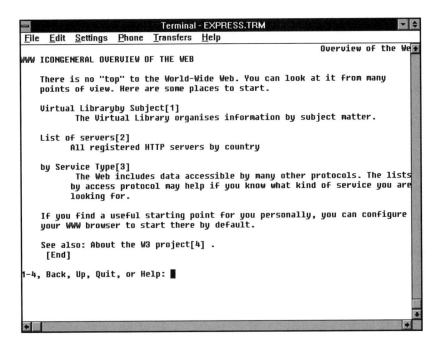

```
┌─────────────────────────────────────────────────────────────────┐
│                    Terminal - EXPRESS.TRM                    ▼│▲│
│ File  Edit  Settings  Phone  Transfers  Help                     │
│                                              Overview of the We▲│
│ WWW ICONGENERAL OVERVIEW OF THE WEB                              │
│                                                                  │
│     There is no "top" to the World-Wide Web. You can look at it from many │
│     points of view. Here are some places to start.              │
│                                                                  │
│     Virtual Libraryby Subject[1]                                │
│           The Virtual Library organises information by subject matter. │
│                                                                  │
│     List of servers[2]                                          │
│           All registered HTTP servers by country               │
│                                                                  │
│     by Service Type[3]                                          │
│            The Web includes data accessible by many other protocols. The lists │
│            by access protocol may help if you know what kind of service you are │
│            looking for.                                         │
│                                                                  │
│     If you find a useful starting point for you personally, you can configure │
│     your WWW browser to start there by default.                 │
│                                                                  │
│     See also: About the W3 project[4] .                         │
│      [End]                                                      │
│                                                                  │
│ 1-4, Back, Up, Quit, or Help: █                                 │
│                                                                  │
└─────────────────────────────────────────────────────────────────┘
```

The Line Mode browser, a simple text-based browser.

And Now, the Browsers

Unfortunately, picking a browser is a "circular" decision. The type of browser you can run depends on the type of account you get, but the type of account you get will (for many people at least) be determined by the type of browser you want to run. So, it's time we looked at the browsers.

Where do you find all these browsers? Look in Chapter 27 for information.

MS-DOS Browser—DOSLynx

The only DOS browser currently available is DOSLynx. This is a text-based browser; that means no nifty graphics. You can use it if you have a SLIP connection from a DOS computer or an Ethernet connection to a network with a permanent connection.

Microsoft Windows Browsers

There are three sorts of Windows Web browsers: those that require any kind of permanent or dial-in direct connection; those that must be used with a particular service provider; and SlipKnot, the only graphical browser designed for use on a terminal connection. Let's start with the first category. (And remember, you can use The Internet Adapter to fool your system into thinking it's on a dial-in direct connection when it's actually a dial-in terminal connection—see Chapter 11.)

> **Mosaic**   The most famous of them all, from the NCSA (National Center for Supercomputing Applications). It's a free system (for noncommercial use) and so well known that many people seem to think that Mosaic *is* the Web. This comes in both 16-bit and 32-bit versions (we'll get into this in more detail in Chapter 13).
>
> **Cello**   This is simpler than Mosaic and, consequently, easier to use. It's also free.
>
> **WinWeb**   This one is published by EINet. It's free for non-commercial use. It's a very nice browser, though again, simpler than Mosaic; that is, it has fewer features. You can find it at the **ftp.einet.net** FTP site in the **/einet/pc/winweb** directory.

Mosaic Netscape   This is a new browser, another modification of Mosaic and much better than Mosaic, according to most users. This one's from Mosaic Communications Corporation, and it's written by some of the original Mosaic programmers. It's a great, fast browser—a real competitor in the shareware "market." (It costs $39 to register it.)

Enhanced NCSA Mosaic   Created by a company called SpyGlass, this is a modification of the original Mosaic. It really is better than the original, but it's not free. SpyGlass is selling it to companies who plan to bundle it with their hardware and software. For instance, DEC PCs will soon come with a copy of the program.

Super Mosaic   This is actually Enhanced NCSA Mosaic, licensed by Luckman Interactive and sold together with TCP/IP and Win32s software (it's a 32-bit program and requires software called *Win32s* to run in Windows 3.1 and Windows for Workgroups). At the time of writing, the program is exactly the same as Enhanced NCSA Mosaic, but it comes bundled with "substantial" Web directories. This product will sell in the software stores for around $49.

Luckman Interactive's Enhanced Mosaic   The same as Super Mosaic, except for the name. This version is being sold to computer and software companies to bundle with their products; it's also being sold to book publishers.

GWHIS Viewer   This is an early version of Mosaic. It's actually *behind* the free version of Mosaic, but that's because Quadralay wants it to match their UNIX version of the product. Quadralay sells this product as part of a larger system designed to help companies publish their documentation online.

Web Navigator (InterAp)   InterAp is a suite of programs (from California Software, Inc.) that contains a browser called Web Navigator. This is a much-modified version of Cello.

AIR Mosaic   Another modification of Mosaic, this one is produced by SPRY. It's sold as part of the AIR Series (to corporations) and as part of Internet In a Box (to bookstore buyers). Internet In a Box is published in conjunction with SPRY, by O'Reilly and Associates.

Tapestry   Tapestry is part of the SuperHighway Access suite of programs published by Frontier Technologies. We bundled SuperHighway Access Sampler in the second edition of *The Complete Idiot's Guide to the Internet*; the Sampler has an FTP program you can use to visit the Frontier Technologies FTP site to download a Tapestry Sampler. The Sampler will also be available at the Macmillan Internet site (see Chapter 27).

Quarterdeck Mosaic   This product is from Quarterdeck, the company that makes the QEMM memory manager. It's due for release in mid-1995, but a beta version is freely available. (It wasn't ready in time for me to talk about it in this book, but I got a copy just before we went to print, and it looks pretty good.)

Internet Chameleon   This is a commercial suite of Internet programs from NetManage. They just recently added a Web browser, WebSurfer, to the set.

Word Viewer   Just before we went to print, Microsoft announced that they were going to release two free products: Word Viewer and Internet Assistant for Microsoft Word (they should be out early in 1995). Word Viewer is an add-on to Word for Windows that lets you turn Word into a Web browser—document text will be imported straight into Word, but you'll still be able to click on the links to travel around. Internet Assistant is an authoring tool that helps you create HTML files (see Chapter 24).

InternetWorks   This one's from BookLink, which, as we went to print, had just been bought by America Online (AOL). The AOL buy-out has changed plans for InternetWorks. Originally, BookLink intended to give away InternetWorks Lite and sell the full version (which would come with an e-mail program and a news reader) and a Web version of the *New Riders' Official Internet Yellow Pages*. At the time of writing, though, they hadn't decided what to do, or whether there will be a InternetWorks Lite version at all. It all depends on how AOL decides to "position" its Internet service. (AOL gives its software away to subscribers, so who knows what they plan to do with their Internet software.) At the time of writing, you could get a free beta version of InternetWorks.

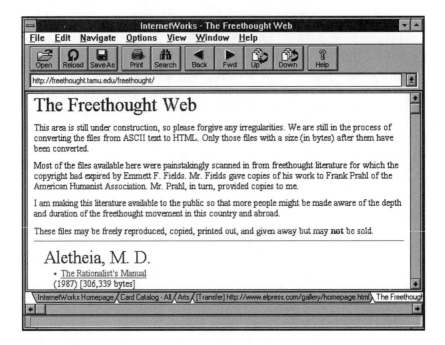

InternetWorks, one of the best browsers available.

It's Mine! Proprietary Browsers

Now, about those "proprietary systems." The following browsers are designed to be used with a service provider that is specially configured to run the software.

> **The Pipeline**   This is an all-in-one system with all the Internet tools you need, including a Web browser. Originally designed for use with a service provider called The Pipeline Network, Inc. (in New York), you'll also find service providers around the country who are licensing the system.

> **NetCruiser**   Another all-in-one system, this only works with NETCOM, a large service provider with access numbers throughout the United States. It's very easy to install and use, with a pretty good—though by no means "full-featured"—Web browser.

InterNav/Delphi   Phoenix Technologies Ltd. makes a product called InterNav for the Delphi online service. It's a Windows program, but it's really only a fancy terminal program. You'll still be using the terminal-based Web browsers on Delphi (Lynx and the Line Mode browser), but with the ability to double-click on a word to use that word as a command.

Graphics for Windows Terminals

Now, about that product that lets you run a Web browser through a dial-in terminal connection:

SlipKnot   This program runs in Windows and lets you browse the Web through a dial-in terminal connection—no need to go to the time and trouble of setting up a TCP/IP connection. It's relatively easy to set up and has some neat features. It's great for Free-Net users and others who can't get SLIP or PPP accounts.

OS/2 Warp Browser

The new OS/2 operating system, Warp, comes with an excellent Web browser:

WebExplorer   This is part of the bonus pack included with OS/2 Warp (the operating system and bonus pack sells for around $80). It's a *very* good browser, and has some neat features. The product also comes with an easy-to-set-up TCP/IP connection to IBM's Internet service, and other programs: Gopher, e-mail, a newsreader, FTP, telnet, and 3270 Terminal.

Macintosh Browsers

There's not quite as much choice in the Macintosh world, but you Mac users are not left out altogether. You'll need a dial-in direct or permanent connection to run these systems, or you can try to use The Internet Adapter to fool your system into thinking it's on a TCP/IP connection (see Chapter 11).

Mosaic for Macintosh This is simply the Macintosh version of Mosaic, from NCSA. It's very similar to the Windows version.

Samba This is a fairly simple browser from CERN, the European Laboratory for Particle Physics in Geneva, Switzerland, the originators of the World Wide Web.

MacWeb This is the Mac equivalent of WinWeb, also from EINet. Again, it's new and fairly simple, but easy to use.

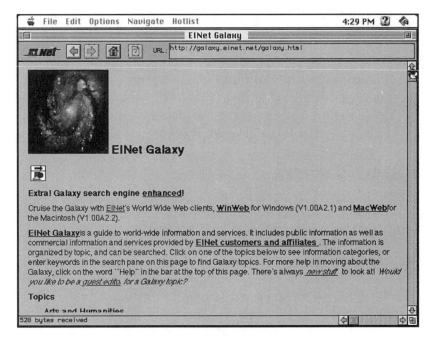

Why should the Macintosh be left out? MacWeb from EINet.

GWHIS Viewer Quadralay claims they'll eventually have a Macintosh version of the GWHIS viewer that's currently available for Windows and UNIX.

Enhanced NCSA Mosaic There's also a version of this program, from SpyGlass, for the Macintosh.

The Pipeline The Pipeline has a Macintosh version of its Internet software available, though it doesn't yet have a Web browser; it should have one by early in 1995.

NetCruiser   There's currently no Macintosh version of NetCruiser, but NETCOM promises to rectify that by early in 1995.

Amiga Browsers

You may have thought the Amiga died out years ago, but it's alive and well, living underground. There are, apparently, enough Amiga users to warrant the creation of a couple of Amiga browsers.

AMosaic   This is based on NCSA's Mosaic, though not published by NCSA. You can use it on older Amigas as well as on the newer machines.

Emacs-W3   A text-based browser that will run under Gnu Emacs running on the Amiga.

Almost Everything: The Line Mode Browser

I'm going to break in here and mention a browser type rather than a particular computer. The *Line Mode browser* is a very simple, easy-to-use Web browser. It doesn't run on DOS, Windows, the Macintosh, or the Amiga, but it does run on all the computer systems we're about to look at (on the NeXT, Sun workstations, all sorts of UNIX machines, VMS, even the Apple).

You can try this system out by telnetting to **nxoc01.cern.ch**. (At the UNIX shell, type **telnet nxoc01.cern.ch** and press **Enter**). Anyone with a terminal connection to the Internet can use this system.

NeXT Browsers

Here's another computer you don't hear much about these days, though it's alive and well: the NeXTStep. These browsers are "native" NeXT browsers actually designed for that computer. The computer also can run X Window browsers if you are using an X-server.

OmniWeb   A World Wide Web browser for NeXTStep. For more information, view the document at **http:/www.omnigroup.com/**.

WorldWideWeb   Another Web browser from CERN. It also contained an editor for modifying Web documents, but the system is reportedly out of date and the editor is not working. The browser was designed for NeXTStep 3.0.

UNIX and VMS: The Neat Stuff

There are many graphical Web browsers designed for UNIX and VMS. While most Internet users are fiddling around with the UNIX shell, the lucky ones actually have a UNIX GUI (graphical user interface).

NCSA Mosaic for X Window A UNIX browser designed to run under the UNIX X Window system. It's very similar to the Windows version, with all the neat stuff: full graphics, forms support, and so on.

GWHIS Viewer This is Quadralay's UNIX version of the GWHIS Viewer (also available in Windows, as we saw earlier). You'll have to pay for this; it's part of an HTML publishing system sold to corporations.

tkWWW Now there's a *real* UNIX name, *tkWWW*. It's designed for X11 and, apparently, includes an HTML-document editor.

MidasWWW This is a beta UNIX/X browser.

Viola There are two versions of Viola: one for Motif and the other for Xlib.

Chimera This is a UNIX/X browser using Athena (it doesn't require Motif). It has lots of the fancy stuff.

Netscape Mosaic Communications also has a version of Netscape for X Window.

FrameMaker If you have a copy of FrameMaker desktop publishing program, you may be able to get a free add-on that will let you browse directly from the program. (It wasn't ready at the time of writing.)

Mosaic There's a version of Mosaic for VMS, although it's not directly from NCSA. It's a modification of NCSA's code, from CERN.

UNIX for the Rest: Text-Mode Browsers

If you don't have a GUI running on UNIX or VMS and you need to install a Web browser, you'll have to use a text-mode browser. You may want to do this if you have a dial-in terminal connection but your service provider hasn't set up a Web browser, or if you don't like the one that's available. You can install a browser on your service provider's system and run it through your connection.

You may also want a text-based browser even if you have a nifty GUI browser. Text-based browsers are much faster, so when you are after nothing but text, they can save a lot of time.

Lynx   This is a very good text-mode browser for VT100 connections; most dial-in terminal connections emulate VT100, so most users can work with this. Unlike the Line Mode browser, Lynx lets you use the arrow keys to move from link to link within Web documents.

Line Mode browser   As we saw earlier, the basic Line Mode browser, a very simple system, is available for UNIX.

Tom Fine's perlWWW   A simple dumb-terminal browser.

VMS for the Rest: Text-Based Browsers

I know about a couple of Web browsers for computers running VMS:

Rashty VMS Client   A full-screen browser for VMS.

Emacs w3-mode   A browser for emacs. You can also run this in Emacs on the Amiga.

The IBM VM/CMS Operating System

There's not much designed for the IBM VM/CMS operating system. There's only one that I know about:

Albert (formerly **UF-WWW**)   A line-mode Web browser from the University of Florida designed for IBM 3270 terminals on the IBM VM/CMS operating system.

A Page at a Time

Finally, there's also a *batch-mode* browser, **url_get**. Well, it's not a true browser, because you're not going to do much browsing with it. Rather, you can type a command at the command line to grab a Web page. It's not intended for real humans; rather, it's for system administrators and other UNIX geek types. Actually, it's really designed for use by programs—for *cron* jobs, which are procedures carried out by the cron command at a specified time and date, often for maintenance purposes.

E-mail "Browsing"

Finally, don't forget the e-mail Web system that lets you transfer Web documents back to your e-mail inbox. So it's not true "browsing," but for many people, it's the only connection to the Web they have (see Chapter 8).

So What Ya Going to Do?

Decisions, decisions. It's difficult to know what to do, isn't it? You have many choices. If you need more information, though, we're going to look at a variety of browsers in the next few chapters. We'll look at Mosaic, plus other PC and Macintosh browsers, to help you compare. In particular, we'll look at Netscape and InternetWorks, probably the two best browsers. Also, see Chapters 6 and 7 for information about Lynx and the Line Mode browser and Chapter 8 for information about using e-mail to grab a Web document. Hey, if all you need is to go out and periodically grab a document on the Web, why bother setting up a browser when you can use e-mail?

My Crystal Ball

I'm going to take a quick look into my crystal ball and tell you what I see. Soon, very soon, installing a Web browser is going to get much easier. The operating systems most of us use (Windows, the Macintosh, and even OS/2) will come with built-in TCP/IP software, the stuff you need to set up a dial-in direct link (we'll look at this in more detail in Chapters 10 and 11). It's going to be relatively easy to make that link, and once you've made the link, installing a Web browser is a breeze.

We're also going to see more easy-to-install, all-in-one packages, such as The Pipeline, NetCruiser, Internet In a Box, and SuperHighway Access. One way or another, you'll be able to install a Web browser quickly and easily. When you buy a computer, you may find a Web browser already loaded on your hard drive.

And those Web browsers are going to get more common, better, and even cheaper (the commercial ones, that is—you can't get much cheaper than freeware). The owner of a company that sells a Web browser (I'd better not say who) told me, "Web-browsing technology is really crude; most browsers are simply toys." As the software business pays more attention to the Web, you'll see browsers that make today's look like something out of the Stone Age.

These are easy prophesies; they may be reality by the time you read this. The last, most difficult prophesy is the other side of the equation. Not "this is how you'll get onto the Web," but "this is what you'll find when you get there." It's easy enough for me to say that the Web will continue to grow. You'll find much more on the Web tomorrow than you do today.

However, I'm not going to make any far-reaching claims, such as "*everything* will be on the Web in five years; bookstores will go out of business," and other such hyperbole. The Web is just one form of communication, and there are others appearing on the scene. (Remember, most people don't have computers, but they do have TVs. The Web on TV? Yes, eventually, but there'll be plenty of other stuff, too.)

All I'm going to say for now is that getting on the Web is going to be easier; you'll have more choice in the way of browsers, and there's going to be lots of really interesting, neat, and weird stuff to see and do. (For a sample of what's already there, see Chapters 25 and 26.)

The Least You Need to Know

➤ There are dozens of browsers for many different computers.

➤ One of the best text-based browsers is Lynx. Most Internet users should be able to find or install this program.

➤ Perhaps the simplest browser is the Line Mode browser; you can try it out by telnetting to **nxoc01.cern.ch**.

➤ If you only need to grab a Web document now and again, you can use e-mail.

➤ There are at least 18 Windows browsers available, and Mosaic is *not* the best!

## Chapter 6

Fast, Cheap, and Easy— Lynx

In This Chapter

➤ Why you may want to use Lynx, a nongraphical browser

➤ Moving around the Web with Lynx

➤ Advanced Web operations

➤ Installing Lynx for yourself—your first step to geekhood!

We're going to start our foray into the Web by using Lynx. Why? Because it's easy to use and available to millions of Internet users. Lynx is available on most UNIX systems connected to the Internet. At first glance, though... well, you may not like what I'm going to show you. It's certainly not as fancy as Mosaic or the other GUI browsers.

Don't get discouraged. There are some very good reasons to use Lynx. Yes, the graphical browsers, such as InternetWorks, Netscape, and Mosaic are neat. Yes, they're fun, but once the novelty has worn off, you'll be left with a big problem: they are very slow, particularly if you're working on a phone line.

Lynx, on the other hand is *very* fast, so even if you have a GUI browser, you may also want Lynx for those jobs that require speed, not pretty pictures. It's fairly easy to use, too. So, let's take a look at what it can do for you.

Let's Look for Lynx

First, where will you find Lynx? Well, Lynx is primarily a UNIX and VMS Web browser. The people who create Lynx distribute many different versions, for IBM mainframes, Ultrix, Alpha OSF/1, Sun 4, and OpenVMS for Alpha AXP (Multinet). There's also a program called DOSLynx, which we'll take a quick look at in Chapter 15. There may be other versions around (for NeXT Step, Linux, SCO, and so on), but these are not directly from the program's creators; they are compiled by other Internet users. If you are connected to a UNIX or VMS host, you'll probably find Lynx somewhere on your service provider's system. (If your system doesn't have Lynx, you can get it and load it yourself. See the "Do-It-Yourself Lynx" section later in this chapter.)

For instance, on Internet Express, one of the services I use, there are several ways to use Lynx. I can select **S>Internet Services** from a menu, then select **W>World Wide Web**. Lynx opens and displays Internet Express' home page, as you can see here.

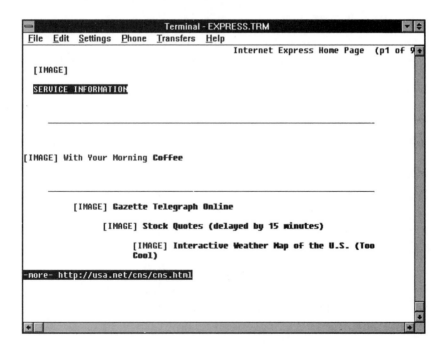

Lynx's home page on the Internet Express system.

I can also start Lynx from the UNIX shell by typing **www** and pressing **Enter**. Again, I find myself in Lynx, reading the Internet Express home page, but there's another command I can use. I can type **lynx** and press **Enter** to open Lynx and view the Lynx default home page (a good place to start if I want to find more information about the program itself). Remember, UNIX commands are case sensitive so you must type lynx with a *lowercase* **l**.

If you can't find Lynx, ask your system administrator where it is. If it *isn't*, then check later in this chapter for information on loading it yourself.

There's another way I can start Lynx; I can include a URL, so when Lynx opens, it displays the document I want to see. For instance, if I type **lynx http://cc.lut.fi/~mega/simpsons.html** and press **Enter**, I'll be visiting the Simpson family Web page (in Finland, of all places).

What's All This, Then?

So, what do you see when you connect? Take a look at the earlier illustration showing Lynx. You'll notice several things. First, there are several lines with [IMAGE] on them. This is simply a "placeholder." Remember, the Web can contain images—pictures—but Lynx can't see them. So, in their place it puts [IMAGE].

Next, notice that some of the text is highlighted. Depending on the terminal you are using, it may appear in "reverse" video (that is, the text takes the normal background color and appears inside a box colored with the normal text color—a black box and white text, for instance). It may be brighter than the text around it. In most cases, these are the *links*. (In some cases, you'll see bright text that doesn't work as a link.)

Moving Around

The first thing you need to know is how to move around. Easy. When you are viewing a large document, you can press the **Spacebar** to move down a page. Press **b** to go back up to the previous page. You can also use the + key and - key to move up and down, but make sure you press **Shift** when you press the + key; otherwise, you'll be using the = command, which we'll look at in a moment.

 Some communications programs, such as Windows Terminal, don't do a good job of emulating a VT100 terminal, so you may find garbage left on your screen when jumping from one document to another while using Lynx. You can quickly "clean up" the page by pressing **Ctrl+W**.

You can also use the numeric keypad, if the NumLock key is on. Use **Home** to go to the top of the document and **End** to go to the bottom. Use **PgDn** and **PgUp** in place of Spacebar and b to move down and up a page at a time.

Now, about those links. You can move the highlight between links by using the arrow keys. **Down arrow** moves down the list, and **up arrow** moves up the list. You can also use **Tab** to go down the list.

Let's say you find a link to a document that you want to read. Highlight it using the arrow keys, and then press **Enter** or **right arrow**. Wrong document? You can move back to the previous document by pressing **left arrow**. Keep pressing left arrow and you'll move through the list of all the documents you've viewed during this session.

Sometimes, you won't be able to use a link, though. The link may not go to a normal HTML document; it may be a link to a sound or video file. Different versions of Lynx handle this in different ways. If you press **Enter** or **right arrow** to select the link, Lynx may transfer the file and then ask you what you want to do with it. One of the options (perhaps the only option) will be to save the file. Also, your version of Lynx may let you highlight the file and then press **d** to download the file. Remember, if you have a dial-in terminal account, the file is being transferred to your service provider's system, not yours.

Those are the basic movement commands you need to know. With these, you can read documents, move to links, select links, and move back to the previous document. Of course, there's more.

How Do I Do That?

Okay, I said Lynx was easy—maybe I exaggerated. It *is* easy to do the basic stuff. Lynx is the fastest thing around for quickly jumping from Web site to Web site.

Unfortunately, it has the same inherent problem that all non-graphical programs have: how do you remember all the commands? With the Web browsers we're going to use later in this book, you don't have to remember exactly what a command is called because, in general, you can find it in a menu. With Lynx, you have to remember the command or read the help file, and then go back to Lynx and execute the command.

> If you spend a lot of time working with Lynx, print a "cheat sheet" with all the commands on it.

So, what are all these advanced procedures? Let's take a look.

View the index   The default index shows the GENERAL OVERVIEW OF THE WEB document (**http://info.cern.ch/default.html**), a "starting point" for beginning work on the Web. It lets you view lists of subjects, Web servers, and service types (FTP, telnet, and so on). However, your system administrator can set up any document he wants as the index, so you may see something different.

See the history list   Press on **Backspace** to see the history list, so you can quickly jump back to earlier documents. (If Backspace doesn't work, try the **Delete** key.)

Return to the home page   Press **m** and then **y** to go to the *main screen*. (Most other browsers call this the *home page*.)

Search the document   Press / and type the word you are looking for; then press **Enter**. If the word is in the document, Lynx will move to the first line containing the word. Press **n** to go to the next occurrence.

Search an index document   Some Web documents are specially set up as index documents that search *index servers*. To search this sort of document, press **s** and then enter the search string.

View the HTML   To see the source document—the HTML codes used to create the document you are viewing—press \. Repeat to return to the normal text.

Clean up the screen   Use **Ctrl+w** or **Ctrl+l** to clear the screen and redisplay, or use **Ctrl+r** to reload the document and then redisplay it.

View file and link information   Press = and you'll see information about the owner of the document, the document's title, and the highlighted link. Repeat to return to the document.

If you can enter your e-mail address but can't write the message, it's because there's no editor defined. See the information about customizing Lynx later in this chapter.

View a particular document   To jump straight to a document, press **g**, type the full URL (including the **http://** bit at the beginning), and press **Enter**.

Send a message to the document owner
Web documents sometimes have "owners." To send a message to the owner, press **c** followed by **y**.

Download a file   To download a file that is pointed to by a link, highlight the link and then press **d**. You'll see the Download Options document, which lets you "Save to disk." Your system administrator can set up other download methods, such as creating a script to download the file to your computer using Zmodem.

Edit a file   If the document you are viewing is a local document (on the system running Lynx), and if you have permission to modify the file, you can press **e** to edit the file.

Cancel a transfer   Press **Ctrl+G** or **z** to cancel a transfer that was a mistake or is taking to long.

Go to the shell   Press **!** and you'll see your shell prompt. You can carry out commands at the shell; then type **exit** to return to Lynx.

Clear your entry   If you make a mistake while typing—entering a search string or a URL—press **Ctrl+u** to clear it so you can start again.

View Help   Press **?** or **h** to see the system Help and User Manual. Press the **left arrow** to return.

Close Lynx   Press **Q** to immediately close Lynx or **q** to display a prompt asking you to confirm.

There are a few more advanced options, but they need a little more explanation. Read on.

Using Bookmarks

As you saw in Chapter 3, bookmarks let you create a list of useful sites, places you'll want to return to. The bookmark list is a collection of document titles and URLs. Select the title, and the browser uses the URL to go directly to the document. Before you can use Lynx's bookmarks, though, you need to create a bookmark file. Press **o** to see the Options page. Select the Bookmarks option (press **B**). Then enter a bookmark name (you'll have to delete the word NONE using the backspace key, and then type the name). **Bookmark** will do. Press **Enter**; then press **r** to return to Lynx.

If Backspace doesn't seem to work, try **Delete**, **Ctrl+h**, or **#**.

Now you can set your bookmarks. When you reach a document you know you'll want to return to, press **a**. Depending on the version you are using, you will now press **y** to create a bookmark that will bring you back to this document, or you may be able to make a choice. Press **d** to create a bookmark for this document or **l** to create a bookmark on the document pointed to by the selected link.

You can view the bookmark list by pressing **v**. The document you see works just like any other Web document, so you can move to the bookmark and press **Enter** to select it.

Your Bookmark file is a text file. Once you understand how HTML documents work, you can, add bookmarks by typing them into the document. See Chapter 21.

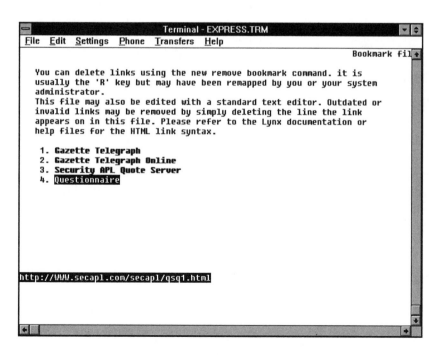

```
─                      Terminal - EXPRESS.TRM                    ▼ ▲
File   Edit   Settings   Phone   Transfers   Help
                                              Bookmark fil ▲

   You can delete links using the new remove bookmark command. it is
   usually the 'R' key but may have been remapped by you or your system
   administrator.
   This file may also be edited with a standard text editor. Outdated or
   invalid links may be removed by simply deleting the line the link
   appears on in this file. Please refer to the Lynx documentation or
   help files for the HTML link syntax.

      1. Gazette Telegraph
      2. Gazette Telegraph Online
      3. Security APL Quote Server
      4. Questionnaire




 http://WWW.secapl.com/secapl/qsq1.html
```

Lynx's bookmark list.

Save and Print

Press **p** if you'd like to save the current document in a file, print it, or e-mail it somewhere. You'll see a document with three links: **Save to a local file**, **Mail the file to yourself**, or **Print to the screen**.

What if you *want* the HTML document, codes and all? First, use the \ command to view the HTML, and *then* use the **p** command.

If you want to save it in a file, you'll be prompted for a filename. Lynx will strip all the HTML codes out of the document, and then save it in an ASCII file. You can use the Mail option to mail the file to anyone, not just yourself. You'll be prompted for the e-mail address. (Again, the HTML codes will be stripped out before the file is mailed.) Finally, the Print option really means "display" on your screen. (Hey, in UNIX-speak, and even old DOS-speak, print means send it to some device—and that device happens to be your screen.) This is a handy way to get a copy of the file onto your computer if you are using a dial-in account. Turn on your communications program's text-capture feature; then "Print to the screen."

By the way, you may *not* be able to save to a file, and you may have *different* save and print options, according to how your system administrator set up the system.

Customizing Lynx

You can set a few customizable options by pressing **o**. (That's the letter o, not zero.) You'll see the Options Menu (see the next figure). To change an option, press its letter. A highlight will appear on the option you selected. Make your change. In some cases, you must type an entry; in others, press any key to select from multiple options. The line at the bottom of the screen tells you which. Then press **Enter**. If you want to save the change for future sessions, press >. Then you can press **r** to return to your Lynx session.

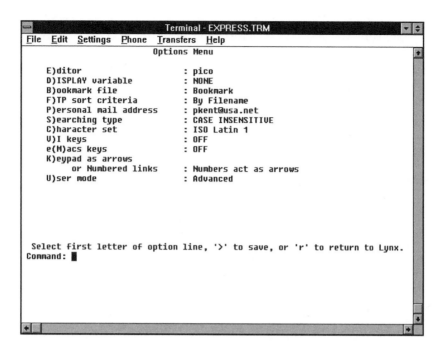

Lynx's Options Menu lets you customize the program.

These are the options:

Editor   Specifies the name of the editor used when editing local HTML files and sending e-mail to document owners. Type the name of an editor you like, such as pico (pico is a relatively good one).

Display variable   You can forget this unless you are using X Window. It should be set automatically.

Bookmark file   You need to create a file that will store your bookmarks. Call it whatever you want.

FTP sort criteria   This option *may* appear in the list. It lets you select how the lists of files will be sorted when viewing FTP sites.

Personal mail address   Enter your e-mail address, so that when you use the **p** command, the e-mail address will be filled in automatically for you.

Searching type   This determines whether you need to type search words in the correct case or not; you'll probably want to leave it set to CASE INSENSITIVE. This only affects searches within a document, not when searching index documents.

Character set   You can select the character set that Lynx will use. You can usually leave this alone, though.

VI keys   If this is ON, the **h**, **j**, **k**, and **l** keys will work as the left, down, up, and right arrow keys.

emacs keys   If this is ON, the **Ctrl+p**, **Ctrl+n**, **Ctrl+f**, and **Ctrl+b** key sequences will work as the up, down, right, and left arrow keys.

Keypad as arrows or Numbered links   Lets you configure your numeric keypad; it either works as arrow keys or lets you type a number to select a link (each link has a number, from 1 for the first link, though the number does not appear).

User mode   You have three user modes: *Novice* (displays two lines of help at the bottom of the screen), *Intermediate* (doesn't display the help lines), and *Advanced* (doesn't display the help lines, but *does* display the URL of the selected link).

Local execution scripts or links   If a script of some sort is connected to a link, it may be run when you click on the link. You can use this option to turn script execution off, allow execution of local scripts, and allow any script, anywhere, to be run.

Working with Forms

Lynx has *forms support*. That means it can work with Web forms, documents with fields into which readers can type information, lists that they can select from, and buttons they can click on.

You're in a form document and can't use the Lynx commands? The commands won't work if you have a text box selected.

Buttons   These look like links; simply press **Enter** or the **right arrow** to activate.

Check boxes and option buttons
These are shown as parentheses: ( ). When selected, they look like this: (*). Select one by pressing the **right arrow** or **Enter**.

Text boxes   These are shown as underlines: _____. You can type into the area above the underline.

Okay, What's the Catch?

Lynx is great for rushing around the Web at great speed. As you'll see later in this book, using some of the graphical browsers we'll look at later can be excruciatingly painful, especially when you are working over a phone line. So why use the graphical browsers?

Well, apart from the fact that Lynx is what might be termed slightly ugly (okay, so I'm a great believer in the GUI—the graphical user interface), there are certain things it can't do. It can't display pictures or video, it can't play sounds, and its bookmarks system doesn't match the sophisticated hotlists used by other browsers.

Also, in general, if you are using Lynx, you are using it on some-one else's computer—not yours, theirs. You are using it through a terminal connection. In the case of a dial-in terminal connection, when you download files using Lynx the files are placed on the other computer. If you want to get the files back to *your* computer, you'll have to take another step and transfer the files using Zmodem, Xmodem, or something similar.

The graphical browsers are designed to run on *your* computer, so files are transferred directly back to your computer; there's no need to take that extra step.

So, do you need all the fancy features, and is the file-transfer thing a real problem? If not, use Lynx for its speed. If so, you're better off with a graphical browser, or you may want to use *both*. Use Lynx when you need speed, a graphical browser when you are after the neat stuff.

Do-It-Yourself Lynx

Maybe your system doesn't have Lynx. Well, you can find and install it yourself. (It's free!—you can't beat that.) There are a number of ver-sions available, so you need to know the type of computer system you are working on.

If you are not sure what you are running, try this. At the UNIX shell, type **uname -a** and press **Enter**. You may see something like this:

```
OS cns 4.1.3 1 sun4m
```

If the **uname -a** command doesn't work on your system, or if you don't understand what you see, talk to the system administrator.

This is UNIX. If you are using a different operating system or version of the program (one for VMS, for instance), the procedure for extracting, renaming, and running the program will be different.

This tells me that I have a version 4 SUN operating system.

Now, go get the version of Lynx that you need (Chapter 27 tells you where to find it). It will probably be in a .Z UNIX compressed file. Simply type **uncompress *filename*** (for instance, **uncompress lynx2-3.SUN4.EXE.Z**) and press **Enter**. Now, you may want to rename the file. Typing lynx2-3.SUN4.EXE each time you want to start Lynx is just a *leeetle* bit tedious. For instance, type **mv lynx2-3.SUN4.EXE lynx** to change the name to lynx. (In UNIX, you have to "move" a file—with mv—to rename it.)

One more thing. You may not be able to run the file yet, because you probably don't have the necessary permissions to do so. Type **chmod u+x *filename*** (for instance, **chmod u+x lynx**) to give yourself permission to execute the program. (Or use **chmod 755 *filename*** to give other people permission to run the program, also.)

That's it. Now you can run the program by typing its name and pressing **Enter**.

The Least You Need to Know

➤ Lynx is available on most service providers' systems.

➤ If your service provider *doesn't* have Lynx, you may be able to load it yourself.

➤ Lynx is a *very* fast nongraphical Web browser.

➤ It's easy to learn the basics, but if you want to use advanced Lynx operations, you may want to create a "cheat sheet."

➤ Some of the Web will be unusable if you work with Lynx because it doesn't work with graphics.

## Chapter 7

Poor Man's Web—The Line Mode Browser

In This Chapter

➤ Using telnet to find the Line Mode browser

➤ Moving around the Web with the Line Mode browser

➤ Using the list of topics

➤ Using the URL to get somewhere

➤ Saving what you find (maybe)

Some systems don't have Lynx. As you saw in the previous chapter, you can always install Lynx yourself or ask if your system administrator will. But what if *you* don't want to and *he* won't? You are left with the Line Mode browser. Your system administrator may have this browser installed, but if not, you can telnet to CERN (the European Particle Physics Laboratory) and use it there.

The Line Mode browser is a very simple system. You won't be able to use the arrow keys to move from link to link, as you can with Lynx; the text is not even underlined or highlighted. Instead, a link is indicated with a number in brackets: [1], [2], and so on. To select a link, you'll type the number and press Enter.

Off to the Alps

If you have the Line Mode browser available on your service provider's system, use it; otherwise, you can take a quick trip to Switzerland to **nxoc01.cern.ch** (that's a zero before the 1, not the letter *o*). You'll use telnet to get there.

At the command line, type **telnet nxoc01.cern.ch** and press **Enter**. Let's watch the session:

```
CNS> telnet nxoc01.cern.ch
Trying 128.141.201.214 ...
Connected to www0.cern.ch.
Escape character is '^]'.


UNIX(r) System V Release 4.0 (www0)
          Welcome to the World-Wide Web
THE WORLD-WIDE WEB


    This is just one of many access points to the web, the universe of
    information available over networks. To follow references, just type
    the number then hit the return (enter) key.
    The features you have by connecting to this telnet server are very
    primitive compared to the features you have when you run a W3
    "client" program on your own computer. If you possibly can, please
    pick up a client for your platform to reduce the load on this
    service and experience the web in its full splendor.


    For more information, select by number:
    A list of available W3 client programs[1]
    Everything about the W3 project[2]
    Places to start exploring[3]
    The First International WWW Conference[4]


    This telnet service is provided by the WWW team at the European
    Particle Physics Laboratory known as CERN[5]
    [End]
    1-5, Up, Quit, or Help:
```

Notice that we didn't have to log in; when you telnet to here, you are placed into WWW automatically. Notice all the numbers in brackets. For instance, if you'd like to take a look at the *Places to start exploring* document, from which you can search through different subjects as a starting point, type **3** and press **Enter**. If you want to see a list of the WWW browser programs, type **1** and press **Enter**, and so on.

The Line Mode Commands

Here are the commands you'll use when moving through the Web. Type each command and then press **Enter**.

Go down one page	Press **Enter**
Go to the previous page	**u** or **up**
Go to the last page	**bo** or **bottom**
Go to the first page	**t** or **top**
Go to a [*number*] reference	Type the number and press **Enter**
Search a document for a keyword when you see FIND on the prompt line	**f** *keywords* or **find** *keywords*
See a list of [ ] references	**l** or **list**
Go to the previous document	**b** or **back**
Go to the first document you saw	**ho** or **home**
List the documents you've seen	**r** or **recall**
Go to a document in the Recall list	**r** *number* or **recall** *number*
View the next reference from the last document	**n** or **next**
Refresh the page you are viewing	**REF**
Go to a particular document	**go** *url*
Display the Help page	**h** or **help**

67

Display the WWW manual   **m** or **manual**

Quit   **quit**

Play with these commands while you're working in the Line Mode browser, and soon you'll get the hang of it. Type the link number and press **Enter** to select a particular link. Then move down the page, whether it's a listing or document, by pressing **Enter**. Move back up a page by pressing **u** and then **Enter**. To go back to where you just came from, use **b** and **Enter**. You'll soon get the idea. Take a look at the chart included here, and try navigating through the Web. Sure, it's not Mosaic or InternetWorks, but hey, some people really like this funky text-based stuff. It's macho. (*Real* men don't use mice.)

Let's Explore

Let's take a look at what we find if you select **[3]** from the page we saw earlier (**Places to start exploring**). You'll see a list of options; select **Virtual Library by Subject [1]**, and you'll see the beginning of a list, like this:

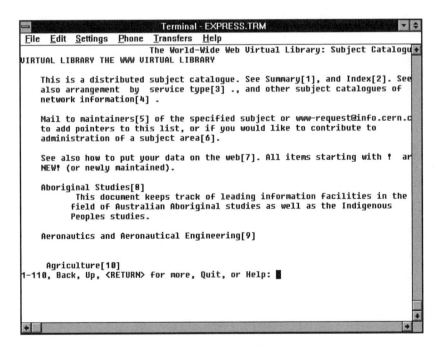

The Line Mode browser—it's not pretty, but it works.

We have nine links or topics in this small area alone. We can see a summary (**1**), an index (**2**), and a list of different services available by selecting **3** (World Wide Web servers, WAIS servers, Network News, Gopher, Telnet, and so on). We can also see other subject catalogues by selecting **4**; we'll see several other types of indexes of information we can work our way through.

Below the header stuff, we see the beginning of the catalogue itself, starting with **Aboriginal Studies** and **Aeronautics**. You'll notice that there are numbers next to both these entries and, below Aeronautics, the words **Separate list** on the description line. This means that if you type **9** and press **Enter**, you'll see a list of aeronautics-related resources: **Embry-Riddle Aeronautical University**, **Aviation and Aerospace Outlook**, **Penn State University**, **Aerospace Engineering**, and so on.

Okay, so maybe you're not interested in aeronautics. Just play with the Web and go where your fancy takes you.

Looking at a Topic List

You can view a list of all the topics or references in the current document. Type **l** and press **Enter**, and you'll see something like this:

```
*** References from this document ***
[1] http://www.biotech.washington.edu/WebCrawler/WebQuery.html
[2] http://rubens.anu.edu.au/prints.xmosaic/inlines.no/Part4.html
[3] http://rubens.anu.edu.au/prints.xmosaic/inlines.no/Part3.html
[4] http://www.eb.com/release.htm
[5] http://www.inhs.uiuc.edu:70/1/edu
[6] http://www.tulips.tsukuba.ac.jp/ndc/200.html
```

If you are in a very big listing or document, you may have dozens of topics, and they'll shoot right by you before you can read them. Still, in smaller documents, the listing may be useful.

On the other hand, it may not. Unfortunately, this is a list of URLs, Uniform Resource Locators, the addresses of the documents, not the document titles. It's kind of like giving you a list of business addresses without including the business names. Sometimes, you'll be able to figure out what all this is, often you won't.

After viewing the list, either type one of the numbers or **u**, and press **Enter** (**u** will just return you to the previous page).

That's the One I Want

Now, let's say you want to go directly to a particular document: the *WebCrawler*, a giant index of WWW resources, for instance. You'll use the **go** *url* command. Simply type **go http://fishtail.biotech. washington.edu/WebCrawler/WebQuery.html** (well, okay, I know it's not *really* simple) and press **Enter**. You'll shoot off across Webspace to the WebCrawler.

Save the Info You Find

Saving information from the Line Mode browser may be a problem. If the Line Mode browser has been set up by your service provider, you can save the data. If you are telnetting to a Web browser, though, you are out of luck.

On UNIX versions of the Line Mode browser, you can use the **print** command to print a document, or the > *filename* command to save the document in a file (use >> *filename* to append it to the end of an existing file).

The Least You Need to Know

➤ You can telnet to **nxoc01.cern.ch** to use a simple line-mode browser or use one set up by your service provider.

➤ With the Line Mode browser, follow references by typing the *number* and pressing **Enter**.

➤ To get back to the first page you saw, use the **ho** command.

➤ Travel around in a document with the **top**, **bottom**, and **up** commands. Press **Enter** to go down one page.

➤ Type **l** and press **Enter** to view a list of the document's topics.

## Chapter 8

Snail Mail?
Web Mail!

In This Chapter

➤ Using a "mail robot" to get Web documents through e-mail

➤ Finding the documents referenced by the links

➤ Asking the mail robot for the linked documents

The World Wide Web by mail? Nah!

Yes, it really is possible, but would you want to? Well, maybe. If you don't have access to a Web browser, you can still get to Web documents using a *mail robot*, a program that does the work for you. I often see e-mail messages in mailing lists from people who only have e-mail access to the Internet, trying to find out how they can get to certain resources working with what they have. Unfortunately, it's not always easy.

If you read *The Complete Idiot's Guide to the Internet*, for instance, you'll know that you can do FTP "sessions" via e-mail. Using an

Even if you have full Internet access, Web mail can sometimes be a handy way to grab a copy of a document without spending much time navigating to it and saving it.

FTPmail server, you can send instructions indicating which file you want and where it is, and the file is returned to you uuencoded—that is, converted to ASCII text. Awful.

If that's the only type of connection you've got, then perhaps it's worth messing with; I'd hate to have to do all my FTPing via e-mail, though. Getting Web documents is quite simple—much easier than using FTPmail.

The Web Mail Robot

To carry out an e-mail Web session, start by sending e-mail to **listserv@info.cern.ch**. Don't enter a Subject line. In the body of the message, enter **SEND *url***. For instance, if you'd like to get the document that lists all the Web browsers available by telnet, type this message:

```
SEND http://info.cern.ch/hypertext/WWW/FAQ/Bootstrap.html
```

(You can use the **www** command in place of **send**, if you want, as in **www *url***.) You can add several SEND lines, one for each document you want to get. Now, send the message.

In addition to **listserv@info.cern.ch**, you might try working with **webmail@curia.ucc.ie**. This is a simpler system than the **listserv@info.cern.ch** one. It uses the **go** command instead of the **send** command and only accepts one command per e-mail message. These are the only Web mail robots I know of right now, though maybe there'll be more later.

At the moment, this system is pretty quick; you may get a message in a few seconds or a minute or two. When you get your response, you'll see something like the figure on the next page.

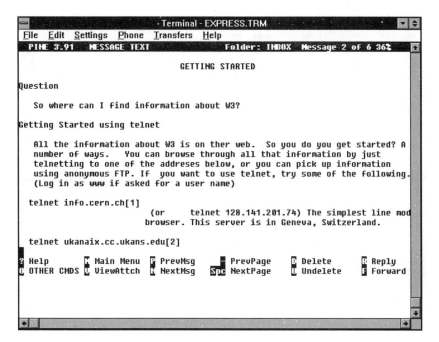

An e-mail response containing a World Wide Web document.

You can see that this document is the Getting Started document. It contains a list of a few telnet sites that have various different types of Web browsers: simple line-mode browsers, Lynx, and a Hebrew/English line-mode browser. Notice also that there are numbers in braces: [1], [2], and so on. These are the hypertext links. You can use these numbers to "navigate" through the Web. (I didn't say this was going to be *quick*, did I?)

Selecting a Link

Okay, you have your first Web document back, and you've found a link you are interested in. You have two options. You could go to the end of the document, where all the link URLs are listed (see the following figure). For each number in braces, you'll see the URL that the link points to. You can copy down this URL and then use a Web browser to go to the document.

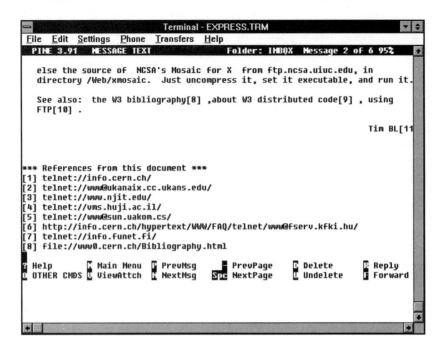

```
─                    Terminal - EXPRESS.TRM              ▼ ▲
 File  Edit  Settings  Phone  Transfers  Help
  PINE 3.91    MESSAGE TEXT            Folder: INBOX  Message 2 of 6 95%   ↑

  else the source of  NCSA's Mosaic for X  from ftp.ncsa.uiuc.edu, in
  directory /Web/xmosaic.  Just uncompress it, set it executable, and run it.

  See also:  the W3 bibliography[8] ,about W3 distributed code[9] , using
  FTP[10] .

                                                        Tim BL[11



*** References from this document ***
[1] telnet://info.cern.ch/
[2] telnet://www@ukanaix.cc.ukans.edu/
[3] telnet://www.njit.edu/
[4] telnet://vms.huji.ac.il/
[5] telnet://www@sun.uakom.cs/
[6] http://info.cern.ch/hypertext/WWW/FAQ/telnet/www@fserv.kfki.hu/
[7] telnet://info.funet.fi/
[8] file://www0.cern.ch/Bibliography.html

? Help        C Main Menu  P PrevMsg  ─ PrevPage  D Delete     R Reply
O OTHER CMDS  V ViewAttch  N NextMsg  SPC NextPage U Undelete   F Forward
```

Each e-mailed Web document lists the links at the end.

You won't be able to get all links. Take a look at the bottom of the document in the preceding figure, and you'll see that some of the links are to telnet sites. If you had a browser, selecting the link would start a telnet session. So you can't retrieve these links. Look for URLs that end with **html**; these are documents that you can retrieve.

Ah, but of course you don't have a Web browser, do you? So your other option is to reply to the message, and ask for information about the link.

Here's how it works. Reply to the message, but don't copy the original message (the Web document) into the reply. Don't touch the Subject line, either; let your e-mail program enter the Subject for you. In the body of the message, type the link numbers you want, separated by spaces. For example: **1 3 6 7**.

That's all that should appear in the body. Now, send this off to the Reply To address and wait for your response.

It Doesn't Work?

Okay, so this might not work. You may get a blank message back or just the top part of the message (the part that contains information about the Web mail system).

Why didn't it work? It may be that the document you tried to get to simply isn't available, the machine that the document is stored on is not available right now, or perhaps the document has been removed; the Web is in a constant state of change, so you'll find that Web documents are sometimes not where they are "supposed" to be.

Is your document missing stuff at the end? There's a 5,000-line limit; documents over that won't be sent.

Also, you may have selected a non-document link. For instance, you may have selected a link that would, if you had the right sort of Web browser, start a Gopher or FTP session. It's not always clear from a URL what a link does. If you select one that ends with **html**, though, you can be sure that it's a document.

Let's Speed This Up

Here's a command you may want to try. On the other hand, you may not, as it can fill your e-mail box with a huge quantity of Web documents. The **deep** *url* command works like the **send** *url* or **www** *url* commands; it sends the document you requested with the *url*, but it also checks all the links in that documents and grabs all the referenced documents, too! You may want to use this if you know that the document you are retrieving has a fairly small number of links. Perhaps there's a particular document you retrieve periodically, and you know its size.

If you are getting a document you've never seen before, using this command may overwhelm your e-mail system. I used it and discovered the mail program I'm working with has an inbox size limit. The document I was retrieving had 373 links!

Still, you won't get more than 5,000 lines back, total, the same limit that applies to the **send** *url* command.

Just a Little Bit More...

Here are a few more commands that may interest you. You can use the **source *url*** command to retrieve the source document. That is, you'll get the original HTML document, including the HTML codes. That's nice if you want to load it into a Web browser to read it; instead of getting plain vanilla text, you'll get a formatted Web document (you'll learn in Chapter 18 how to load documents from your hard disk into a browser).

You can also use the **rsource *emailaddress url*** and **rsend *emailaddress url*** commands to send the requested files—whether source files or "rendered" text files (the text without the HTML codes)—to a different place.

Don't forget the **help** command. This will retrieve information about using the system. You may want to do this now and again to see if the capabilities have improved.

Don't Overdo It!

This is a test system. The people who run the system have asked that you don't overdo it. Don't use it to regularly read newsgroup messages. In fact, don't use it regularly at all. Now and again is okay, but don't make a habit of it. Don't use it for very large documents. Don't try to transfer computer files from FTP sites (it won't work, anyway).

The Least You Need to Know

➤ Yes, you really *can* get Web documents via e-mail.

➤ Send a message to listserv@info.cern.ch; leave the Subject line blank.

➤ In the body of the message, type **SEND *url***; you'll get a reply containing the document.

➤ Links are numbered, so you can reply to the message asking for the linked documents.

➤ When you reply, let your e-mail program enter the Subject, and don't include a copy of the original. Type the numbers of the links you want to read, separated by spaces.

Part 3
Getting Ready for Work

In this Part of the book, you'll learn how to get ready; how to set up a TCP/IP connection on a Mac or Windows machine; and why you may want to work with SlipKnot or The Internet Adapter if you can't get a TCP/IP connection.

By the time you finish this Part of the book, you'll be ready to get down to work, or you'll at least have a connection to the Internet sorted out and be ready to pick a browser.

OH **THAT**, HE'S BEEN ACTING THAT WAY EVER—
SINCE HE GOT HIS PASSWORD TO FINALLY WORK...

## Chapter 9

Making the Connection

In This Chapter

➤ How to fool your software—TIA

➤ A graphics browser for non-TCP/IP connections—
SlipKnot

➤ TCP/IP "stacks"

➤ Finding different stacks

Most of the really nice Web browsers require a dial-in direct or permanent connection to the Internet: a TCP/IP connection (Transmission Control Protocol/Internet Protocol). If you are not working with a large company or organization that provides you with a network connection to the Internet, that means you'll need to sign up for a SLIP or PPP account if you want to run InternetWorks, Mosaic, Netscape, Cello, or one of the other new browsers. (Okay, there are exceptions, as you'll see in a moment.)

Unfortunately, you may find it difficult to set up these accounts. It's not just a matter of running a short setup program to load the program onto your hard disk; there's important information that you must enter to tell the program how to run.

First, there's the configuration data; you have to enter your service provider's IP number, and perhaps yours, too. There's a domain name to plug in, and, as we'll see in the next two chapters, various other numbers here and there that tell the program how to act once connected.

The second problem is the login script. Each service provider has a different login procedure—a different sequence of events that occurs when you dial into their system. So you have to create a login script that tells your program what it has to do to log in; what login and password prompts to wait for; whether it has to send a special command to change to SLIP or PPP mode (some systems require this, some don't); and so on. Setting up these accounts can be tricky, but there are ways around these problems. In this chapter, I'm going to explain a little about:

➤ How to fool a browser designed for a dial-in direct or permanent connection into working with a terminal account.

➤ A Windows graphics browser designed specifically for terminal accounts.

➤ Installing a TCP/IP "stack" (the program that makes the connection to the Internet) on both Windows and a Mac.

Fool It!

Let's say you can't or won't, for some reason, get a dial-in direct or permanent connection. Perhaps you are working with a Free-Net or a college, and there's no way your system administrator will give you a SLIP or PPP account. Maybe your service provider wants to charge you a little extra—a setup fee and perhaps a higher hourly rate—and you don't want to pay.

Well, there is a way around this problem; use The Internet Adapter (TIA). This is a special program that you place on your service provider's system. Each time you want to run your Web browser, you start TIA and then start your TCP/IP software. Your TCP/IP programs think they are running on a dial-in direct connection. You've fooled them into running across a dial-in terminal account—something they weren't designed to do.

You still have to set up the normal TCP/IP programs on your own computer. That is, in addition to the Web browser you want to use, you still need the TCP/IP "interface." On the Macintosh, that means you need MacTCP and MacPPP (or perhaps InterSLIP, or another such program). See the rest of this chapter for information. On Windows machines, you still have to install the TCP/IP stack that comes with InternetWorks, or whatever other TCP/IP stack you want to use (we'll discuss this in a moment).

Here's a poor reason for using TIA: *You don't want the hassle of setting up a SLIP or PPP account.* Setting up TIA is actually more work than setting up a normal dial-in direct account—not only do you have to set up TIA itself, but you *still* have to set up all the SLIP or PPP software on your system.

If you want more information about setting up TIA, send e-mail to **tia-info@marketplace.com**; you can leave the subject and body of the message empty. You'll get an automatic reply containing the *About The Internet Adapter* document: "an overview of what it is, who should use it, how it is sold, how you can evaluate or order it, and so on."

Easier Yet—SlipKnot

Here's an even easier method (for Windows users only, sorry), if setting up TIA and SLIP or PPP software is too much of a hassle. Use SlipKnot. It's a Windows Web browser designed for terminal accounts, yet it's a graphical browser—yes, you'll get pictures!

SlipKnot is a great system for people condemned to using terminal accounts, though it's a poor substitute for the top Web browsers, such as InternetWorks, Netscape, Enhanced NCSA Mosaic, and so on.

It's a little slow, and the windows in which the Web documents appear tend to be small. It's relatively easy to install, though. You have to write a short logon script, but it's not too painful. If you want to find out more about this browser, see Chapter 15.

Going the Whole Hog: TCP/IP

Okay, then, you want to go the whole hog and install TCP/IP. Where are you going to start? There are several ways to do this. The most preferable, of course, is to get someone else to do it. If you have a connection through your employer or college or some other sort of system with a system administrator whom you can finagle into doing it for you, then do so.

The next best method is to get someone to at least help you. I suggest that you check with your service provider—some are very helpful, others are about as useful as gills on a rabbit. Some will send you the software you need, or at least tell you where you can download it, and then "hold your hand" as they walk you through what you need to do to get your TCP/IP connection up and running. Others will take your money and expect you to be able to master the complexities of a TCP/IP hookup by yourself. (Well, not quite by yourself—in the next two chapters I'll help you set it all up.)

What's next? Well, you could try one of the simple-to-install proprietary systems: Internaut or NetCruiser. Or you could buy a suite of programs such as Internet In a Box, SuperHighway Access, or Internet Chameleon. These vary in complexity, and the ease of installation depends to a great degree on the service provider you are trying to connect to. You may be lucky and get everything up and running in an hour or so, or you may give up in disgust after a day or so.

Another method is to use the software that comes with your operating system. OS/2 Warp now ships with the TCP/IP software that's very easy to set up, especially if you are connecting to IBM's own service provider. When Windows 95 (or 96, or whatever it is) finally ships, that, too, will come with a TCP/IP stack built-in. As for the Mac, the latest operating system now comes with at least *part* of the software you need (as you'll see in Chapter 11).

Finally, you can install the shareware TCP/IP software. That's right, there's software waiting for you right now: programs that will help you connect your Mac or PC to the Internet.

So, before we can continue with this book, you have to get your connection sorted out. I can't help you with most of these methods; check the documentation, talk to technical support, call your system administrator, and so on. I can, however, help you install the shareware TCP/IP software. If that's the route you want to take, turn to the next chapter (to install the software on a Windows machine), or Chapter 11 (for the Macintosh). As for the rest of you, I'll see you in Chapter 12.

Good luck!

The Least You Need to Know

➤ If you want to run TCP/IP software but don't have a TCP/IP account, use The Internet Adapter to fool your software.

➤ If you don't want all the hassle of setting up TCP/IP but want a graphical browser, use SlipKnot.

➤ If you want real TCP/IP, you'll have to install a TCP/IP "stack," a program that sets up a connection to the Internet.

➤ If possible, get someone else to set up the software for you—it's tricky! If you can't do that, at least get someone to help.

➤ If you want to install TCP/IP software on a Windows computer, turn to Chapter 10; for the Macintosh, turn to Chapter 11.

TCP/IP for You and Me: Windows Connections

In This Chapter

➤ A word about WINSOCK.DLL

➤ Installing Trumpet Winsock for a dial-in direct connection

➤ Writing a Trumpet Winsock login script

➤ Setting Trumpet Winsock options

You've decided to take the plunge and install a shareware TCP/IP stack. I hope you won't regret this decision (I'll be honest, many people do!). I'll do my best to help you, but I can't cover every eventuality. Remember, if you can get help from your service provider, turn back now and do so!

Okay, here we go. We have to install a file called WINSOCK.DLL to run Windows on the Internet. WINSOCK.DLL is a *dynamic link library*, a system from which programs can "borrow" when they want to carry out some common task.

WINSOCK.DLL provides a way for Windows programs to communicate across a TCP/IP link. That makes it much easier for software writers to create new Internet programs. Instead of writing a program that contains the necessary tools to transmit data over a TCP/IP link, all a programmer needs to do is write a program that can talk to WINSOCK.DLL. Although various programmers have created different versions of WINSOCK.DLL, there's a set of standards—the *Windows Socket* standards—that define what the file should do. A program that can work with one version of WINSOCK.DLL should be able to work with any of them.

The TCP/IP stack that we're going to install is called Trumpet Winsock. This is the most popular and capable shareware TCP/IP stack (the registration fee is $20). In fact, it's become a de facto standard and is probably simpler and easier to use than a number of the commercial stacks. See Chapter 27 for information on where to find this program.

But How Do I Get It?

There's a catch to setting up a TCP/IP connection, though. You need Trumpet Winsock, which is available online, but you can't get to it unless you have a connection to the Internet. If you already have a dial-in terminal connection to the Internet, no problem. Use that connection to get Trumpet Winsock, and then install it and change over to your TCP/IP connection. If you don't have an Internet connection, it's more complicated.

Many service providers give their subscribers both dial-in terminal and dial-in direct (TCP/IP) connections at the same time, for one price. This, it seems to me, is the ideal. You can use your dial-in terminal account (often known as a "shell" account) to grab your software; then switch to your dial-in direct account. So when you shop for a dial-in direct account, ask if you'll get a dial-in terminal account, too. (Be careful, though; some service providers will be happy to give you both accounts but will charge extra!)

 Never used basic dial-in terminal Internet? Don't know how to use FTP? Take a look at *The Complete Idiot's Guide to the Internet* for a back-to-basics introduction to the Internet.

If you don't have a connection and will be getting a dial-in direct account but no dial-in terminal account, you have a problem. Ask your service provider how you can get hold of Trumpet Winsock. Ask about WS_FTP, too, because once you have your TCP/IP connection up and running, you'll need a program that will let you grab the Web browser of your choice (and WS_FTP is the best Windows FTP—File Transfer Protocol—program there is).

> You can't just install TCP/IP software and then connect to your service provider; they have to set up a SLIP, CSLIP, or PPP account for you first. Call and ask about it.

Perhaps they can send you a disk. If not, ask a friend to get it for you, or look for it on local bulletin boards. Anyway, I can't help you with this. I'm going to move on to explaining how to install Trumpet Winsock.

Installing Trumpet

You can use Trumpet Winsock to connect in either of two ways: to a dial-in direct account using SLIP or CSLIP, or to a network with an Ethernet *packet driver* already installed and a permanent connection to the Internet.

If you are planning to install on a network, you'll have to look elsewhere for help. There are many different configurations, and how you install Trumpet Winsock will depend on how you are running your network. If you are the network's system administrator, you'll probably be able to figure it out from the Trumpet Winsock documentation relatively easily. If you are not, talk with the administrator and find out if he can help. An ordinary user shouldn't be messing with this sort of thing, anyway. If you know nothing about network software, don't touch it.

> **Packet driver** A program that sends out "packets" of data through your network card and across the network. Ethernet is a common form of Local Area Network.

Okay, if you want to install Trumpet Winsock for use with a dial-in direct account, follow these steps:

1. Start by creating a directory from which you will run Winsock. Call this something such as **C:\WINSOCK** or **C:\TRUMPET**.

2. Copy the Winsock files to the directory; you'll probably have these files:

> **BUGS.LST**   A text file containing information about Winsock versions and bugs.
>
> **BYE.CMD**   A text file containing the commands sent to your modem to end a session.
>
> **DISCLAIM.TXT**   A text file containing a disclaimer and copyright notice.
>
> **HOSTS**   A sample text file containing a list of host names. Some TCP/IP programs may refer to this list, but most don't, so you can forget about it for now.
>
> **INSTALL.DOC**   A text file containing the Winsock user manual.
>
> **INSTALL.TXT**   A Word for Windows file containing the Winsock user manual.
>
> **LOGIN.CMD**   A text file containing the commands sent to your modem to begin a session.
>
> **PROTOCOL**   A text file containing a list of Internet protocols. Not used for dial-in direct connections.
>
> **README.MSG**   A short text file providing the software author's e-mail address.
>
> **SERVICES**   A text file containing a list of Internet services. Not used for dial-in direct connections.
>
> **TCPMAN.EXE**   The program that you run to set up and use the WINSOCK.DLL program.
>
> **WINSOCK.DLL**   The Windows dynamic link library that is the "guts" of TCP/IP driver.

Later, after running setup, you'll find a **TRUMPWSK.INI** file in this directory. This is a text file containing the initialization information used when starting a Winsock session. It's created the first time you enter setup information.

3. Use Windows Notepad or Windows Sysedit to change the PATH statement in your AUTOEXEC.BAT file to include the name of the directory you put the Winsock files into. For example, if you put them in **C:\TRUMPET**, make sure the path statement contains **C:\TRUMPET** (such as, PATH C:\DOS;C:\WINDOWS;C:\TRUMPET). (You can find the AUTOEXEC.BAT file in your root directory.)

I'm going to assume you understand a few basics such as how to create directories and copy files, and how to edit an AUTOEXEC.BAT file. If you don't, you may find Winsock a little more of a problem than you imagined. Pick up *The Complete Idiot's Guide to DOS* for a quick education on the subject.

4. Reboot your computer and then restart Windows.

5. Start the **TCPMAN.EXE** program. You can create an icon if you want to, and start the program by double-clicking on the icon. Or select **Run** from the Program Manager or File Manager **File** menu, and then type **TCPMAN** and click on **OK**. The program will start. (If it doesn't, you didn't put the path information into AUTOEXEC.BAT correctly.) The Trumpet Winsock Network Configuration dialog box should appear (see the following figure).

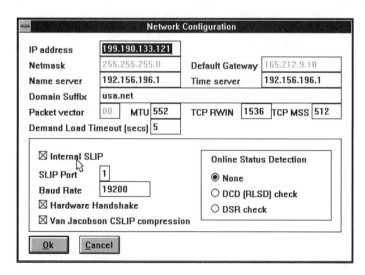

The Trumpet Winsock Network Configuration dialog box, after you have entered all the data.

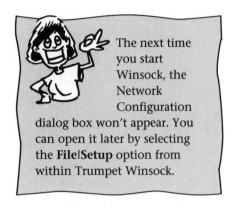

The next time you start Winsock, the Network Configuration dialog box won't appear. You can open it later by selecting the **File|Setup** option from within Trumpet Winsock.

6. Find out how to log into your system. It's a good idea to run Windows Terminal, or another simple serial communications program, and try to log in- to your SLIP or PPP account with that. Of course, you won't get all the way in, but you should be able to get up to the point where your service provider's system switches over to SLIP or PPP. Record the session so you can see exactly what happens when you log in. You're going to need this data to set up Trumpet Winsock.

7. Click on the **Internal SLIP** check box. This disables certain options you don't need, and enables others that you do need. (If you were connecting to a network with a permanent connection, you would leave the Internal SLIP check box cleared.)

8. Type your Internet Protocol address into the **IP address** text box. This is the address by which your computer will be identified on the Internet once connected. (In some rare cases, you may have to type **bootp** instead of a number. Only do so if instructed by your service provider.)

9. Now enter your service provider's domain nameserver IP address into the **Name server** text box. If you have more than one nameserver IP address, you can enter them one after the other, leaving a single space between each one.

10. The **Time server** option is, at the time of this writing, unused, though future versions may use it. If so, your service provider will give you the time server address.

11. Enter the domain name given to you by your service provider. For instance, if you connect to Internet Express, and your e-mail address is jbloe@usa.net, you'll type **usa.net** in the **Domain Suffix** text box. You may be given several domain names to put in here; separate them with spaces.

12. **MTU** is the *Maximum Transmission Unit*. (Yes, another one.) This is usually the TCP MSS value plus 40; 552 for SLIP and 294 for CSLIP.

13. **TCP RWIN** means *Transmission Control Protocol Receive Window,* another esoteric network term. Make this value about three to four times the TCP MSS value; say, 1536 for SLIP and 765 for CSLIP.

14. **TCP MSS** means *Transmission Control Protocol Maximum Segment Size*—some network thing (measured in bytes) you don't need to worry about. If you are using a SLIP account, enter 512; if you are using a CSLIP account, use 254. If your service provider suggests certain values for this and the next two items, use those instead.

15. The **Demand Load Timeout** is the number of seconds that the Trumpet Winsock program remains loaded after an application has finished with it. You can leave this set to 5 seconds.

16. Enter the port number of your COM port that your modem connects to in the **SLIP port** text box. Enter **1** for COM1, **2** for COM2, and so on.

17. In the **Baud Rate** text box, enter the modem speed you want to use. If you have a 14,400 bps modem, try entering 19,200.

18. If your service provider's system supports a *hardware handshake,* also known as *hardware flow control* (a method for two modems to keep synchronized during transmissions), check the **Hardware Handshake** check box. Also, if your modem does not use hardware handshake as the default, you need to turn it on in the login script. See your modem's documentation for information for the correct command.

19. If you have a CSLIP connection, check the **Van Jacobsen CSLIP Compression** check box.

20. If your modem can use DCD (Data Carrier Detect) or DSR (Data Set Ready), click on the appropriate **Online Status** option button. These are methods that modems use to tell a program their on-line status. You may need to turn on the feature if it is not the modem's default. In the script, you would have to use the modem command for turning it on (generally, AT&C1 for DCD and AT&S1 for DSR).

21. Click on the **OK** button. You'll see a message telling you to restart Trumpet Winsock.

22. Click on the **OK** button in the message box; then select **File|Exit** to close Trumpet Winsock.

23. Reopen **Trumpet Winsock**.

Whew! You made it. But no, the TCP/IP hell week isn't over yet. It's time to set up your login script. Read on.

Script Writing 101

It's time to write (or, at least edit) the script that Trumpet Winsock will follow when connecting. First, find the sample login session you recorded earlier in this chapter (remember, I told you to log on using Windows Terminal or another such program). Then select **Dialler|Edit Scripts** in Trumpet Winsock. A typical File Open dialog box appears. Double-click on the **login.cmd** file, and the login script appears in a Notepad window. Here's the script you'll see:

```
# initialize modem
#
output atz\13
input 10 OK\n
#
# set modem to indicate DCD
#
output at&c1
input 10 OK\n
#
# send phone number
#
output atdt242284\13
#
# my other number
#
#output atdt241644\13
#
# now we are connected.
#
input 30 CONNECT
#
```

```
# wait till it's safe to send because some modems hang up
# if you transmit during the connection phase
#
  wait 30 dcd
#
# now prod the terminal server
#
    output \13
#
# wait for the username prompt
#
input 30 username:
username Enter your username
output \u\13
#
# and the password
#
input 30 password:
password Enter your password
output \p\13
#
# we are now logged in
#
input 30 >
#
# see who's on for informational reasons.
#
output who\13
input 30 >
#
# jump into slip mode
#
output slip\13
#
# wait for the address string
#
input 30 Your address is
#
# parse address
```

continues

continued

```
#
address 30
input 30 \n
#
# we are now connected, logged in, and in slip mode.
#
display \n
display Connected.  Your IP address is \i.\n
#
#  ping a well known host locally...  our slip server won't work
#  for a while
#
exec pingw 131.217.10.1
#
# now we are finished.
```

All the lines that begin with # are simply comment lines: they don't do anything. Let's break down the script, piece by piece.

output atz\13   First, at the top, you have the initial message sent to the modem. The line means "send the ATZ command." This command resets the modem, clearing out any settings that it may have picked up from an earlier communications session. (\13 means "send a carriage return," the same as pressing **Enter** or **Return**.)

input 10 OK\n   This means "wait 10 seconds to see if the modem sends the OK signal back." OK means that it's ready to receive more commands.

output at&c1   This is a message being sent to the modem; at&c1 turns on the Data Carrier Detect feature of your modem, if available. DCD sends a signal to the program when connecting to or disconnecting from another modem. In some cases, you may have to modify this line, if your modem can't seem to connect to the service provider's. If so, talk with the service provider's technical support about what you should use.

input 10 OK\n   Again, the script waits for up to ten seconds for the modem to respond.

output atdt242284\13   This line sends the telephone number to the modem; the modem dials the number. Replace the number (after the **t** and before the \) with the number you need to dial to connect to your service provider. If you need to add a number to get an outside line, precede the phone number with that number and a comma or two for a pause, for example, **9,,5551212**. If you are dialing long distance, include all the necessary numbers (such as **18005551212**). If you have call waiting on the line you are using, use the correct code to turn it off, along with a comma or two to create a pause (usually ***70** as in **9,,*70,,5551212**).

 # my other number and **#output atdt241644\13**   This is a sample script, and below where you change your telephone number is space for an additional number, in case the first is busy. If you have two numbers, place the second number in this space. Remember to remove the **#** sign from the start of the line.

input 30 CONNECT   The script now waits up to 30 seconds for the message from the modem informing the program that it has connected to the other modem. That message is, for most modems, CONNECT, so it's unlikely that you will have to change this line.

wait 30 dcd   This tells the script to wait for 30 seconds, to make sure you fully connect before continuing. When you've established a connection for the first time, you may want to experiment with this number, to reduce it and speed up your connection time. The **dcd** at the end of the line means "wait for a Data Carrier Detect single from the modem." You can remove this if you want.

output \13   This is a sample script, and the way your service provider's system works will probably differ from this sample system. In this sample, after connecting, a user has to press **Enter** to send a carriage return to get the host's "attention." This line sends the carriage return. Your system may not require this.

input 30 username: This line tells the script to wait for up to 30 seconds for the **username** prompt. Your system may not have such a prompt, though. The prompt may be **login:**, for example. If so, replace the word **username** with **login:**.

username Enter your username   This line tells Trumpet Winsock to display a dialog box at this point. The dialog box will say, "Enter your username." (You can change that to "login", if you want.) You will have to type your name and then press **Enter**.

95

Make sure you enter the text exactly like it appears on the screen. If your service provider's system displays the word *username*, don't enter **Username** or **USERNAME**. The case of each letter must be correct. If there's a colon at the end of the word, include that. Make sure you don't add any spaces after the word.

You wouldn't want to break the first rule of security—*Don't write down your password!*—would you?

If you would rather have the script enter your username automatically, remove this line.

output \u\13   This tells the script to send the username you typed into the dialog box. If you removed the previous line, though, you should replace the **\u** with your username, leaving a space between **output** and your username. For example, **output pkent\13**.

input 30 password: This time we're waiting for the password. Same warning applies; make sure you get the case of the prompt correct (Password or password or PASSWORD). Include a colon if necessary; don't add extra spaces.

password Enter your password   Again, this tells the program to display a dialog box into which you can type your password. If you don't want to type it—if you want to automatically send your password—remove this line.

output \p\13   This tells the script to send the password you just entered. If you deleted the previous line, you must use your actual password, replacing the **\p**. For example, **output** *password*\13.

input 30 >   This tells the program to wait for the > prompt. There's a good chance that your system won't display a > prompt. (In a moment, I'll show you what my script does after the password.)

output who\13   This line sends the word **who**, to run the UNIX **who** command (which shows you who is logged on).

input 30 >   Again, we're waiting for the > prompt.

output slip\13   Now we send the word **slip**, the command that puts the system into slip mode.

input 30 Your address is   We're waiting here for the words **Your address is**. That's the line where the service provider tells you your IP address.

address 30   This means "take a look at the IP address that's about to be sent, and store the address."

input 30 \n   This says, "wait for the IP address."

display \n   This says, "display a carriage return and line feed on the screen." That is, move all the previous text up a line.

display Connected. Your IP address is \i.\n   This says "display the words **Connected. Your IP address is**," followed by the IP address that has just been stored, followed by a carriage return and line feed. The term **\i** is the IP address that has been stored. **\n** is a carriage return and line feed.

exec pingw 131.217.10.1   This executes the **pingw** program, which automatically pings another site for verification that you are up and running. You should remove this; it's really not essential.

My Sample Script

I modified the script we just looked at so it would work on my system. Here's what I ended up with:

```
output ATZ&H1\13
input 10 OK\n
output atdt7582656\13
input 45 CONNECT
input 30 sername:
output kent\13
input 30 ssword:
output not.my-real-password\13
input 30 continue
output slip\13
input 30 Your address is
address 30
input 30 \n
display \n
display Connected.  Your IP address is \i.\n
```

This is similar to the sample script we just looked at. Notice these differences, though:

output ATZ&H1\13   I changed this line and used the commands advised by my service provider. This tells my modem to use hardware flow control.

input 30 sername: Notice that I have **sername** instead of **username**. This is common practice in the writing of such scripts, just in case the case of the word is changed (from Username to username or vice versa).

output kent\13   Notice that I'm not using the dialog box to ask for my username, I'm entering it automatically.

input 30 ssword: Again, I've knocked off the first letter (okay, the first two, so I didn't upset anyone) of the prompt the program is looking for.

output not.my-real-password\13   Okay, so I'm breaking a security rule by putting my password in here instead of making Trumpet Winsock prompt me for it. I live in a concrete bunker with one door and no windows and I never leave home, so I figure I'm safe.

input 30 continue   My service provider's system prompts me to "Type 'c' followed by <RETURN> to continue." Instead, I have to type **slip** and continue to get into slip mode.

Now Let's See If It Works...

Save your login script. Then select **Dialler|Login** and the script begins. You can follow through, and if you run into any problems, you can figure out more or less where in the script the problem lies. If you reach the **Script completed   SLIP ENABLED** lines, you've succeeded. You are logged in with your SLIP account running (see the figure on the following page). However, if your script just hangs up, you'll need to log out. First, press **Esc**. Then select **Dialler|Bye**. This runs the BYE.CMD script, which tells your modem to hang up. (You may have to try several times to close the script.)

Go examine your script and see where it hung. If you can't find anything obvious, check all your Trumpet Winsock configuration settings, too. Try a different baud rate, perhaps. Make sure you entered the correct IP addresses. Check the script for spelling errors.

If you still can't get it working, talk with your service provider. Maybe you need a particular modem setup. You may need to change the Packet Vectors in the Network Configuration dialog box. You may need to use the **bootp** command somewhere in the script. Your service provider should be able to tell you exactly how to set up your script and configuration. If you register Trumpet Winsock, you can contact the program's publisher for technical support.

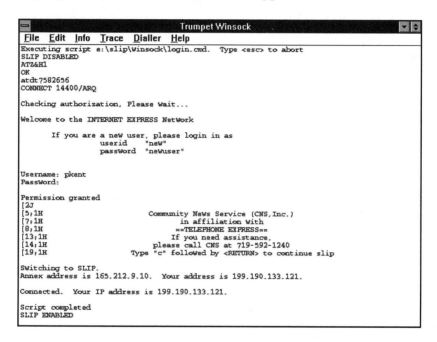

Logging into my SLIP account with Trumpet Winsock.

Getting Out of Cyberspace

To close Trumpet Winsock, first make sure you close all your other TCP/IP programs: your FTP program, your e-mail program, and so on. Then use this method to close:

 If you don't have the **Automatic login and logout on demand** option set, and you close the window without using **Dialler|Bye** first, Trumpet Winsock will close but will not hang up the connection. Your Internet TCP/IP programs won't be able to run without Trumpet Winsock, even though you are connected to the service provider. Reopen Trumpet Winsock, press **Esc** a couple of times, select **Dialler|Bye**, and then close the window.

➤ Use the **Dialler|Bye** command to run the BYE.CMD script, which hangs up the modem.

If you have the **Automatic login and logout on demand** option set (explained later in this chapter), you can also use these options:

➤ Double-click on Trumpet Winsock's **Control** menu.

➤ Press **Alt-F4**.

➤ Select **File|Exit**.

If you have any TCP/IP programs running, you'll see a warning message. Also, you'll find that in some circumstances Trumpet Winsock can't close. You'll have to press **Esc** first, then use one of the above methods to close.

Some More Details Before We Leave

There are a few more things to know about Trumpet Winsock. Let's look at some of the other menu options.

Edit|Copy   Highlight text in the Trumpet Winsock window, and then select this option to copy it to the Clipboard. This can be very useful when using the Trace menu commands, if you understand what the text means.

Edit|Clear   Clears all the text from the window.

Info   This isn't in the current Trumpet Winsock documentation. It gives you some sort of strange network stuff. See *Trace*.

Trace|all sorts of weird stuff   This has a variety of options that you can use to diagnose network connection problems. If you understand what all the terms on the menu mean, you'll know how to use them. If you don't, leave them alone; they can crash the system in some cases.

Dialler|Bye   Runs the BYE.CMD script, which hangs up the modem.

Dialler|Other   You can create other types of scripts that run from this option. For instance, if you have two SLIP accounts, you could run one with the **Dialler|Login** menu option and the other from **Dialler|Other**.

Dialler|Options   This is handy. Select **Automatic login on start-up only** to run the LOGIN.CMD script each time you start the Trumpet Winsock application. Select **Automatic login and logout on demand** to automatically run the script when you start the application, and to close Trumpet Winsock automatically after the **SLIP inactivity timeout (minutes)** value. For instance, let's say this value is 5. That means that if you go for five minutes without a TCP/IP program running, Trumpet Winsock will close automatically. It does not mean that if you have a TCP/IP program open and don't use it for five minutes Trumpet Winsock will close—only if there are no such programs open. Also, when you have **Automatic login and logout on demand** selected, closing the Trumpet Winsock window will automatically run the BYE.CMD script, hanging up the phone. (If you want to use this feature but not the inactivity timeout, put 0 in the **SLIP inactivity timeout** text box.)

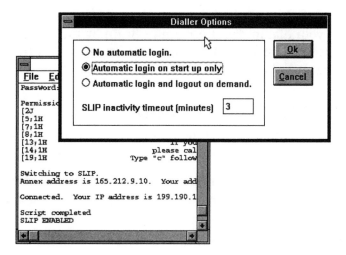

The Dialler Options dialog box lets you automatically start and close Trumpet Winsock.

Dialler|Manual Login   Lets you log into your SLIP account manually, by typing commands into the window. Press **Esc** to end this mode.

Help|About   Displays the Trumpet Winsock version number.

Be Ethical—Register the Program!

If you use Trumpet Winsock for 30 days or more, please register it. You receive a registration number that will remove the UNREGISTERED VERSION signs that appear here and there. You'll also get technical support, and Trumpet Software International says that it will give registered users preference for requests for bug fixes and enhancements.

Working on the Internet with a dial-in terminal account is like writing a book with a typewriter. Working on the Internet once you have Trumpet Winsock installed is like writing a book with a word processor. Pay the registration fee. (See the end of the INSTALL.TXT or INSTALL.DOC file that came with Trumpet Winsock.)

Where Next?

Once you have your Trumpet Winsock up and running, all you have to do is run your dial-in direct programs. Begin by finding and loading WS_FTP (see Chapter 27). Then learn how to use it so you can grab one of the great Web browsers just waiting for you.

The Least You Need to Know

➤ Don't be intimidated. Installing Trumpet Winsock can be relatively easy if you follow these instructions.

➤ You need a login script to automate your connection to your service provider. It's reasonably easy to create one—with patience.

➤ This program is shareware; remember to register it (it only costs $20).

➤ Once Trumpet Winsock is up and running, get WS_FTP; then you're ready to get your Web browser.

## Chapter 11

TCP/IP for You and Me: Macintosh Connections

> **In This Chapter**
>
> ➤ Finding the software you need
>
> ➤ Extracting from archive files
>
> ➤ Installing MacTCP
>
> ➤ Installing MacPPP

Most of the really nice Web browsers require a dial-in direct or permanent connection to the Internet. If you are not working with a large company or organization that provides you with a network connection to the Internet, that means you'll need to sign up for a SLIP or PPP account if you want to run InternetWorks, Mosaic, Netscape, Cello, or one of the other new browsers. (Okay, there are exceptions, as we'll see in a moment.) Unfortunately, you may find it difficult to set up these accounts. It's not just a matter of running a short setup program to load the program onto your hard disk; there's important information that you must enter to tell the program how to run.

If you want to use a Macintosh browser, don't worry. True, there aren't nearly as many Mac browsers as there are Windows browsers. However, you can still get a free one—you can use Mosaic, MacWeb, or Netscape—you'll learn about these in Chapter 15. But first, you have to install your TCP/IP connection.

Now, the information from Chapter 10 about TIA applies to you, too; you can install TIA on your service provider's system and then run the Mac TCP/IP software connected to TIA. You still have to set up your Mac as if you were going to connect to a real SLIP or PPP account first.

There's a catch to setting up a TCP/IP connection, though. You need TCP/IP software, plenty of which is available online, but you can't get to it unless you have a connection to the Internet. If you already have a dial-in terminal connection to the Internet, no problem. Use that connection to get all the software you need, and then install it and change over to your TCP/IP connection. If you don't have an Internet connection, it's more complicated.

Many service providers give their subscribers both dial-in terminal and dial-in direct (TCP/IP) connections at the same time, for one price. This, it seems to me, is the ideal. You can use your dial-in terminal account (often known as a "shell" account) to grab your software; then switch to your dial-in direct account. So when you shop for a dial-in direct account, ask if you'll get a dial-in terminal account, too. (Be careful, though; some service providers will be happy to give you both accounts but will charge extra!)

 Never used basic dial-in terminal connection to the Internet? Don't know how to use FTP? Take a look at *The Complete Idiot's Guide to the Internet* for a back-to-basics introduction to the Internet.

If you don't have a connection and will be getting a dial-in direct account but no dial-in terminal account, you have a problem. Ask your service provider how you can get the software (this chapter tells you what software you need); perhaps they can send you a disk. You can also ask a friend to get it for you or look for it on local bulletin boards.

Anyway, I can't help you with this little problem. So I'm going to move on to explaining how to install a Macintosh TCP/IP connection. (And I'll assume you have some kind of terminal connection from which you can download the software you need.)

You can't just install TCP/IP software and then connect to your service provider; they have to set up a SLIP, CSLIP, or PPP account for you first. Call and ask about it.

What Is All This Stuff?

As with PC software, you'll find that most Macintosh software on the Internet is not stored in its normal, executable format. That is, you can't just download it and run it. The three most common formats are *filename*.**sea**, *filename*.**sit**, and *filename*.**hqx**. Yes, that's right, file extensions. This may be Mac software, but you'll find that on bulletin boards it's often stored with DOS-style filenames; up to eight characters in the name, a period, followed by a three-character "extension." (On some Mac bulletin boards and FTP sites, it will be stored with more Mac-like names.)

Anyway, what are these three file types? The **.sea** files are "self-extracting archives." Place the file on your Mac desktop, double-click on it, and the compressed files within will be "extracted" automatically. The **.sit** files are StuffIt files, which are files that have been compressed using a StuffIt program (but not converted into self-extracting archives). In order to extract these you'll need a program such as StuffIt Expander, StuffIt Deluxe, DropStuff, or another such program—they are usually shareware.

Some Macintosh communications programs have this stuff built in, so when you transfer files, they are automatically converted from the .sit or .hqx format to their original format. The *Fetch* FTP program, for instance, automatically converts these files when it downloads them.

The **.hqx** files are *BinHex* files, the equivalent of uuencoded files, which are files converted to ASCII format so they can be sent across the Internet via e-mail. The files then have to be converted back to their original format, using a utility such as StuffIt Expander or Compact Pro.

There are other formats you may run into. There are files with the **.ins** extension, for instance. These are installer files; double-click on them and they install a program. Then there's the **.cpt** extension (files compressed using Compact Pro); they can be uncompressed by Compact Pro or StuffIt Expander. This whole Macintosh file-extension thing can get very confusing. I thought Macs were supposed to be *easier* than PCs!

Track down one of these utilities. You should be able to find them somewhere on your service provider's system, on local bulletin boards, or on many FTP sites. Look for one with the **.sea** or **.ins** extension, so you can just double-click on the file to get started.

Now you can look for the TCP software you need and convert it to the format it has to be in to run. Simply drag the **.sit** or **.hqx** file onto the utility, and it will convert the file to the correct format.

Building the Foundation—MacTCP

Now, let's get on with it. First, you need something called MacTCP. This is produced by Apple. If you have a Macintosh with System 7.5, then you have MacTCP (there's an incentive for you to upgrade, eh?— it's about $90). If you are using an earlier operating system, you'll have

For information on finding the software mentioned in this chapter, see Chapter 27.

to find MacTCP elsewhere. Some Macintosh Internet books have it, though it's not the latest version and doesn't come with full documentation. If it's a good book, that shouldn't be a problem. Otherwise, you can buy it from an Apple dealer (you need *TCP/IP Connection for Macintosh*, which is around $100, so you may as well just upgrade to System 7.5!).

Loading MacTCP

MacTCP is not loaded automatically when you install System 7.5. It's on the installation disks, but you'll have to use the Custom Install to get to it. Follow these instructions:

1. Place the first installation disk in the disk drive. The Mac will load the disk. You'll see the Installer in the Install Disk 1 window open on your desktop.

2. Double-click on the **Installer** icon to start the program.

3. When you see the Welcome to System 7.5 window, click on the **Continue** button.

4. When the System 7.5 Installation window opens, select **Custom Install** from the pop-up menu in the top right of the window. Your window will list the different components that you can install.

5. Click on the triangle to the left of the **Networking Software** entry, and the networking options will appear.

6. Click on the **MacTCP** entry (see the following figure).

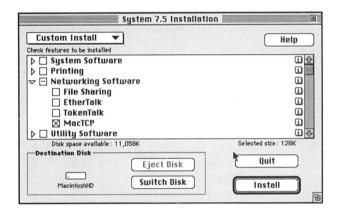

Select MacTCP in the System 7.5 Installation window.

7. Click on the **Install** button and the program begins installing MacTCP. Follow the instructions.

If you don't have System 7.5, follow the instructions that come with the MacTCP program. The MacTCP program will appear in the Control Panels folder.

Now for the Walls—MacPPP

Now that you have MacTCP built, you need to add a PPP or SLIP program. Remember, you can use TCP/IP on a network or on a dial-in line. MacTCP provides the basic TCP/IP interface, but not the dial-in stuff—the SLIP and PPP dialer. So you'll have to get another program. I'm using MacPPP, freeware from Merit Network Inc., at the University of Minnesota, and there's a program called InterSLIP, also freeware, from a company called InterCon.

Let's take a look at how to work with MacPPP. If you are using an operating system earlier than System 7.5, the procedure may be slightly different; carefully read the documentation that comes with the program.

If you are using System 6.x, place both icons in the System folder.

1. Place the PPP icon in the Extensions folder (inside your System folder).

2. Place the ConfigPPP icon in the Control Panel folder (inside your System folder).

3. Reboot your machine.

4. Open the MacTCP program; double-click on the MacTCP icon in the Control Panel folder, or select **Control Panels|MacTCP** from the Apple menu.

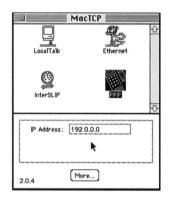

The MacTCP Control Panel, showing the PPP icon.

5. When the MacTCP Control Panel opens, click on the **PPP** icon. Then click on the **More** button to see the box in the following figure.

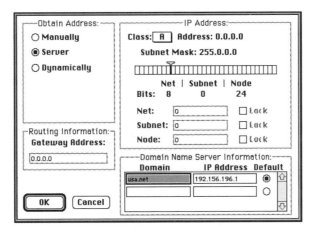

Here's where you set up the MacTCP Control Panel.

You need to talk to your service provider about these items. Call and talk to your service provider's technical support line while you have the program in front of you. Make sure you get through to someone knowledgeable about TCP/IP connections!

6. Select the **Server** radio button under the **Obtain Address** options. This tells that program that your service provider's system will assign an IP (Internet Protocol) number to you when you log on.

It's unlikely that you will have to select **Manually** or **Dynamically**. The local server you are dialing into will normally assign you an IP number. (If your service provider tells you that you *do* need to use the **Manually** option, you'll have to click on the **Config** button in the Config PPP Control Panel—which we'll look at later—then on the IPCP button, and enter an IP Address.)

7. In the **IP Address** area of the box, select the correct **Class** (your service provider should be able to tell you which one).

8. In the **Domain** column, near the bottom of the box, type your service provider's domain name: usa.net, cscns.com, csn.org, or whatever.

9. In the box next to the domain name you just entered, type your service provider's nameserver IP number.

10. Make sure the **Default** radio button is selected next to your entry, and then click on the **OK** button.

109

11. Close the MacTCP Control Panel.

12. Open the Config PPP Control Panel.

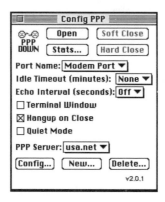

The Config PPP Control Panel.

13. Select the correct **Port Name** for the modem you have installed (you will generally select the **Modem Port** entry).

14. Select the **Hangup on Close** check box, but clear the Terminal Window and Quiet Mode.

The Terminal Window check box tells the program to let you run a manual login. You'll see a window into which you have to type all the commands; then click on the **OK** button when it appears that the connection is complete (it's not always obvious, though). We're turning the Terminal Window *off*, because we're going to create a script that will log on automatically.

15. At the **PPP Server** pop-up menu, select the domain you entered into the MacTCP Control Panel.

16. Click on the **Config** button.

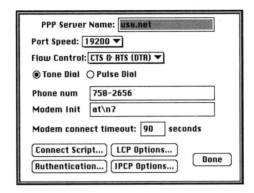

Here's where you set up your PPP connection.

17. Select the **Port Speed** for your modem. If you are using a 14,400 modem, select 19,200.

18. Select the **Flow Control** method advised by your service provider.

19. Make sure the correct dialing-method radio button is selected; in most cases it will be **Tone Dial**.

20. Under **Phone num**, type the phone number you have to dial to connect to your service provider. Remember to include **9**, if that's what you dial to get an outside line. Include ***70** to turn off call waiting (or whatever code is used in your area), if necessary.

21. Under **Modem Init**, enter the correct modem initialization string. This may be as simple as ATZ. Take a look at other communications programs that you've used to connect to your service provider, to see what initialization string they use (if you're not sure), or talk with the service provider's technical support people.

22. Click on the **Connect Script** button. You'll see the box (it will look like the box in the figure on the next page) where you have to tell the program what it will see when it connects to your service provider. Call and ask them what prompts they send and the necessary responses.

```
┌─────────────────────────────────────────────────┐
│  Wait timeout: │60    │ seconds                   │
│                                              <CR> │
│  ○ Out ⦿ Wait  │Username:                     │ □ │
│  ⦿ Out ○ Wait  │pkent                         │ ⊠ │
│  ○ Out ⦿ Wait  │Password:                     │ □ │
│  ⦿ Out ○ Wait  │%^hg81we                      │ ⊠ │
│  ○ Out ⦿ Wait  │continue                      │ □ │
│  ⦿ Out ○ Wait  │ppp                           │ ⊠ │
│  ⦿ Out ○ Wait  │                              │ □ │
│  ⦿ Out ○ Wait  │                              │ □ │
│                          ┌────────┐  ┌────────┐   │
│                          │ Cancel │  │   OK   │   │
│                          └────────┘  └────────┘   │
└─────────────────────────────────────────────────┘
```

Here's where you create your login script.

Creating the Script

Look at the script box carefully. Notice that next to each box are two radio buttons: **Out** and **Wait**. You are going to enter information that will tell the program what to expect to see when you log onto your service provider's system, and then tell it what to send in response. Each line that is a system prompt (something the computer is waiting to see) has the **Wait** radio button selected. Each line that the program has to send to your service provider has the **Out** radio button selected.

In the preceding figure, you can see that we begin by waiting for the prompt *Username:* (make sure you enter this in the correct case). If you are not sure if it starts with an uppercase U, you can simply enter **sername:**. (Of course if *your* prompt is different, such as *Login:*, for instance, enter that.)

In response to the *Username:* prompt, I send my login name, pkent. Then we wait for the *Password:* prompt, and I send my password. Next we wait for the word *continue* (because my service provider sends the line Type "c" followed by <RETURN> to continue). If I type **c**, I go into my shell account. If I type **ppp**, though, I start my PPP connection.

Notice also the <CR> column. For each of the outgoing boxes, you'll normally check the <CR> check box. This simply means, "send this text and then send a carriage return," which is the same as pressing the **Return** key.

Now, close the script and return to the ConfigPPP dialog box. Click on the **Open** button and your system will start to dial.

You'll see a small message box showing your progress. When you see the "PPP Phase: Establishment" and "Network" messages and the message box then disappears, you'll know you are connected.

Done! You're up and running!

To close your PPP session, you'll use the **Soft Close** or **Hard Close** buttons in the Config PPP Control Panel. **Soft Close** disconnects the modem, but leaves your applications "connected;" that is, when you restart your PPP connection, you should find that applications are connected to the same Internet sites they were when you closed. (You might use this method if you have a modem problem.) **Hard Close** disconnects your application's connections to whatever tools you were using *and then* disconnects the modem.

Still can't get the system running? Read the documentation carefully, and try to find someone in your service provider's tech support who will tell you exactly what to enter where.

Now What? Go Shareware Hunting!

Once you have your PPP (or SLIP) connection up and running, you need one more thing: a good FTP program. The PPP or SLIP connection does nothing for you without a program that will run across the connection. The first program you'll probably want is a program that helps you get all the neat software you can find on the Internet (in particular a Web browser, of course).

First, get a program such as *Fetch*; this will let you run FTP sessions across your PPP or SLIP connection (start the connection and then run Fetch). How are you going to

Once you have your TCP/IP applications installed (programs such as Fetch, Mosaic, MacWeb, and so on), you don't need to use the MacPPP Control Panel to start your connection. Simply start the application you want to use, and it will start MacPPP for you.

get Fetch? Well, ask your service provider where you can find it online, or see Chapter 27 for information. You'll still have to use a normal terminal connection to your service provider to get the software. Once you have Fetch, though, you can kiss the terminal connection goodbye, go grab your Web browser (see Chapter 15), and move on.

The Least You Need to Know

➤ Get MacTCP; it's bundled with the System 7.5 operating system.

➤ You'll also need MacPPP, InterSLIP, or another shareware program to make the connection.

➤ Once you have your Mac connection running, get Fetch, an FTP program.

Part 4
The Browser Catalog

Browsers, browsers, everywhere. If you've finished Part 3 of the book, you'll know how to set up your connection to the Internet. Once you've done that, you have a plethora of browser choices. But, no browser can do everything. Some browsers are better at one thing; others are better at another.

You may find that you want two or more browsers on your system. I like InternetWorks and Netscape—they're both excellent browsers. Cello and InterAp's Web Navigator are useful because they let you save documents to your hard disk. Slipknot is handy if you want to use a graphical browser or a terminal connection. Read on and try them out!

## Chapter 12

A Window on the World: Viewers and Helpers

In This Chapter

➤ Displaying various file formats in a browser

➤ Using internal and external viewers

➤ Installing viewers for Mosaic—on Windows and the Mac

➤ Installing viewers for InternetWorks

➤ Installing viewers for Netscape

➤ Finding more viewers

Once you have your browser installed, you can wander all over the Web, clicking here, clicking there, reading this, listening to that... or can you? Well, you can always do the basics (read the Web documents), but in order to work with some of the fancier stuff, you may have to install some more programs.

Browsers use what are known as *viewers* (sometimes called *external viewers* or *helpers*). These are programs that can display or run file types that the browser itself can't deal with, such as sounds, video, specialized graphic formats, and so on.

It May Be There Already! Built-In File Support

Each browser is different, of course. As you've already learned, there are two basic types of browsers:

➤ Text-based browsers, which can display the text in the HTML documents but can't display any images.

➤ Graphical browsers, which can display the text and include the inline .GIF and .XBM pictures (as we'll see in Chapter 19).

Within this second group, there are more variations. Some graphical browsers have built-in support for other file formats. InternetWorks, for instance, has built-in support for these file formats:

.JPEG and .JPG   A compressed image file, common for storing large color pictures and photographs.

.GIF   An image format common in the PC and Mac world.

.XBM   An image format common in the UNIX world.

.BMP   A Windows bitmap.

.WAV   A Windows sound file.

.AU   A sound file common in the UNIX world.

In other words, if you transfer one of these files from the Web back to InternetWorks, the program will display or play the file for you.

You can see in the following figure the pages shown after transferring a .WAV file and a .BMP file from my WINDOWS directory (using the **File|Open Local File** command). In the first case, InternetWorks transferred the file, played the sound, and displayed a sound icon and filename; in the second case, it displayed the picture. (You'll learn how to split the InternetWorks window like this in Chapter 18.)

Other graphical browsers may not be so helpful. They will display HTML and any text files they find, and they'll display inline images, but they won't display other formats, or even let you open .GIF files directly (most inline images are .GIFs). For instance, Mosaic won't play a .WAV file for you or load a .BMP bitmap. (It *will*, however, play an .AU sound file.)

The sound plays...

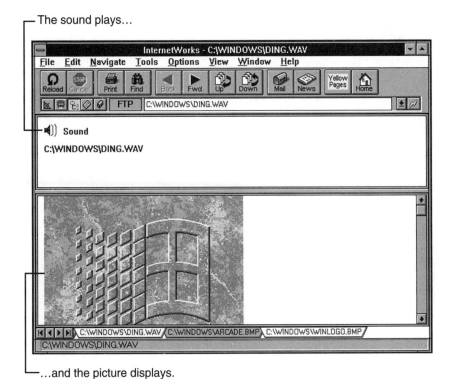

...and the picture displays.

InternetWorks supports .WAV and .BMP files, among others.

When Your Browser Needs Some Help: Using Viewers

Most graphical browsers will let you tell them what to do with files they can't handle. In other words, you find a program that can run videos, play sounds, or display certain file formats, and then you tell the browser where the program is located and which file types should be sent to it.

You almost certainly already have viewers for various file types. For instance, Microsoft Windows comes with Multimedia Player, an application that will play sound files (.WAV), MS Multimedia Movie files (.MMM), Musical Instrument Digital Interface files, known as "MIDI" (.MID and .RMI), and video files (.AVI). Windows also comes with Paintbrush, which will display .PCX (a common bitmap format),

.BMP (a Windows bitmap), .MSP (Microsoft Paint, an early bitmap), and .DIB files (a special Windows "device independent bitmap" format).

 IBM did a really nice job with the OS/2 Warp WebExplorer; all the viewers are included and preconfigured for you. If WebExplorer comes across a file format it can't handle, it sends it on to one of the OS/2 Multimedia pack applications.

You may have added other programs that you can use, too. For instance, if you have loaded a good graphics program that lets you open .BMP, .JPG (JPEG), .CGM, .DRW, .TIF, and other graphics files, you can tell your browser to use this program for those files. If you've loaded a Windows file-compression program such as WinZIP, you can tell your browser to send all .ZIP files to that application.

But if you don't have viewers for some file types, you may be able to find them online—I'll tell you where in a moment. First, though, let's look at how to configure viewers.

Viewers in Mosaic

Mosaic is not as helpful as InternetWorks. To configure viewers for this program, you'll have to fiddle around in the MOSAIC.INI file, which is probably in your WINDOWS directory. Open this file in a text editor such as Notepad. Go down to the [Viewers] section of this file, and you'll find that a number of formats have been defined. For instance, you'll see this:

```
[Viewers]
TYPE0="audio/wav"
TYPE1="application/postscript"
TYPE2="image/gif"
TYPE3="image/jpeg"
TYPE4="video/mpeg"
```

These are the file types, but you don't really need to worry too much about these. Further down in this section, you'll find a piece that starts like this:

```
application/postscript="ghostview %ls"
image/gif="c:\windows\apps\lview\lview31 %ls"
image/jpeg="c:\windows\apps\lview\lview31 %ls"
video/mpeg="c:\winapps\mpegplay\mpegplay %ls"
```

Mosaic has made some assumptions about these (and other) file types. It's assuming, for instance, that you have the LVIEW31 graphics viewer in the C:\WINDOWS\APPS\LVIEW\ directory. All you need to do is change this path (and, if necessary, the filename) to show where LVIEW32 is, or if you are not using that program, where the one you *do* want to use can be found.

Further down in the MOSAIC.INI file, you'll find the [Suffixes] section, with entries like these:

```
application/postscript=.ps,.eps,.ai,.ps
application/zip=.zip
video/qtime=.mov
video/msvideo=.avi
```

This section tells Mosaic what each file extension is. For instance, it says that a file that ends with .PS, .EPS, .AI, or .PS is a PostScript file. If you look further up in the [Viewers] section, you'll find this line:

```
application/postscript="ghostview %ls"
```

This tells Mosaic to send PostScript files to the Ghostview program (you can replace **ghostview** with the correct path and filename).

Helpers in Mosaic for the Mac

Mosaic for the Macintosh is, true to form, easier to set up than the Windows version. Instead of messing around in a text file, you'll open the Preferences dialog box, and then click on the **Helper applications** button to see the Helper Configuration box. This works more like InternetWorks; you have to select or add an extension and document type and then tell Mosaic which program to use.

121

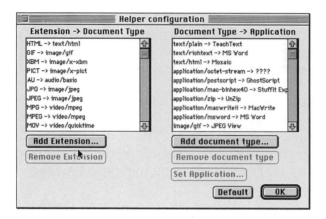

Setting up helpers (the Mac Mosaic term for viewers).

If you look at the picture, you'll see that there are two list boxes. We'll work first with the one on the left, **Extension -> Document Type**. Click on the **Add Extension** button to see another box in which you can type a file extension, and then select one of the MIME file types. For instance, you could type **1ST** (as in README.1ST) and then select the **text/plain** MIME type. So when Mosaic transferred a README.1ST file, it would assume that it was text. The second list box, **Document Type -> Application**, is where you define which program is used to open the files. After you've created the new extension, click on the **Set Application** button to associate the new extension with a program.

Setting Up Your Viewers in InternetWorks

To begin setting up your viewers in InternetWorks, select **Options|Viewers**. You'll see the External Viewer Configuration dialog box.

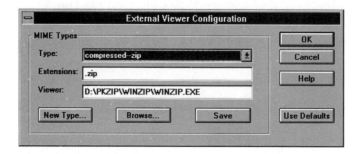

Setting up InternetWorks' external viewers.

You can see that the first option (**Type**) contains a drop-down list box. Open this list, and you'll see that it contains file types: text/plain, text/html, image/gif, image/jpeg, image/x-bitmap, and so on. Select one of these, and in the Extensions box, you'll see the file extensions for this type of file. For example, if you select **image/x-tiff** in the Type box, you'll see **.tif,*.tiff**. This is for the TIFF image format; on PCs, it uses the .TIF extension, on other systems, it uses .TIFF.

If you'd rather send one of the file formats that InternetWorks can handle to a different application, you can do so. For instance, you could define Windows Paintbrush as the program to launch when InternetWorks downloads a .BMP file.

In the **Viewer** box, you'll see the path and filename of the program you want to send this file to. Well, right now the Viewer box will be empty. That's okay for several of these formats, anyway—remember, InternetWorks can handle .WAV, .AU, .BMP, .GIF, .JPG and .JPEG files, without any help.

Here's a quick way to check if a viewer's working. Use the **File|Open Local File** command to open a file of that format from your hard disk; it will work in just the same way as it would if you transferred it from the Web.

For the other programs, you'll have to enter your own viewer. Let's take a look at the **application/rtf** format, for instance. This is the .RTF, Rich Text Format, a word processing format that many Windows word processors can open. I have Word for Windows, so I can define Word as the program to open, as you can see in the following illustration. I can either type the path and name into the Viewer box, or I can use the **Browse** button to see the typical Windows Browse dialog box.

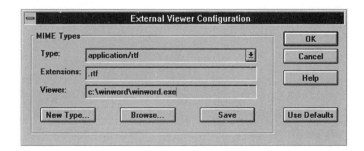

Word for Windows, set up as my .RTF viewer.

So what happens the next time I click on a Web link that takes me to an .RTF file (which, admittedly, isn't very often)? InternetWorks transfers the file to my computer, launches Word for Windows, and opens the .RTF.

Adding a New Viewer to InternetWorks

Let's look at how to create a new reference to a viewer. I want to set up InternetWorks so that if it transfers a .ZIP file—a PKUNZIP compressed file—it automatically opens WinZIP.

First, I click on the **New Type** button. In the New Type dialog box, I type **compressed/zip**, and click on the **OK** button. Then I type **.zip** into the Extensions box, and type **D:\PKZIP\WINZIP\WINZIP.EXE** into the Viewer box (or use the **Browse** button to specify the file). I click on **Save**, and that's it—the viewer's configured.

Helpers in Netscape

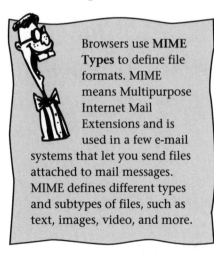

Browsers use **MIME Types** to define file formats. MIME means Multipurpose Internet Mail Extensions and is used in a few e-mail systems that let you send files attached to mail messages. MIME defines different types and subtypes of files, such as text, images, video, and more.

Netscape has a pretty easy way to set up viewers; it even lets you set up viewers "on the fly." That is, when you try to download a file type that Netscape doesn't recognize, you'll see a dialog box asking you if you want to set up a viewer for it.

You can still set up viewers beforehand, though. Select **Options|Preferences**. In the Preferences dialog box, select **Helper Applications** in the drop-down list box at the top. This looks very different from InternetWorks and Mosaic for the Mac's systems, but the principle is the same; you are going to associate a file type with an application.

Netscape lets you select one of four different file-handling options.

To enter a new one, click on the **New** button, and type a Mime Type and Mime Subtype. For instance, you could enter **compressed** and **zip**. (You can get an idea of the types from the list box in the Preferences dialog box; type in any kind of subtype.) Click on **OK**, select the new entry in the list, and then enter the extension into the Extensions text box (**.zip**, for example).

You then have a few options (select the appropriate option button): you can select Prompt User, Save, Launch Application, and, in some cases, Use Mosaic [Netscape] as Viewer. These options affect how a file is handled when Netscape transfers it.

➤ If you select the **Prompt User** option, a dialog box appears when Netscape tries to work with this file type, asking you what to do (you can save directly to disk, cancel the transfer, or configure a viewer).

➤ If you select the **Save** option, files are saved to disk rather than opened in the viewer.

➤ If you select **Launch Application**, the files are opened in the viewer you specify; you'll have to enter the path and filename for the viewer in the text box next to this option.

➤ If you select the **Use Mosaic as Viewer** option, files are loaded into Netscape itself; you could view .GIFs or .XBMs in the browser, for example. This option is available only for file types that Netscape supports.

I Want More—Finding Viewers

Where are you going to find all these viewers? Well, as I mentioned before, you may have some on your system already. Windows and Macs have programs such as Windows Paintbrush, Multimedia Player, Sound Recorder, SimpleText, TeachText, Simple Player, and others. You may have loaded others, too. If you need more, take a look on the Net.

Where Do I Get Windows Viewers?

Try these sites for Windows viewers:

```
http://www.ncsa.uiuc.edu/SDG/Software/WinMosaic/viewers.html
http://www.law.cornell.edu/cello/cellocfg.html
ftp.cica.indiana.edu
```

Also, get the **viewers.zip** file, a bundle of viewers from **ftp.law.cornell.edu** in the **/pub/LII/Cello/** directory (this is from the people who created Cello).

Here are a few freeware and shareware programs you may want to find for Windows:

GhostScript and Ghostview   Display PostScript files.

GV057, WinGIF, WinJPEG, and Lview   Programs that display .GIF and .JPEG graphics files, and others.

VIDVUE   For .MPG and .AVI animation files.

Mpegplay, MFW, and MPEGW   Play MPEG video files.

PC Speaker Driver   A Microsoft driver to play sounds through a computer's speaker.

WHAM   Plays .AU and .AIFF sound files.

Wplany   W-play-any, plays almost any kind of sound file.

Adobe Acrobat Reader   Views and prints .PDF files.

And for the Mac?

For the Macintosh, try these sites:

```
http://www.ncsa.uiuc.edu/SDG/Software/MacMosaic/HelperApps.html
ftp://ftp.ncsa.uiuc.edu/Mosaic/Mac/Helpers
```

You'll find programs such as:

StuffIt Expander and Drop Stuff   Extract compressed files in various formats (also UUDECODEs).

Fast Player   Plays QuickTime movies.

Gif Converter   Displays .GIFs and other formats including JPEG, PICT, TIFF, RIFF, MacPaint, and Thunderscan.

Graphic Converter   Another, more extensive, graphics program.

JPEGView   Displays JPEG files and others.

Sound Machine   Plays various sound files.

Sparkle   Plays several types of movie files.

Adobe Acrobat Reader   Views and prints .PDF files.

The Least You Need to Know

➤ Browsers display some file formats, but not others.

➤ At the least, browsers can display text and HTML documents.

➤ InternetWorks and some other browsers can display .GIF, .XBM, JPEG, and .BMP files, and can play .WAV and .AU sound files.

➤ If a browser can't display or play a file type, you can configure an *external viewer* (sometimes called a *helper*) to handle the file.

➤ You already have programs that can act as viewers— word processors, simple graphics programs, and so on.

➤ You can find plenty of free and shareware viewers online.

My Oh My! Mosaic!

Mosaic has been so incredibly hyped in the press that almost everyone's heard of it… but almost nobody knows what it is. Here are a few misconceptions:

➤ Mosaic is an Internet navigation tool, similar to Chameleon or Internet In a Box. No! Mosaic is specifically a Web browser.

➤ Mosaic is a giant hypertext system with documents all over the world. No! That's the World Wide Web. Mosaic is simply one of many Web browsers.

➤ Mosaic is the best Web browser available. No! There are better commercial and freeware browsers.

➤ Anyone can install and use Mosaic, even on a dial-in terminal account. 'Fraid not. You have to have a very specific setup (we'll get to that in a moment).

➤ Mosaic will make your coffee, sweep your floors, and find you a date. Well, maybe the last, but it *won't* do housework.

There's another misconception: Mosaic is widely used. After all, the NCSA (National Center for Supercomputing Applications) has counted two gazzilion Mosaic downloads, so everyone must be using it, right? I doubt it. There are plenty of downloads of Mosaic for several reasons:

➤ NCSA releases a new version every few weeks, so the people who do have it running, or are trying to get it running, often have several versions.

➤ There are various versions; for Windows, for instance, there's a "released version," a 16-bit alpha version, and a 32-bit alpha version. Users often try out two or three versions.

➤ Users often download Mosaic and then try to load it on their dial-in terminal account—only to find it won't work.

➤ Users often download Mosaic, try to get their dial-in direct account running, and give up in frustration before they ever get around to installing Mosaic.

When you take all this into consideration, you'll probably find there are about 15 Mosaic users in the northern hemisphere, and another two or three in the southern. Let's see if we can remedy that.

So What's It Take?

First, let's consider what it takes to get Mosaic running. We discussed this in Chapter 4, of course, but let's quickly reiterate:

➤ You need a TCP/IP connection to the Internet: a dial-in direct or a permanent connection.

➤ You *cannot* run Mosaic on a simple dial-in terminal connection, so if you get access from a Free-Net or BBS, you probably won't be able to install it.

➤ However, you *can* fool your software into thinking it's on a TCP/IP connection when it's really on a dial-in terminal connection. (To do that, you need The Internet Adapter—see Chapter 9.)

➤ You can get PC and Macintosh versions of Mosaic, as well as the Amiga and X Window (UNIX).

➤ If you are using the Windows version 2.0 alpha 3 or later, you must either run it in Windows NT or Windows 95, *or* install Win32s so that your 16-bit version of Windows (Windows 3.1) can run a 32-bit program.

Installing Mosaic is actually very easy. It's setting up the TCP/IP connection that's the tricky thing. (We've covered that already, in Chapters 9 through 11.) In this and the next chapter, though, we'll take a look at Mosaic, so you can see if it's really the program for you.

For information on finding Mosaic and other programs, see Chapter 27.

Which Version Do You Need?

Mosaic is from the National Center for Supercomputing Applications, the NCSA. This organization has created different versions of Mosaic for different computers and made them available for *free* use, as long as that use is "noncommercial." (So if you employ 500 people and give them all a copy of Mosaic, you're breaking the law.) You don't have to pay to use Mosaic; though if you pay taxes, you've already paid to create it, as it's funded by the National Science Foundation.

There are various flavors of Mosaic:

➤ Microsoft Windows (Windows 3.1, Windows for Workgroups, and Windows NT) on a PC running the Intel 386, 486, or Pentium.

➤ Microsoft Windows NT on a DECpc (which uses the aXP processor).

➤ Microsoft Windows NT on a workstation running the MIPS processor.

➤ The Macintosh—there are two versions: one for the Power Macintosh and one for the plain old Macintosh (anything that runs System 7.x).

➤ Computers running X Window (a UNIX graphical user interface): there are about eight different versions for various different computers.

➤ VMS computers: there's a version from CERN that has been modified to run on these computers.

➤ Amiga: (this version is called *AMosaic*, though it's not published by NCSA).

Want to goof around with Mosaic and create your own version? NCSA will release the source code to any nonprofit academic or government organization promising not to distribute the program commercially. See **http:// www.ncsa.uiuc.edu/SDG/Software/WinMosaic/source.html**.

There's another thing to consider: how stable you want the program to be and how much you're prepared to sacrifice stability for features. Every now and then, the NCSA posts new versions of these programs, but it has three classifications. There's a *released* version, which means they figure it's pretty stable and more or less bug-free (there's no such thing as *completely* bug-free software!). Then there's *beta*, which means the version is pretty much finished, but there are a few rough edges that need smoothing before it's actually "released." Finally, there's the *alpha* version. This means, "Hey, check out these neat new features… but watch out for the bugs!"

The term *released* is a bit misleading; all versions are released in the sense that they can be downloaded from the NCSA site. The "released" version, though, is regarded as the official version. Get one of the others and all bets are off.

However, I'm going to refer to the latest version at the time of writing; for Windows, that's Version 2.0 alpha 7, for the Macintosh, it's Version 2.0 alpha 8. If you use anything earlier, some of the features I describe won't be present.

Windows Has to Be Difficult!

Is anything *ever* simple with Microsoft Windows? Well, in this case it's not! The very latest Mosaic for Windows is a *32-bit* operating system. That means it will run on Windows NT or Windows 95 (both of which are 32-bit operating systems) but, normally, not on Windows 3.1 or Windows for Workgroups 3.11 (which are 16-bit systems). If you have one of these 16-bit systems, you have three options. You can run Mosaic Version 2.0 alpha 2, the last 16-bit version. If you prefer to use the "released" version, you can work with Version 1.0, also a 16-bit version. Or you can install Microsoft Win32s, a special program that fools Mosaic into thinking it's running on a 32-bit system.

What's all this 16-bit and 32-bit stuff? It refers to the way in which data is transferred along a computer's *bus*. (That's simply a piece of hardware that data can be transferred along.) The components in your computer are connected to the bus, so they can pick up data as needed. A 16-bit bus can, not surprisingly, transfer 16-bits of information at a time. A 32-bit bus transfers—yes, you guessed it—32 bits.

There are also three different versions of the 32-bit software because Windows NT runs on several different computers. There's a version for Intel-based PCs (386, 486, or Pentium), for Windows NT running on a DECpc (the Alpha aXP processor), and for Windows NT running on a MIPS workstation.

If you want to install Win32s, look in Chapter 27 for information on where to find it. The installation program is generally quite straightforward. (However, if you have a LaserMaster printer, you'll have to disable the WINSPOOL driver by removing the LMHAROLD.386, LMCAP.386, and LMMI.386 lines from your SYSTEM.INI file before extracting the Win32s files from the archive file. You can put the lines back in once you've installed the Win32s software.)

Is installing Win32s so you can run Mosaic worth it? Personally, I don't think so. Not when you can use Netscape or InternetWorks. Still, if you really *have* to see what Mosaic is all about, carry on. Be warned, though, the word on the Net is that Win32s makes your system a little unstable.

Enough Talk, Let's See It

Enough talk about installing Mosaic. Let's take a look at how to *use* it now, so you can see if it's a program you want to work with, and so we can compare it with more browsers in the next two chapters. The rest

133

of this chapter is based on Mosaic for Windows V2.0a7 (that's short-hand for Version 2.0 alpha 7, okay?). In the following chapter, we'll look at more advanced Mosaic for Windows features and the Macintosh Mosaic V2.0a8.

The Home Page

If you are using Mosaic V2.0a7, you'll see the home page when you start the program. By default, that's set up as one of the NCSA Home Page documents; there's one for Windows, one for the Macintosh, and one for X Window.

Okay, in Chapter 3, I told you that the home page was not the main page at a Web site; rather, it's the first page you see when you open your browser. Now we come across a Web document with the *title* NCSA Home Page! It's called the NCSA Home Page because it's the page that the NCSA defines as the home page; it's the first page seen when it starts up.

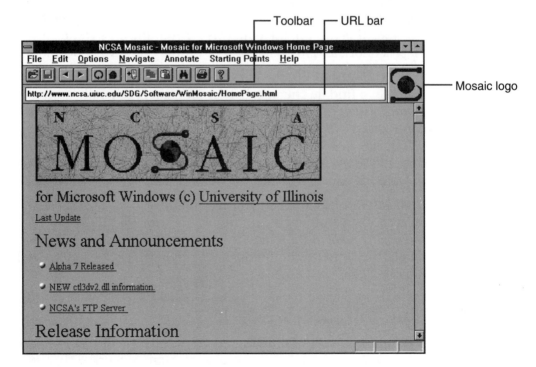

Mosaic, at the default home page.

If you plan to use Mosaic regularly, you should change your home page rather than continue to use the NCSA one; it takes a long time to load, and it may not be accessible every time you start. The best thing is to create your own (see Chapter 21).

The Mosaic Window

Let's take a quick look at the Mosaic Window. At the top is, of course, the title bar. Notice, however, that it contains not only the program title (NCSA Mosaic), but also the title of the document currently displayed in the window.

Below the title bar, you see a typical Windows menu bar. You can modify the Starting Points menu and create your own menus (see Chapter 14). Below the menu bar is the toolbar, containing buttons; these duplicate some of the menu commands.

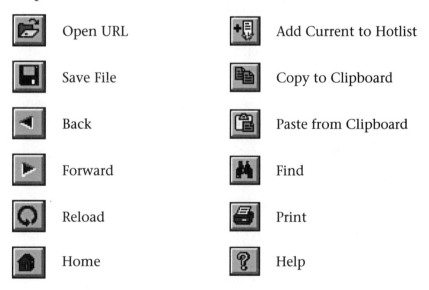

	Open URL		Add Current to Hotlist
	Save File		Copy to Clipboard
	Back		Paste from Clipboard
	Forward		Find
	Reload		Print
	Home		Help

Then there's the URL bar. This contains a text box into which you can type a URL. When you press **Enter**, Mosaic begins to download the document referenced by that URL. Notice to the right of the toolbar and menu bar is the NCSA Mosaic logo. This is actually a button.

While Mosaic is transferring data, the button is animated; "lights" move along the bars above and below the globe. You can click on this button to *stop* the transfer—if you click on a link accidentally, for instance, or if the transfer is taking too long.

The main workspace is where the Web documents will appear. You can move around in this area using the scroll bars and keyboard; try **PgDn**, **PgUp**, **End**, and **Home**.

Finally, the status bar at the bottom shows you, er, status information, such as the URL of the link you are pointing at with the mouse pointer (which, incidentally, changes to a hand when it crosses a link), and progress information when transferring data.

Starting the Journey

Now, notice the links (sometimes known as *anchors* in WWW-speak). Most colored text is a link (now and again, you'll notice colored text that is *not* a link, though it's usually by accident). The text is, by default, blue, and it's underlined. (You can change the color, though, by editing the MOSAIC.INI file.) Clicking on the text gets another document (or some other kind of data).

In most cases, clicking on the big globe button should stop the transfer. However, the TCP/IP software used by Windows NT may not allow the button to work.

Where should you start? Just fool around, clicking on items that look interesting to see where they take you. You can also select from the **Starting Points|World Wide Web Info** menu. This leads you to several useful documents, including directories of Web resources. And use the **Starting Points Document** and the **NCSA Mosaic Demo Document**, both on the **Starting Points** menu.

More Getting Around Stuff

Here are a few more ways to move around hyperspace with Mosaic. Use these menu commands or the equivalent toolbar buttons.

Navigate|Back   Returns to the previous page.

Navigate|Forward   Goes forward to the next page in sequence, assuming you have used the Back command (this is *not* the "browse sequence" that is used in some hypertext systems, such as WinHelp). The Back and Forward commands move you through the *history list*, the list of documents you've seen in the current session.

Navigate|Reload   Redisplays the current document, getting the information directly from the Web, not from the cache. (We'll come back to this in a moment.)

Navigate|Home   Returns you to your home page.

Navigate|History   Displays the history list in a dialog box, a list of all the documents you've been to in this session.

Today's Itinerary... The History List

Mosaic has a very simple history list—a list of the documents you've been to during this session. Select **Navigate|History** and a dialog box pops up. Unfortunately, this only shows URLs, not document titles, so you'll have to look closely to figure out what each URL refers to. As you'll see later (Chapter 18), InternetWorks and some other browsers show the title, which is much clearer.

You can keep the history list displayed if you want, as it's an "always on top" box; it won't disappear under the Mosaic window.

Mosaic has online documentation that's very good. If you have a recent version, you can select **Help|Online Documentation**. Or go to **http://www.ncsa.uiuc.edu/ SDG/Software/Mosaic/ NCSAMosaicHome.html** to find a Web page that leads to documentation for all the versions of Mosaic.

So, I Have This URL Thing...

You've been given a URL and told that you really need to check it out. How do you use it? How do you get to the document identified by that URL? There are several ways:

➤ Type or copy it into the URL text box at the top of the Window (if this isn't there, select **Options|Show Current URL** to turn it back on). Then press **Enter**.

➤ Select **File|URL**, type the URL into the **URL** text box, and then click on **OK**.

➤ Add the address to one of your menus. Then you can get to it whenever you need it, without remembering the address. We'll look at working with menus in Chapter 14.

Save This for Me—Document Caching

We'll look at caching in detail in Chapter 18. The cache is where a browser stores Web pages that you've just seen, so it doesn't have to get them from the Web if you want to see them again.

Caching is very useful but can cause strange results. For instance, if you save a cached page—one you viewed, left, then returned to—you'll find the file you saved is empty. The answer is to *reload* the page before saving. See Chapter 18 for more information.

Mosaic's cache is a memory cache; the pages are stored in RAM. And by default, it's only set up for four pages, which really isn't enough. You should experiment to see how many pages you can store; you'll have to modify the MOSAIC.INI file, though, to adjust the cache.

Want to see a list of features planned for Mosaic? It's continually changing, so what I've written here will not be exactly what you see (unless you have V2alpha7). Go to **http://www.ncsa.uiuc.edu/SDG/Software/WinMosaic/future.html** to see the Mosaic "Wish List."

Stop the Presses!

Just before we went to press, NCSA released Version 2.0 alpha 8 of Mosaic for Windows. Most changes are minor, but there is one significant improvement. There's now a Preferences dialog box in which you can modify information that used to be set in the MOSAIC.INI file; also, some of the options from the Options menu have been moved into this dialog box. (Select **Options|Preferences** to get there). You can use it to set the home page, change the way links appear, modify the window background color, enter your e-mail address and e-mail server address, change the number of cached documents, and set up how annotations and tables work.

The Least You Need to Know

➤ Mosaic is a free program (for noncommercial use) from the National Center for Supercomputing Applications.

➤ There are lots of different versions: several for Windows, two for the Mac, and several more for the X Window system (UNIX).

➤ Click on a link to travel to the referenced document. Use the **Back** button to return.

➤ Select **Navigate|History** to see a list of where you've been in this session.

➤ You can use **Edit|Find** to search documents.

➤ Use **Navigate|Reload** to bypass the document *cache—* Web documents saved in memory.

## Chapter 14

Much, Much More Mosaic

In This Chapter

➤ Printing from Mosaic

➤ Using the Annotations feature

➤ The Kiosk mode

➤ Saving files to your disk

➤ Creating menus and hotlists

➤ Speeding up Mosaic

➤ Working on the Macintosh

As you saw in the last chapter, the basics of navigating Mosaic around the Web are really quite simple. In this chapter, we're going to get into the more advanced stuff. Don't worry, nothing horrendous (it's just that the last chapter was getting too big and I knew my editor would complain if I didn't break it up a little). So, let's start with something quite easy.

Printing

Printing a Web document is pretty simple. You have the usual three File menu print options: **File|Print**, **File|Print Setup**, and **File|Print Preview**. These work in the way they usually work, such as in a

Windows word processor. Use the Print Setup command to select your printer, the Print Preview command to see what the document will look like once you print it, and Print to actually go ahead and get it on paper.

Annotations

Here's a feature that few other browsers have: annotations. Wouldn't it be neat if you could add notes to the documents you view? For instance, you are viewing a Web page and have to run (some trifling interruption, such as picking up the kids from school). You could add a note to the document, telling you what you need to do next in that document, so when you return, you can start back where you left off.

Well, use the **Annotate|Annotate** command. You'll see a dialog box into which you can type any kind of notes you want. Click on **Commit**, and the notes are saved on your hard disk, in an .HTM file.

Now, the next time you enter this document, you'll see a *Personal Annotation* link at the bottom of it. Click on the link to go to the notes you made. Unfortunately, the feature isn't fully implemented or working correctly. The **Delete** and **Include File** buttons don't do anything, yet, nor do the **Annotate|Edit this annotation** and **Annotate|Delete this annotation** commands.

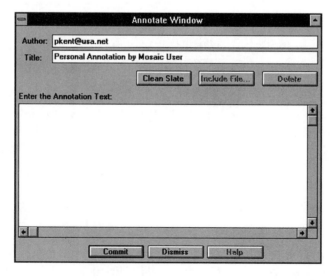

The Annotate Window dialog box.

There's also a "group annotations" feature that can be used by companies and workgroups to let groups add annotations that will be available to other group members.

Get Yer Hands Off!—Kiosk Mode

Here's a useful little "hidden" feature that can come in handy if you want to let lots of novice users play around with Mosaic, such as in a company lobby, in a library, or at a trade show. It's called *kiosk mode*.

To start the kiosk mode, you'll have to add **/k** to the Command Line in your Program Properties dialog box (hold the Alt key while you double-click on the icon to open this box). For example, the Command Line will look like this:

```
C:\MOSAIC\MOSAIC.EXE /k
```

When you start Mosaic, it will look similar to normal mode, except you'll find that various controls have been removed. Instead of 12 toolbar buttons, you only have 6; the Back, Forward, Reload, Home, Find, and About buttons. Most menu options have gone; you can't create bookmarks, modify menus, load files from the hard disk, print, and so on. You just have the basic navigation controls, and that's it.

But I Want It on My Hard Disk—Saving Data

How do you get stuff from the Web onto your hard disk? Some Web documents have links to files that are intended to be transferred to your hard disk, not displayed in your browser (we'll look at this in detail in Chapter 19). Some browsers will automatically figure this out and save the file on your disk for you. Mosaic, however, has to be told.

For instance, let's say a link points to a file containing the latest version of Mosaic. Just hold the **Shift** key and click on the link. A Save As dialog box appears. Click on **OK** and the file is transferred to your hard drive.

You may want to transfer a whole series of items. In this case, you can select **Options|Load to Disk**. Now, each time you click on a link—no need to hold Shift—it will be transferred to your disk; again, you'll see the Save As dialog box so you can tell Mosaic where to place it and what to call it.

By the way, although you can't currently copy the text out of the document into the Clipboard or a file, NCSA is working on this, and future versions should let you use the **File|Save As** and **Edit|Copy** commands to do so. (Some other browsers *do* let you save the text.) Mosaic, will, however, let you use the **File|Save** command to save the document you are looking at as an .HTM file.

Building Menus and Hotlists of Favorite Places

Mosaic lets you build and modify *personal menus* (also known as *user menus*). Most of the menus on the menu bar are fixed, but the **Starting Points** menu is a personal menu. There's also the *QUICKLIST*, a list of places you want to go. It doesn't appear on the menu bar; you get to it using the **File|Open URL** command and select it from the **Current Hotlist** drop-down dialog box.

So what's the *hotlist*? It's a list of bookmarks, really. You can quickly and easily add the addresses of WWW documents. For instance, let's say you've found an interesting document, one you know you'll want to return to. You select **Navigate|Add Current to Hotlist** and the document's address is placed in your hotlist—whatever that happens to be at the moment. You can make any of your personal menus the hotlist; you may want to have several hotlists, each for documents about different subjects.

Selecting the Hotlist

There are two ways to select your hotlist.

> **Method One**   Click on the first toolbar button or select **File|Open URL**. Open the **Current Hotlist** drop-down list box. This shows all the personal menus and submenus (strictly speaking, *cascading menus*, menus that come off other menus). Select the one you want to work with. The top line of the Open URL dialog box has two drop-down list boxes: the first contains the URLs of the items in the selected hotlist, the second contains the corresponding document titles.

> **Method Two**   Select **Navigate|Menu Editor**. In the Personal Menus dialog box, select the menu you want to use from the **Current Hotlist** drop-down list box. Click on **Close**.

A document title, strictly speaking, is the text that appears between the <TITLE> and </TITLE> codes in the HTML source document. That's not necessarily the same as the heading you see at the top of a document (which uses the <h1> and </h1> codes). Not all authors include a title in their documents, so in some cases, you'll only see a URL in the top line of the Open URL dialog box.

Adding Your Own Menu

Here's a quick and easy way to create a menu of places on the Web that you like to go to often. First, select **Navigate|Menu Editor**. You'll see the Personal Menus dialog box in the following illustration.

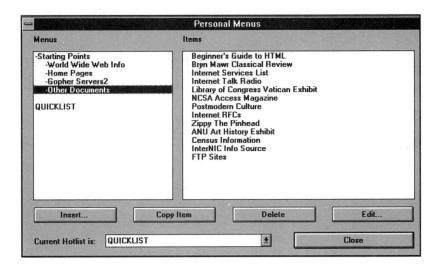

The Mosaic menu editor.

The Menus list box displays all the personal menus, both top-level and cascading menus. At the bottom, it shows the QUICKLIST. There are several ways to modify the menus.

New top-level menu Click in the space immediately above the QUICKLIST. Click on the **Insert** button. Type the name of your new menu (for instance, ****MY STUFF****) and click on **OK**.

New cascading menu Click on the menu to which you want to add a cascading menu. For instance, you may want to create

145

several submenus of the menu you have just created, so click on **MY STUFF** or whatever you called it. Click on the **Menu** option button, type the name of the menu, and click on **OK**. The new menu is added to the end of the menu, after all the existing items and submenus.

Place a menu item   Click on the menu to which you want to add an item. Type the title of the WWW document you want to link to this menu. Then type the URL address and click on **OK**.

Place a separator   Click on the menu to which you want to add the separator. Click on the **Separator** option button and click on

You can't reorder items in this dialog box yet. If you want to do that, you'll have to adjust the order in the MOSAIC.INI file.

OK. When you open that menu, you'll see that a line has been added to the bottom of the menu. The next things you add will be placed after the line.

You can use these same techniques on the QUICKLIST, with the exception that you can't add submenus to the list (because QUICKLIST is not a real menu).

But It's Slooooow!

If you are using Mosaic over a dial-in direct line, rather than a permanent connection, you'll find it rather slow. It's neat, it's fun, but *Lord,* it's slow. Text pages transfer quickly, but pictures transfer very slowly. They really draaaag sometimes. There are a few things you can do to speed up your system, though.

Did you turn off inline images but decide that you want to see a particular picture? Click on the picture with the **right mouse button**. Mosaic will go get it for you. You can also turn **Options|Display Inline Images** back on, and then use the **Navigate|Reload** command to get all of the images in the document.

The first thing you should do is turn off **Options|Display Inline Images**. With the check mark removed from here, Mosaic won't bother transferring a document's pictures.

There's another important change you can make to your MOSAIC.INI file that will speed things up, too. Open the file in Windows Notepad, and look for this:

```
[Document Caching]
Type=Number
Number=2
```

This section relates to what Mosaic does with information that it displays on your screen. It "caches" documents. That is, instead of throwing a document away when you leave it, it keeps it in memory so that if you want to return to it, the page can be redisplayed very quickly—Mosaic doesn't have to transmit it again. By default, it caches two to five documents, depending on the version

Stop Press! If you are using Mosaic Version 2 Alpha 8 for Windows, you'll use the Preferences dialog box to change the Inline Images and Cache settings.

you are using, but you may experiment with increasing the number. If you have lots of memory, you can cache more pages; if you have very little memory, you may even want to turn caching off. See what works best.

Have It Your Way!

Earlier in this chapter, I told you that *markup language* documents are displayed according to how the program wants to display them. The documents are simple text, so the actual fonts, sizes, and colors depend on the program—and you. You can change all sorts of things in Mosaic.

Select the **Options|Choose Font** command to change any of the font styles. You'll see the typical Windows Font dialog box that lets you choose a typeface, style, and size.

You can also modify various other items in the Options menu, such as removing the toolbar and option bar, and turning on Extended FTP Parsing. That means, when Mosaic is displaying available files on an FTP server, it gives you file icons and file sizes, instead of just filenames. There are more things you can modify in the MOSAIC.INI file, too. As you saw in Chapter 12, if you want to install Viewers, you need to do so by modifying the MOSAIC.INI file, for instance. Read the installation documentation that comes with the Mosaic program files for more information.

Mosaic for the Mac

Mosaic for the Macintosh is not exactly the same as the Windows version; there's no MOSAIC.INI file, for a start. Mac users wouldn't put up with that sort of nonsense! And the user interface looks different in a number of ways. There are fewer buttons, for instance, as you can see from the following illustration, and the current document's title is not shown in the program's title bar. Instead, it appears in a drop-down list box in the toolbar (which also serves as a history list). Also, when you point at a link, the URL of that link doesn't appear in a status bar; it's placed in a bar immediately below the URL box.

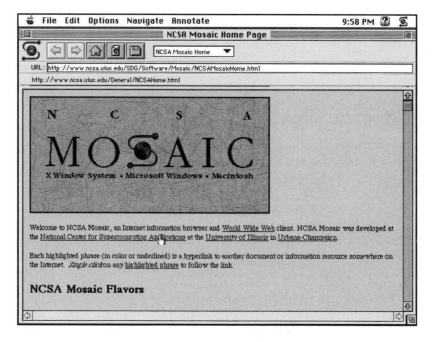

Mosaic for the Mac.

Of Course It's Better!

As any Macintosh owner will tell you, Mac programs are always better. Actually, this is not a theory to which I subscribe; I've seen some pretty bad Mac programs, but as far as Mosaic goes, it does have some important advantages over the Windows version.

First, you can save the document you are viewing as a text file, without the HTML tags; the Windows version only lets you save it as HTML. (The current Mac version won't let you save text to the Clipboard, though.)

Configuring the Macintosh is easier, too. Everything is done through its Preferences box. If you think it's crazy to have to set up a home page by going to an .INI file, you'd be okay with the Mac version, because the home page is set up in the Misc. section of the Preferences box.

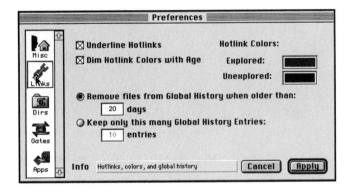

Mosaic for the Mac has more preferences, and they're easier to select.

You also have *more* choices with the Mac version. You can make the program change the color of links that you've used, for instance; tell the program to keep history lists for a specific number of days; change the text size of all types of text with one command; and superscript and subscript particular types of text.

The hotlist system is very different from the Windows version. There's an actual hotlist box that displays all the Web titles you've saved. You can add the hotlist to the menu bar and create other menus, too, but the hotlist and menu system are two separate systems and easier to work with.

The Annotations feature is more advanced, also; not only can you add notes, you can record a verbal message to be attached to a particular Web document, too. Another nice feature: instead of making you wait until all of the document you are retrieving has been received, the Mac version will display information within a few seconds so you can begin reading. Then it retrieves the rest in the background. All in all,

149

the Mac version has a nicer user interface than the Windows version, but if you are a Mac user, you probably expected that, didn't you?

That's enough of Mosaic. As I've said before, it's not the only game in town. In the following chapter, we're going to look at some other shareware browsers, some of which may suit you better. Then we'll look at the commercial options, which are sometimes *free* when you subscribe to a particular service provider.

The Least You Need to Know

➤ The Annotations feature is nice but not working correctly yet.

➤ Kiosk mode lets you remove some important controls from Mosaic.

➤ Click on link while holding **Shift** to load the referenced file to disk, or use the **Options|Load to Disk** command to load each time you click on a link.

➤ The Menu Editor lets you create your own menus and hotlists.

➤ Speed up transmission by turning off **Options|Display Inline Images,** or in V2.0 alpha 8, turn it off in the Preferences dialog box.

➤ Grab a single image by clicking with the **right mouse button** on the picture.

➤ The Macintosh version has a lot of improvements over the Windows version.

Free and Shareware Browsers for the Masses

Mosaic is not the only player in the free-browser world. There are several other browsers you may want to at least goof around with—they all have their strengths and weaknesses. In fact, the "power browsers" among you may even want to have several browsers. For instance, you might use Lynx for the really fast work (see Chapter 6), InternetWorks for day-to-day browsing, and Cello for saving documents from the Web (you'll see why later in this chapter). If you have a permanent connection at work, but a dial-in terminal connection at home, you could use SlipKnot in the evenings and weekends. All of the browsers in this chapter are either free or shareware—you can download them directly from the Internet.

Yes, There's Even a Browser for DOS!

Remember, these programs will vary slightly from the descriptions here. These comments are based on the latest versions *at the time of writing*. Still, you'll get an idea of the relative strengths of the products.

I'm going to start with a DOS Web browser, for those of you who use PCs and don't like Windows. (Yes, there are a few such people—hard to believe, isn't it?) We'll cover this browser first so you don't skip this chapter thinking it's nothing but GUIs.

DosLynx is a very simple Web browser that hasn't been "released" yet. (As with Mosaic, you can still download the alpha version; it's just not regarded as "finished.") It's provided free for "instructional and research educational use" by the University of Kansas. You'll need DOS TCP/IP software to run this browser; you might try UMSLIP, a program from the University of Minnesota.

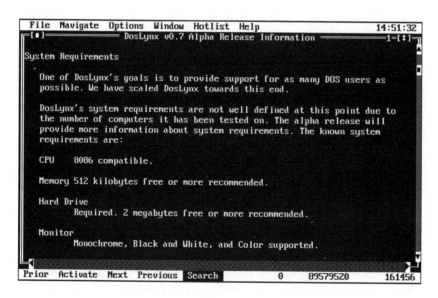

DosLynx provides a simple Web browser for Windows haters.

DosLynx has mouse support, so you can select links by double-clicking on them. You can move around using the keyboard, too. It also allows you to open multiple windows. Each time you use the **Window|Close Window** or **File|Open URL** command, a new window opens. In the first case, it contains the same document as the original; in the second, it has the document referenced by the URL you entered. This is something Mosaic can't do, though some other browsers can.

> You've heard it before and you'll hear it again—see Chapter 27 for information on finding these programs.

Most of the features are fairly normal browser features. You can define a home page, open an HTML document that's on your hard disk, print a document, and search the current document. There's a way to see the URL of the selected link, though it's awkward. Unlike most browsers, which automatically display the URL in some kind of status bar, with DosLynx, you have to select **Navigate|Show Destination URL**.

DosLynx has one nice feature that Mosaic V2.0a7 *doesn't* have. It can save the *plain* text, that is, the text in the document *without* the HTML codes—Mosaic saves codes and all.

There's no history list in DosLynx, but there is a hotlist; DosLynx automatically places all your "bookmarks" into an HTML document called Hotlist, which you can view by pressing **F1**. Not a bad way to do it really, as it provides a quick way to create a home page—you can edit the hotlist HTML document, and create different ones by changing document names.

> Most browsers can't save the displayed HTML document as plain text (without the HTML codes). DosLynx, Cello, and MacWeb *can*. However, most browsers do let you save text as HTML, which you can then convert to a word processing format with a special utility (see Chapter 19).

All in all, a nice little browser, but without the cool tools Windows and Mac browsers have. But whaddya expect, for DOS, for free?

Cello

For a while, it seemed that the only real competition to Mosaic was from Cello, so we'll look at that next. Cello is actually more than just a Web browser. It also lets you run a Gopher, FTP, or telnet session, and send e-mail. However, these tools are very basic, and most people will want the "real thing" of each of those components, a real FTP program (such as WS_FTP) for instance.

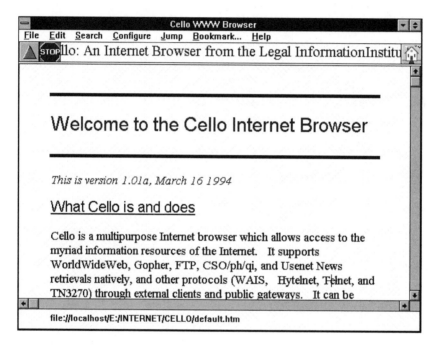

Cello—it's a little clunky but it has some useful features.

The clunky dotted-line boxes around the links in Cello are pretty ugly. Luckily, you can remove the box, leaving just the underline. Select **Configure/Links underlined only.**

Cello certainly beats Mosaic on ease of configuration. It lets you do virtually all setup from within the program itself, so there's no running to the .INI file to mess around. It also has a few nice features that other browser publishers should consider adding. For instance, you can copy the URL from a link in a document directly to the Windows Clipboard, so you can paste them into e-mail or a word

processor. (You can do this with
InternetWorks, too, but I think those are
the only two browsers that let you do so—
with the exception of InterAp's Web Navigator, which was developed from Cello.)
And Cello has a clever way to create HTML
files of useful sites. You can copy your
hotlist—your list of "bookmarks"—to an
HTML file.

If you want to
see where a link
points to, and
copy the URL to
the Clipboard,
click on the link with the right
mouse button.

Another way that Cello beats Mosaic is in its capability to save the
document in text form, without the HTML codes. Cello can open the
HTML document in Windows Write (or another word processor if you
prefer), and then you can save it from there. You can also *e-mail* an
HTML file to someone else on the Net, in theory at least. (I'll admit it; I
could never get this feature to work!) That might come in handy, as
that person can then load the document into their browser and use the
links. Cello also comes with a pretty good Windows Help file.

Web purists will say that it's sacrilege to use the Windows
Help system in a Web browser program—the files should be
HTML! Personally I don't agree. The WinHelp format is in
many ways more flexible than the HTML format, and anyway,
people don't want to view help files in the application they are trying to use
at the time. They want to see them in a separate window, so they can follow
the instructions while working in the main application.

There are some significant problems with Cello. It doesn't display
the URL of the document you are pointing to (you have to right click
on the link to see the URL). There's no Forward button, and it provides
no easy way to open a local file (an HTML file you've saved to your
hard disk). Though, you can set one of these documents as your home
page.

Although Cello was Mosaic's only real competitor for a while, that
is no longer the case. However, it may catch up again. A new version of
Cello should be out soon. It was being alpha tested at the time of
writing, but unlike most Internet products, it was a *true* alpha test; that
is, it's a small, private test that didn't include me, so I can't show it to
you here. The new Cello may be out by the time you read this and will
have a completely new look and feel.

WinWeb

Here's a nice new addition to the Web world, WinWeb from EINet, a service provider in Texas. I took a look at Version 1.0 Alpha 2.1.

WinWeb has a few advantages over Mosaic. For a start, you can change your home page from a dialog box, rather than messing around in the .INI file. Its history list displays document titles rather than the URLs, a big improvement over Mosaic's history list. And it has a progress display during document transfer. A small dialog box shows you what proportion of the transfer has been completed.

But WinWeb has more things *missing*. It doesn't show you the progress of a file transfer, that is, how many bytes you've transferred so far. There's no way to save an HTML file or view the source. No way to copy text to the Clipboard, either, or save a text file. There's no Forward button or command, you can't define the size of the cache, and the Find command isn't working. Unlike some of the more recent browsers, WinWeb won't let you work with any of the document until it's finished transferring data, so you do a lot of waiting (InternetWorks and Netscape handle transfers particularly well).

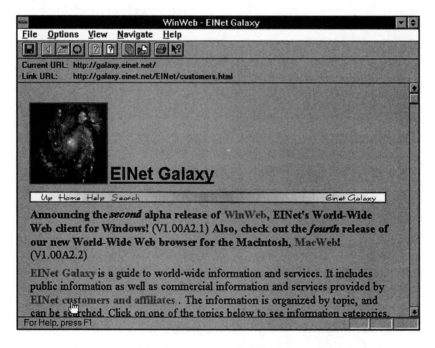

EINet's WinWeb is a nice start, but nowhere near finished.

That said, WinWeb is still a nice little browser. One great advantage is that it's very easy to learn, certainly easier than Mosaic. And it's still in an alpha phase—not truly "released"—so things should change.

MacWeb

MacWeb is the Macintosh version of EINet's Web browser. It's very similar to WinWeb, of course, though not exactly the same. It's a little more advanced than WinWeb, with more features than its Windows sibling.

The Mac version *will* let you save a document as HTML or text, and it also lets you view the source. MacWeb lets you quickly and easily set up "helpers" (viewers for different file types) through a dialog box; in WinWeb, you have to edit the WINWEB.INI file, a real pain.

The history list works differently, too, with MacWeb putting the list in a submenu (in WinWeb, it's in a dialog box).

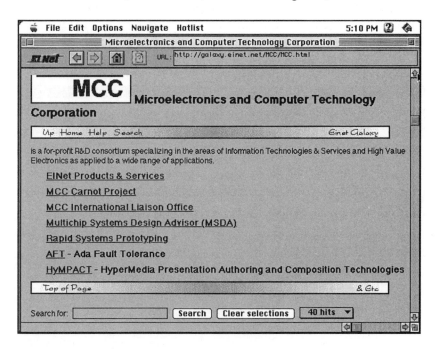

MacWeb, WinWeb's Apple equivalent.

Netscape Navigator

Netscape is a dramatic improvement over Mosaic, and it's getting a lot of attention online, with many users throwing away Mosaic and picking up Netscape. It's actually created by some of the original Mosaic programmers, though they've left NCSA and started a company called Mosaic Communications. At the time of writing, Netscape was in beta. The final version, 1.0, should have a few more features than those in the beta; there are versions for Windows, the Macintosh, and UNIX's X Window.

The big thing you'll notice about Netscape is that it's much faster than Mosaic. The Netscape programmers speeded the program up in a variety of ways, but perhaps the most important method they used has to do with the way it transfers and displays data. Instead of transferring all the data and then displaying it on your screen, it transfers the first page or two of text, and then it displays that text. You can start reading very quickly. While you are reading, it starts filling in the pictures and transferring more text. It shows you how much has transferred and how much is still left to go; there's a little **xbytes of totalbytes** message in the status bar.

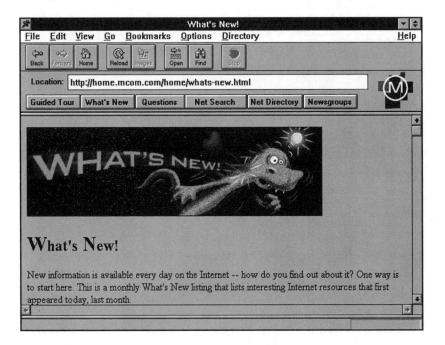

Netscape—Mosaic redux, and a little better this time.

The program is similar in many ways to Mosaic—not surprisingly. It has many improvements, though. First, there's less messing around in the .INI file. (Okay, some of you may enjoy playing with your .INIs, but most of us don't.) Instead, there's a dialog box that lets you set everything up just the way you want it: pick the type of toolbar (pictures, text, or pictures and text), pick a home page, set up the size of the cache, and so on. It won't let you set up every document font, though. Instead, it provides three styles: Small, Medium, and Large. (If you want to modify individual fonts, you can still edit the NETSCAPE.INI file, though.)

> The *cache* is where a browser saves a document; it's either in memory or on disk (in Netscape's case, it's in memory). If a document is in the cache, returning to that document is very fast because the browser just pulls it out of the cache.

Netscape also does something that few other freeware browsers do: it marks your links as used. That is, if you click on a link and come back to that document later, you'll see that the link is a different color, indicating that you've already used it. (You can turn this feature off or give it a time limit—mark links for 30 days, for instance. You can also clear the indicator at any time.)

You still can't copy from a document to the Windows Clipboard or save a plain text document to your disk (you can only save the .HTML format). Right now there's no way to print a file (though that should be added before the 1.0 release; I'm using beta 0.9). Strangely, though, you *can* e-mail a document, with the HTML codes removed, to anyone, including yourself, so this provides a way for you to get clean text.

> *Kiosk mode* lets you quickly remove all or some of the controls (menus, toolbars, and so on). See Chapter 18. The *Annotations* feature of Mosaic lets you create notes linked to any Web document you find; see Chapter 14.

I haven't figured out yet why so many browsers make it difficult to get text out of the document, and into a file or Clipboard. After all, if the program *renders* the HTML document (converts it to plain text you can see on your screen), it has a clean, tag-free version. Can't this be used to create a clean copy of the file? I've been told by one developer that it's fairly easy to do so, and some browsers, in fact, do.

Netscape also comes with a series of directories: HTML files on your hard disk that are displayed when you click on the button bar near the top of the window (you can remove this bar if you'd rather have the room). There's Guided Tour, What's New, Questions, Net Search, Net Directory, and Newsgroups.

There are a few things that Netscape *doesn't* have. There's apparently no Kiosk mode and no Annotations, but the Netscape programmers are probably aware that few people use these features anyway. The Bookmark system is different from Mosaic's; it's actually much easier to work with. You can't create your own menus, but you can create submenus that are connected to the Bookmarks menu.

Finally, note that Netscape allows multiple sessions. It doesn't simply open another document window (a small window within the main window) as some browsers do. It opens a completely new Netscape window, menu bar, toolbar and all.

Stop The Press!

As we went to press, Netscape 1.0 was released, and it has some very nice features. You can now select text and copy it to the Clipboard. And there's a new security feature. If you are connected to an https:// server (a secure Web server), Netscape can communicate in encrypted form. So, for instance, you could send a credit card number securely. Right now Netscape Communications is the only company that has an https:// server, but expect them to start popping up soon.

Oh, and that's the other thing—they've renamed the product and the company! It's now the Netscape Navigator, from Netscape Communications Corp. And they've insititued a $39 registration fee (it's free for academic and non-profit use.)

Netscape for the Mac, Too

There's a version of Netscape for the Macintosh, too (and one for the UNIX X Window system). It's very similar to the Windows version. Obviously, it has a different "look and feel" to it, but otherwise, you'd think you were using the Windows version. The toolbar is almost exactly the same (the Mac version has a Print button, though I suspect the Windows beta is simply a little behind the Mac beta), there's the same button bar, and the dialog boxes all seem to have many of the same components and functions. It's clear that the Mosaic Communications programmers have been trying to match the programs as much as possible. Perhaps the major difference is that the Mac version can save a document in a text file.

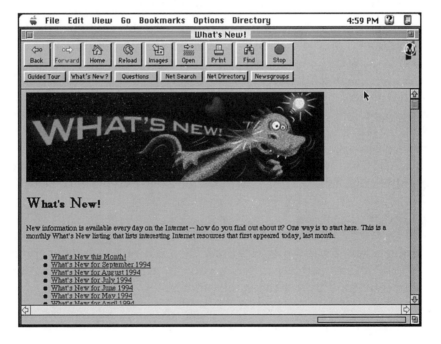

"Is it Windows or is it Memorex?"—Netscape for the Macintosh.

Internet Works

InternetWorks is a very unusual browser. I'm not going into much detail in this chapter, because we're going to look at InternetWorks in detail later in this book, as it's one of the best browsers available. (The only other comparable browser is Netscape.)

This browser has a lot of nice features. Like built-in drag-and-drop OLE support. Drag a document from the browser into, say, Word for Windows. Later, you can run the browser from within Word for Windows. It also has an unusual system for caching and retrieving documents, the ability to split panes vertically and horizontally, a system that lets you click on multiple Web links so the browser downloads several documents at the same time, and much more. The full version of InternetWorks has a few advantages. It comes with a full-featured graphical e-mail and newsreader programs. It also has a Web version of an Internet "yellow pages" book. And its OLE supports is more advanced—it's possible for an enterprising programmer to write Internet applications using InternetWorks OLE interface.

There's some confusion over InternetWorks, though. The publisher, BookLink, was recently bought by America Online, who can't seem to decide what to do with it. I've included it in this chapter because it is currently free; you download it from the BookLink FTP or Web site. That doesn't mean it will remain free. Who knows how it will be distributed by the summer of 1995, the projected "release" date. Still, even if the final version is not free or shareware, you may be able to get hold of one the beta versions. And as I write, the current InternetWorks beta (beta 5) is better than all other browsers, commercial, freeware, or shareware (with the possible exception of Netscape).

A Very Simple Dance—Samba

Samba, a Macintosh browser from CERN, is moribund; development of the product stopped late in 1993. You can get hold of the program and run it, but don't expect to see any updates.

It's a simple text-only program: you won't get any graphics with this one. It's simple in many other ways, too. You have the basics, of course: double-click on links (not single-click), use the Home, Back, Forward, and Open by DocID (Open URL) commands. There's a simple Hotlist feature, too, that lets you add documents to a menu (the document titles, not the URLs). But there's no history list; no reload; no View Source; and very few ways to customize the program.

So what *does* it have? Well, it allows multiple sessions, in effect, because each time you select a link, a new window opens. You can save data to the Clipboard, too, and save documents as Samba files (though I could never figure out how to open these files, and there's no documentation to explain it). You can print documents, too.

Here's a neat feature I haven't seen elsewhere: use Samba's Trace feature to watch the program rendering the HTML document into a text document. When you select a link, you'll see a "console" window appear and you'll be able to watch the program at work.

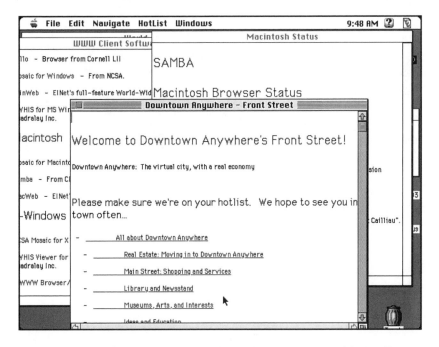

Samba will fill your screen with windows (sans graphics), allowing multiple sessions.

SlipKnot—Graphics for the TCP/IP-less

Here's a way to get Web graphics (on a Windows computer) even if you don't have a dial-in direct or permanent connection; use *SlipKnot*.

This browser's designed around its own terminal program. Start Windows, start SlipKnot, and then dial into your service provider's system. The program will log in, just like any other serial communications program, such as ProComm, HyperACCESS, or whatever. Then click on a button and SlipKnot starts your service provider's Lynx browser, but feeds all the data through its own Web screen, graphics and all.

It's true! You really can have a graphics browser without SLIP or PPP—just get SlipKnot!

This is a simple application. If you are used to working with one of the SLIP or PPP browsers, you'll find SlipKnot a little slow, but SlipKnot has a few features that make it more bearable, and perhaps even preferable for some people.

For instance, you can save complete Web documents, graphics and all, in a folder. Some browsers let you set up hotlists, each one stored in a separate folder. This is the same idea, except that SlipKnot saves the actual document, not just a reference to the file! So when you want to retrieve a document, just get it from the folder.

Also, when you click on a link, SlipKnot displays a small dialog box showing the URL. You can then click on **Retrieve from Internet** (to get it from the Web) or on **Search in other folders** to retrieve it from a folder.

There's also a true Bookmark (hotlist) system that creates folders, and stores related bookmarks in the folders. The history list lets you see not only where you've been in *this* session, but even in the last! The history list is a very good one, too; it shows both URLs and titles, which is more than can be said for Mosaic. You can transfer entries from the history list to a bookmark folder so you can place bookmarks on documents even after you've finished your session.

SlipKnot also lets you run multiple sessions, because when you open a document, it opens in a separate window (my only complaint about the SlipKnot interface is that these windows can't be sized). SlipKnot has many of the features of a full-blown dial-in-direct browser; you can open HTML files on your hard disk, modify screen and font colors, select document fonts, turn inline graphics on and off, save documents on your hard disk as HTML files, and more. There are a few things that the program can't do right now; there's no forms support, and it can't work with gopher yet, either. Both these are planned for later versions.

This browser is so good that many users may wonder why they need to set up a SLIP or PPP account.

165

Decisions, Decisions...

Which of these browsers would *I* use as my primary browser? If some-one held a gun to my head and said I *had* to pick a freeware browser, which would I pick? Well, it wouldn't be Mosaic, for all the misin-formed media hype. I don't want to criticize the Mosaic programmers; they've done a good job and made a great start at graphical browsers. But now the market is changing, and browsers are appearing that are *better* than Mosaic.

I use both Netscape and InternetWorks. They're both excellent programs, neck and neck in the browser race. They're easy to set up and use, with same very good features. I believe InternetWorks may be slightly better than Netscape, but the latest Netscape lets you copy text to the Windows. Clipboard, a very handy feature that InternetWorks doesn't have.

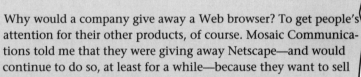

Why would a company give away a Web browser? To get people's attention for their other products, of course. Mosaic Communica-tions told me that they were giving away Netscape—and would continue to do so, at least for a while—because they want to sell their Web *server* software. Stop Press! As we went to print, Mosaic Communi-cations became Netscape Communications and began requesting a $39 registration fee.

The Least You Need to Know

➤ Mosaic is *not* the best browser around; it's just the most famous!

➤ If you have a PC and hate Windows, you can use DosLynx.

➤ Cello is a multifunction application, based on a Web browser; you can run FTP, telnet, and Gopher sessions, and send e-mail.

➤ Netscape is probably the best of the bunch, fast and easy to use.

➤ InternetWorks is possibly the best browser around.

➤ WinWeb and MacWeb are good new browsers but don't match Netscape.

➤ Samba is a simple text-based browser for the Macintosh.

➤ SlipKnot provides a sophisticated graphics browser for Windows users with dial-in terminal accounts.

Chapter 16

If You Want to Pay: Commercial Browsers

In This Chapter

➤ Using service-provider specific browsers: The Pipeline, NetCruiser, and InterNav

➤ Working with commercial versions of Mosaic

➤ Unusual new browsers: WinTapestry and Web Navigator

Business has been rushing to the Internet like flies to a dead pig. Late in 1993, it was hard to find good Internet software. Late in 1994, it was hard not to trip over it.

In this chapter, we're going to take a quick look at the Web browsers available from commercial-software publishers, that is, software you'll have to pay for rather than simply download from the Internet and use for free.

That's not to say you'll necessarily have to fork over large sums of money to get these programs. In some cases, the software will be given to you when you

Where do you find info about getting these programs? Come on, you know by now! Chapter 27.

sign up with a service provider. We'll also look at software that is almost, sort of, kind of free—programs you may get free of charge when you buy a new computer, for instance, or that come bundled with another program.

The Pipeline and Internaut

The Pipeline Network is a service provider in New York—but wait! Even if you are not in New York, you may want to hear this, because The Pipeline's software is being licensed to service providers all over the country—boosted by the high praise the software is getting from the computer press. Even if you can't find a service provider in your area running the software, you can still dial into The Pipeline through SprintNet as a local call.

Recently, The Pipeline changed its product name. The *Pipeline* now refers to the service provider in New York. The software itself is now known as *Internaut* and may be used by other service providers.

You won't sign up with an Internaut service provider just for the Web browser, though; you would sign up because the software is an easy-to-install, easy-to-use, complete Internet package with e-mail, newsgroups, FTP, telnet, Gopher, and more. The Web browser that comes with the package is actually a very simple system, with few but the most basic features and little in the way of configuration options. (At the time of writing, though, the Web browser was in beta testing, so future versions of the software will probably have more features.)

By the time the software is released, it will have forms support (the capability to work with Web forms) and will allow you to print documents and to save them, though probably only HTML files. There's a bookmark system (integrated with The Pipeline's system-wide bookmark system) and a history list. You can run multiple sessions in separate windows by opening different URLs. The Web browser is integrated with The Pipeline's other tools: click on a link that takes you to a Gopher menu, and The Pipeline's Gopher window opens; click on a link to an FTP site, and the FTP box opens; click on a link to a telnet session, and the telnet window opens, and so on.

The Pipeline's Web browser should be fast, as the programmers are adding the new speed features that are turning up in browsers these days—transferring the first page and letting you work with it, while transferring the rest in the background.

There are both Windows and Mac versions of the Pipeline software, though currently the Mac version doesn't have the Web browser (it probably will by the time you read this).

NetCruiser

NetCruiser from NETCOM is another proprietary system. In other words, if you want to use the NetCruiser software, you'll have to get a NETCOM Internet account.

The big advantage of NetCruiser is that it's incredibly easy to install. You're installing a PPP account, though you'd never know it; the entire process takes about 10 minutes.

NetCruiser's Web browser is easy to use, but it's bordering on too simple. It's definitely not in the InternetWorks or Netscape league, though it probably has enough features for many Web users (maybe not for us power browsers, though, eh?).

I like the big chunky buttons and the "look" of the program. There are very simple bookmark and history systems, and a couple of built-in viewers: one for text and one for graphics (.BMP, .GIF, .JPG, and .XBM). But you won't be able to add your own viewers for other file formats.

The system has forms support, and you can save the document you are viewing (in HTML format only). There's no way to print it, though.

NetCruiser at the FedWorld site (a great "gateway" to government documents—http://www.fedworld.gov).

NetCruiser is a nice looking, reasonably quick browser, though definitely not a top-of-the-line model. Also, I've heard a lot of criticism of NETCOM's access (not enough local telephone numbers, too many busy lines) and technical support. I've usually been able to get through reasonably quickly, though, and have found the system so simple that I've never needed technical support anyway.

InterNav/Delphi

This is a weird one: InterNav. It's created by Phoenix Technologies Ltd. for the Delphi online system. It's a Windows program that lets you use Delphi's dial-in terminal connection. This is nothing like The Pipeline and NetCruiser systems set up by other service providers, though. InterNav is simply a communications program designed for use with Delphi's terminal connection. Nothing fancy; you are still working with simple text-based menus and the command line.

You can use a Web browser at the Delphi site, or telnet to a browser elsewhere on the Internet (you get to the Web options through the Delphi gopher). But these are text-based browsers—Lynx and the

172

Line Mode browser. InterNav automates navigating, just a little, by letting you double-click on a word, any word, with the mouse. It assumes that when you double-click you want to use that word as a command. So, for instance, when you are working in the Line Mode browser, instead of typing the number of a link and then pressing Enter, you can double-click on the number.

Because you can only double-click on what you can see on the screen, if you want to use a command that isn't displayed, you have to type it, and you end up jumping from mouse to keyboard. Sometimes when you double-click on a word, it picks up the word *next* to it. (No, I *didn't* move the mouse during the click!)

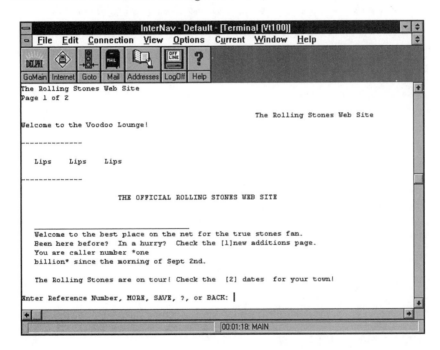

Where are the pictures? (There aren't any!) InterNav's terminal window for the Delphi online service.

However, Delphi told me that the browser they are using is a customized version of Lynx, and it did have some advantages (it looks like a customized version of the Line Mode browser, actually, but I let it pass). It lets you save Web documents by e-mailing them to yourself. It automates the downloading of files (from an FTP site, for instance); it will download a file to the Delphi site and then prompt you for the form of data-transmission you want to use. InterNav has built-in

Zmodem, so it can automatically pick up and transfer to your hard disk. There's also a simple bookmarks system.

I found the program a little "buggy." I closed a Web browser I telnetted to, and the program just hung. There are other non-Web-specific bugs, too. The installation program didn't create an icon for InterNav (though it did give me one for the Help file), and it didn't set up the modem correctly.

InterNav is actually a very good front end to a text-based terminal connection. It's *not* a huge step forward into the GUI world, though.

AIR Mosaic: Internet In a Box/AIR Series

AIR Mosaic is a commercial modification to NCSA Mosaic, published by SPRY. It's sold as part of SPRY's AIR Series of Internet applications and also in the Internet in a Box product from O'Reilly & Associates.

Internet In a Box is probably the easiest non-service-provider-specific product to install. SPRY spent lots of effort to help you config-ure your dial-in direct connection and create a log in script, and the result is a very easy connection.

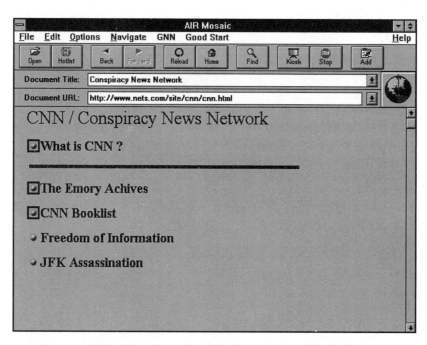

AIR Mosaic, visiting the Conspiracy News Network (http://www.nets.com/site/cnn/cnn.html).

The browser is quite a bit better than Mosaic. One of the nicest features is how the program handles hotlists. As you can see in the following figure, there's a Hotlists dialog box that lets you create a hierarchical system of hotlists, folders, and bookmarks. The program comes with three hotlists, with dozens of interesting sites. You can add your own lists, offload them to your hard disk, and then give them to friends or colleagues. Using a hotlist to create a menu option is as easy as clicking on the check box at the bottom of the dialog box. And if you've been using NCSA Mosaic, you can import the menus you created in that browser as AIR Mosaic hotlists.

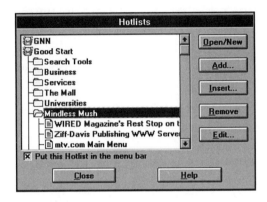

AIR Mosaic's hotlist system is one of the best.

AIR Mosaic makes configuring the application much easier, too, by putting all the controls in a dialog box—no more playing around in the .INI file. You can set up your viewers, configure the document cache, remove the underline from links, and plenty more.

AIR Mosaic even has a kiosk mode, and it's easier to work with than Mosaic's: simply click on the **Kiosk** button to remove the browsers controls, and press **Ctrl+K** to replace them. It's a great way to create a "safe" browser in a public place, and also a great way to expand a Web document to take up all the available space.

All in all, this one's a nice, easy-to-use browser with plenty of features.

GWHIS Viewer

GWHIS Viewer is another browser that is part of a suite of applications. This one's from Quadralay and is part of the Global-Wide Help and Information Systems applications. These are sold to corporations that want to create online documentation systems, available on a company network or on the Web itself.

GWHIS Viewer is way behind the other browsers around. Quadralay said they wanted GWHIS Viewer to have the same features as its UNIX X Window version, which meant keeping it back to the Mosaic 1.0 set of features. That means the program is way behind the latest Mosaic—which is way behind Netscape, InternetWorks, Enhanced NCSA Mosaic, and others. Strangely, even though GWHIS is based on an old version of Mosaic, it's still a 32-bit application. That means if you are using Windows 3.1 or Windows for Workgroups, you'll have to install the Win32s software (it comes bundled with the program; see Chapter 13 for more information about Win32s).

If you get the GWHIS system, I'd recommend that you dump the viewer and use InternetWorks, or even download Netscape.

Enhanced NCSA Mosaic (a.k.a. SpyGlass Mosaic)

Enhanced NCSA Mosaic is a version of Mosaic—in both PC and Mac flavors—with a few (significant) changes. It's a program from SpyGlass, the people who bought the right to license Mosaic to other companies who want to modify it and create their own browsers from it.

This program has been simplified in some ways and had capabilities added in others. Some of the changes I'm not sure I like; others are a definite improvement.

First, there are a lot fewer menu options. I don't like the fact that the toolbar is gone (I *like* toolbars, darn it!), though the Back and Forward buttons are now on the URL line. The Mosaic icon below the menu bar is not a button; clicking on it *won't* stop a transfer, though pressing Esc will normally cancel a transfer. The mouse pointer doesn't change into a hand shape when you point to a link, though you can still see the URL in the status bar. That sounds like a small thing, but I found it irritating.

SpyGlass also did something strange with the file-download function. In Mosaic, if you want to download a file that is pointed to by a link—perhaps the link points to a large picture, or a sound—you turn on the download using the **Options|Load to Disk** command, and then click on the link. But in *Enhanced* NCSA Mosaic, this is gone; you just have to remember to press **Ctrl** when you double-click the link.

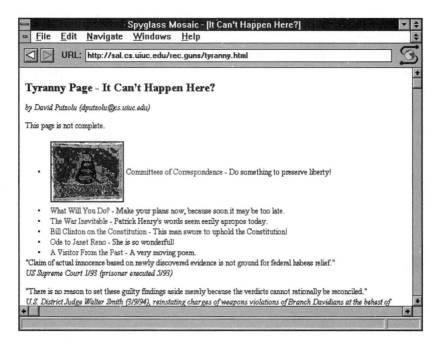

Enhanced NCSA Mosaic—visiting the Tyranny Page (http://sal.cs.uiuc.edu/ rec.guns/tyranny.html).

Still, it's not all bad. In fact, there are some definite improvements. This browser lets you save documents as text files and even copy them to the Clipboard, something Mosaic and many other browsers won't do. It also lets you open multiple windows at once so you can run multiple Web sessions. The hotlist system is much simplified (Mosaic's can get a little confusing), though you can't place hotlists onto the menu bar. (You can, however, save hotlists to an HTML file, so you can mail them to friends and colleagues.) You can also export the history list, which includes documents from previous sessions.

Early versions of NCSA Mosaic don't let you change the home page, a really strange omission that Spyglass has been forced to fix— later versions *will* let you do so. And you can't directly change a particular font in a document. Instead, you have to select from one of several *style sheets* (though you can go into the SMOSAIC.INI file and change fonts there).

Enhanced NCSA Mosaic is okay, but it's really nothing special. It's not up to Netscape's or InternetWorks' level, with the exception of the capability to save documents and copy them to the Clipboard.

177

Super Mosaic and Luckman Interactive's Enhanced Mosaic

These are, currently, the same as Enhanced NCSA Mosaic, though they come with extensive directories—useful HTML files that help you find your way around the Web. In other words, the Super Mosaic home page contains links to a number of other Web pages (on your hard disk) that contain links to all sorts of stuff on the Web.

Later versions of Super Mosaic and Luckman Interactive's Enhanced Mosaic will start to diverge from Enhanced NCSA Mosaic, as the Luckman Interactive program begins to add its own—"significant," they say—new features.

WinTapestry

WinTapestry is one of the applications in the SuperHighway Access suite. It's a very unusual Web browser; it's really a combination of different tools, accessed through a sort of "card file." Click on a tab, such as **Entertainment**, **Food**, **Best of the Web**, **Legal**, **Religion**, or whatever, and a list of folders and items appears.

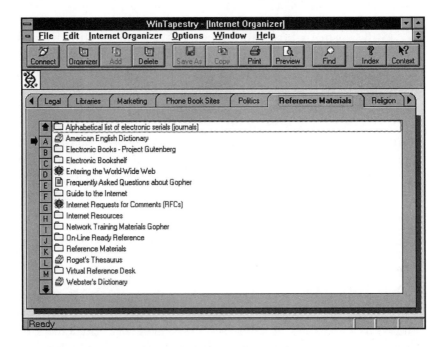

The WinTapestry Internet Organizer—a kind of "card file" of Internet sites.

Some of the items are Web sites, but others may be Gopher sites, telnet sessions, FTP sites, files of various kinds, and so on. Click on one of the Web icons and another window opens; this is where you do your actual browsing. It's a pretty good browser, too. You can add bookmarks; you'll get a chance to select the category (there are about 30, and you can create your own), and the document is added to the card file.

There's no history list, though, nor can you search a document, at least in the version available at the time of writing. There is an option to turn off the loading of images until all the text has been transferred; the same sort of thing that InternetWorks and Netscape do to speed up transfers. You can also do all the normal configuration stuff, such as select font types, change link and background colors, and so on.

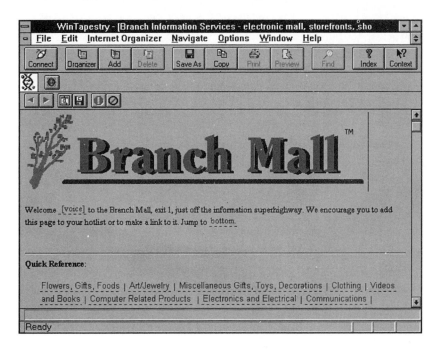

WinTapestry's Web browser, shopping at the Branch Mall (http://www.branch.com).

The interesting thing about WinTapestry, of course, is how it integrates Web sites with all other Internet resources. The program is supposed to organize your work around your interests, rather than the various tools.

Web Navigator (InterAp)

Web Navigator is one of the programs included in California Software's InterAp Internet suite for Windows. The other programs are for e-mail, newsgroups, FTP, and telnet. There's also a special scheduler to run programs at a particular time.

Get *The Complete Idiot's Guide to the Internet*, load the SuperHighway Access Sampler bundled with that book, double-click on the **Get More Demos** icon, and the program will take you to the SuperHighway Access FTP site, where you can download a fully functional Tapestry demo. You may also be able to find a demo of WinTapestry elsewhere on the Net; use Archie to search for **SHADEMO2.EXE** or some variation of SHADEMO.

The browser is actually derived from the freeware Cello browser, so there are some similarities. (Web Navigator doesn't have the "clunky" look that Cello has, though.) It has many of the advantages that Cello has: the capability to save a document as a text file, to copy the document to the Clipboard, to launch an FTP or telnet session directly from the browser, and so on. See the description of Cello in Chapter 15, and you'll get a good idea of what Web Navigator can do. If you've used Cello, you'll find most of the menu options are the same.

There are some more important features. The suite comes with NetScript Manager, a program that lets you write Internet "macros" to automatically retrieve information. For instance, you can create a script that will automatically run out to a particular Web site and grab the latest version of a specified document. (I looked at an InterAp beta, though, and this feature wasn't functioning yet.)

The program should also have OLE functions, though they weren't included in the beta version I looked at. Windows' OLE (Object Linking and Embedding) lets you link different applications together. InterAp will let you "drag and drop" Web documents from the browser to another Windows application.

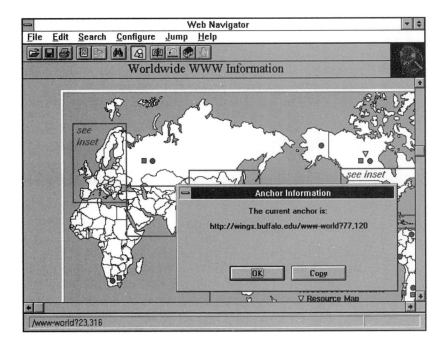

Like Cello, Web Navigator lets you copy a link to the Clipboard—right-click on it. (This is the Virtual Tourist page—http://wings.buffalo.edu/world/.)

There's also a Previous Session history list, and Edit|Select All and Edit|Copy commands to let you copy directly to the Clipboard (Cello makes you open the file in a viewer first). It also has a very good online help system and a better toolbar than Cello.

There's a rather unusual feature: the Jump|Launch hypertext session command. This lets you enter a host name, rather than a URL, and open that host's main Web document. For instance, if you know the wings.buffalo.edu host has a Web document you want to find, but you don't have the full URL, you can enter **wings.buffalo.edu** and Web Navigator will find that host's main Web document; you can dig around from there. (With other Web browsers, you can usually do the same thing, though, by simply opening the http://wings.buffalo.edu/ URL—Web Navigator simply provides a small shortcut.)

181

One thing I didn't like was that you have to double-click on links, rather than single-click.

Web Navigator is a good little Web browser, but not the best. Its real advantage, though, is that it comes as part of a suite of applications and has OLE and scripting capabilities.

OS/2 Warp's WebExplorer

IBM recently released a new version of their OS/2 operating system— they're calling it OS/2 Warp. The product comes with a "bonus pack" that includes a great set of Internet tools: e-mail, newsreader, FTP, telnet, 3270, and Gopher. At the time of writing, the bonus pack didn't include a Web browser, though one should be added by early 1995.

The browser is called WebExplorer, and it really is very good. It has loads of viewers already configured: OS/2 also comes with a Multimedia package, so the Web browser sends the appropriate files over to these programs. There's a great history list (it's actually called a Web Map, at least in the beta version). You'll see a Web document showing you where you've been—you don't just see a list of document titles or URLs, but you see, using indented folder icons, the path you took to get to each document you've visited. IBM is right, it's more than just a list, it's actually a map of where you've been.

The same system is used to show you the links you've used. Not only does WebExplorer color links that you've already used, but it also adds links to documents, showing where you've been from that document—the additional links are shown indented from the one you took from that document.

There's also a very good kiosk mode; WebExplorer calls it Presentation mode. IBM seems to have realized that this mode (discussed in more detail in Chapter 18), is useful to all Web users, not just people wanting to set up browsers in public places. Press **Ctrl+P** and all the controls are removed, displaying the Web document full screen.

The whole package (operating system and Internet tools) is around $80, which seems really good. If you are a confirmed OS/2 user, then you'll probably want to upgrade and get all these tools. If you're not, though... is it really worth it? You have to install the OS/2 operating system. It seems a bit drastic, changing operating systems just to get hold of some good Internet tools, especially when Windows 95 will be out in a few months. (Here's my prediction: Microsoft, which has already added a TCP/IP stack and PPP dialer to the Windows 95 beta, will start to add the basic Internet tools soon, to match OS/2.) And it seems that installing OS/2 is not always an easy job; people have reported spending a day or two to get the thing working.

Did I Miss Any?

Well, yes, I guess I did. I missed the non-PC and Mac packages, for a start, though many of them are versions of packages we just looked at—GWHIS has a UNIX version, for instance. I also missed Quarterdeck Mosaic and Microsoft's Word Viewer, as neither was available while I was writing.

I'm sure I missed others, too. Browsers are sprouting up like long-lost relatives at a rich man's wake, so expect to see plenty more appearing soon. What we've looked at here covers the field pretty well for most people (at least as much as possible at the time of writing), and should give you a good idea of what's available and what it can do for you.

The Least You Need to Know

➤ The Pipeline: An all-in-one Internet package with a very simple browser.

➤ NetCruiser: NETCOM's all-in-one Internet package with a glitzy but fairly simple browser.

➤ AIR Mosaic: A really nice browser, with a great hotlist system and a convenient kiosk mode.

➤ GWHIS: Old. Clunky. Forget it.

➤ Enhanced NCSA Mosaic: Mosaic improved in some ways, over- simplified in others.

➤ Super Mosaic & Luckman Interactive's Enhanced Mosaic: Enhanced NCSA Mosaic plus neat directories on your hard disk.

➤ InterAp: Cello redux, with scripting and OLE.

➤ WinTapestry: Provides an unusual "card file" interface that stores Internet resources of all kinds, including Web sites.

➤ InterNav: Delphi's front end to a simple text Web browser.

➤ OS/2 Warp's WebExplorer: Very nice Web browser. It's a shame it only runs in OS/2!

Part 5
Working on the Web

Now, down to work. In this Part of the book, you'll learn how to work on the Web. You'll learn the basics, of course: clicking on links; using Back, Forward, Home; and so on. But you'll get more, oh, so much more.

I'll explain how you can save things you find: how to save documents as text or in the original HTML format, how to extract inline images from a document and save them, how to copy text to the Clipboard, save computer files, even how to save complete "hypermedia" files. I'll also tell you about working with other Internet resources: FTP, Gopher, telnet, newsgroups, finger, and loads more.

## Chapter 17

Getting Down to Work: Browsing on the Web

In This Chapter

- ➤ Getting started—the home page
- ➤ Basic navigation
- ➤ Things that go wrong
- ➤ Fast transfers
- ➤ Canceling transfers
- ➤ Multiple sessions
- ➤ Moving around in a document

It's time to do some work on the Web. In the next few chapters, I'm going to explain how to work with your browser. I'll be explaining primarily how to work with InternetWorks, Netscape, and Mosaic, but all graphical browsers share some features, so many of the techniques will be common to other browsers. I'll also mention important features in other browsers, and talk about how different browsers use different methods to accomplish the same thing. When you finish these chapters, you'll have not only a good working knowledge of how to get the job done, whether you are working with one of the "big three" or another browser, but you'll also have an idea of what other browsers can do for you; so if you have a special need, you'll know where to go.

So let's get started. We'll begin with the basics in this chapter, and then move on to more advanced stuff in subsequent chapters. I'm going to assume that you've connected to your service provider and have started your browser.

Starting at Home (Page)

The first document you'll see when your browser opens is a home page. Which home page? Well, it depends on which browser you're using and how it's set up. In the case of InternetWorks, for instance, it's the DEFAULT.HTM document.

InternetWorks' home page—the page that appears when you first open the browser.

InternetWorks' home page contains a large graphic which nearly fills the entire screen. This graphic has hotspots on it that will take you to various other documents. For example, the area around the word "Humor" is a hotspot. If you clicked on the word Humor, you would be taken to a Humor page.

Different browsers come set up with different home pages, of course. Early versions of Mosaic came with the home page turned off. So when you open your browser, you don't see any kind of home page at all, just a blank workspace inside the window. Later versions of Mosaic use a page at the NCSA site as the home page, and Netscape uses a page at the Netscape Communications site. Later on, in Chapter 21, you'll learn how to specify which home page appears when you start your browser.

The Basic Moves

The simplest Web move is to click on a link. As you've probably figured out by now, clicking on a link takes you to another document, maybe something closely related to the first document, or maybe something completely different halfway around the world.

For example, when you click on the words **Arts & Lit** in the InternetWorks home page, you go to the Arts and Literature page. No surprise there. Click on **Electronic Books** in that page, and you go to the Electronic Books page. Click on **Index of Online Books** and you'll go to the Online Books Page.

Most graphical browsers are designed to be used with a mouse and have no corresponding keyboard actions for selecting links. So if you don't have a mouse, you'd better go get one!

What Goes Where, and What Goes Wrong?

It's common for Internet writers, myself included, to think of and write about working on the Web as if somehow you are traveling around from computer to computer ("the document you are taken to," "when you go to this site," and so on), and in a sense you are. But what is happening in a literal sense?

Well, a link in a Web document contains two parts: the text you can read, and a Web address (a URL) that your browser can read. When you click on the link, your browser reads the URL, finds the host name, and then sends a message to the Web server at that host requesting the document referenced by the link. If you're lucky and the Web server responds, it transmits that document across the Internet to your computer.

Sometimes clicking on a link won't work; the referenced document won't appear. Why? For one of these reasons:

➤ The host computer containing the document is not working.

➤ The host computer containing the document is working, but it's too busy to respond to your browser's request for the document.

➤ The host computer is working and willing, but the document is not there anymore.

➤ You've lost your Internet connection. Perhaps your service provider's system has dropped the phone line, or maybe your program or computer has dropped the line.

➤ The URL in the link is incorrect; perhaps the document author made a typo.

If your browser is unable to contact various different hosts, one after another, then your connection has probably been broken. If you have another application (Ping or FTP, or whatever), try to use that to see if the connection is working. Or simply disconnect and reconnect; if you are using a dial-in direct connection, hang up and then dial again.

Most browsers have status messages you can watch. You won't want to watch these things all the time, but if you have trouble getting to a document, click on the link again and then watch carefully. You may see a message saying something like **Unable to locate host**, (either the host address is wrong, or the host is not working); or **Cannot find this file**.

InternetWorks has a little symbol you can watch, too. In the top left of the window, you'll see a plug pointing toward a socket, with the word **Connecting** next to it. When the browser contacts the host, the plug goes into the socket, the word changes to **Connected**, and then the icon changes to a picture of a truck and the word changes to **Transferring**. If the word

Connecting doesn't change to **Connected**, and you see a message box saying **Cannot find this file**, it means that, for some reason, InternetWorks could not reach the host.

InternetWorks opens a new window for each Web page you go to, but if you can't get through for some reason, there's nothing to put in the window. Instead, InternetWorks displays the **Document not accessible** message. You can remove this by right-clicking on the window and selecting **Close Document** from the pop-up menu that appears.

Not All Are Equal—Fast Transfers

Some browsers transfer data more quickly than others, and some simply make it appear that way. Up until recently, browsers would transfer all the data in a document—including inline images, if you have them turned on (more about that a little later in this chapter)— and then display the data in the window. That's fine for fast browsers on fast systems. For instance, Lynx working on your service provider's system works so quickly (and doesn't transfer images), that you don't have much of a wait. It's fine for small documents, too. But if you are working on a slow system, such as a dial-in direct connection, and if you are transferring large documents with lots of images, that's a real problem because you may have to wait and twiddle your thumbs while all the data gets transferred.

Newer browsers (notably Netscape and InternetWorks) have a better way to do this. They transfer the text first and display a page or two of text almost immediately, so you can begin reading right away. The thumb-twiddling stage is just a few seconds rather than the minutes that you might wait with, for example, Mosaic.

Once the text has been transferred, these browsers then begin filling in the graphics. In InternetWorks, you'll notice that, at first, the pictures are replaced with the InternetWorks wave icon. As the images are transferred (while you are reading), the icons disappear and the actual inline images appear.

Let Me Get Off!—Canceling Transfers

Sometimes, you'll want to stop what you started. Perhaps you clicked on the wrong link; or maybe you have inline images turned on, clicked on a link, and then realized that the document you are transferring may take a week or two to arrive (or at least several minutes)! Also, when using InternetWorks or Netscape (browsers that begin displaying data before all of it has arrived), you may want to stop a transfer once you've found what you need in the document.

Other ways to cancel a transfer: select the **Window|Cancel Transfer** command, or use the **Window|Close Document** or **File|Close** command to cancel the transfer and remove the document window at the same time.

In InternetWorks, you can quickly stop a transfer by clicking on the **Stop** (Cancel) button in the toolbar, or by right-clicking on the window and selecting the **Cancel Transfer** command in the pop-up window that appears.

─Stop button

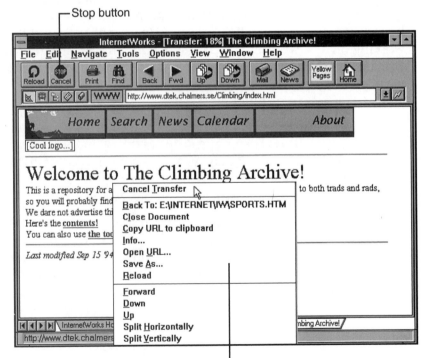

This menu pops up when you right-click on the window.

Canceling a transfer with InternetWorks' right-mouse-click pop-up menu.

Other browsers use different methods. In Netscape, just press **Esc** to cancel a transfer. In Mosaic and some derivatives, click on the **Globe** icon in the top right corner. Other browsers sometimes have a toolbar icon or a menu option that cancels. In AIR Mosaic, for instance, you can click on a Stop button in the toolbar.

> Mosaic's cancel feature is a little flaky. It may not always work, and it may *never* work with some TCP/IP stacks. It may even lock up the program.

So Where's This Go?—Examining the URL

Most browsers let you see where a link will take you. In InternetWorks, Mosaic, Netscape, and most other graphical browsers, you simply point at the link and then look in the status bar. You'll see the URL displayed there. Cello 1.0 and InterAp's Web Navigator are a little unusual. To see the URL, point at the link and press the right mouse button; a message box pops up, with the URL inside it.

Remember, the URL is the address of the item referenced by the link; it's where you will go if you click on the link. URLs take a number of forms; here are a few indicators of what the link will do if you click on it:

➤ If the URL starts with http://, it will take you to another Web resource.

➤ If the URL starts with something else, such as ftp://, file://, gopher://, wais://, news:, or whatever, it will take you to another type of Internet resource, which will only work if your browser has been set up correctly. (We'll look at this in detail in Chapter 20.)

> How do you know which parts of the document are links? Text links are usually underlined and colored. Pictures, when the entire picture is a link, have a colored line around the picture. If it's a *hypergraphic*, though (a picture with multiple links inside it), there's no direct way to tell. Most browsers change the mouse pointer to a small hand when you point at a link, whether on text or a picture, and they usually show the URL of the link when the mouse pointer passes over the link.

The news URL is currently a little unusual. It's **news:** not **news:/** /. Unlike other URLs, it doesn't have the // immediately after it.

➤ If the URL starts with #, it's taking you to a target that has been set somewhere else in the same document, that is, when you click on the link, you'll move to another part of the document.

➤ The file extension at the end of the URL indicates what sort of resource it is. The .HTM and .HTML extensions mean that the file is a text file; .GIF and .JPG are graphics files; .AU and .WAV are sounds, and so on.

➤ If the URL is a filename without a hostname and directory path, then it's a link to another file in the same directory as the one you are currently viewing.

➤ If the URL is a filename without a hostname, it's a file on the same disk, but not in the same directory. This and the previous link are relative links (we'll look at these later in this Chapter 18).

One Is Not Enough: Using Multiple Sessions

Some browsers let you run more than one session at a time. For instance, browsers such as SlipKnot, Netscape, Samba, and DosLynx let you open more than one window or panel, so you can have more than one Web document open at a time. So, you could follow one route through the Web in one window, another route in another window.

InternetWorks takes this a step further. It lets you actually click on multiple links and download information from those links simultaneously.

To use this feature, first split the InternetWorks window; use the **Window|Split Horizontally** or **Window|Split Vertically** command to break the current window into two panes. Then hold the **Ctrl** key down while you click on a link in the top or left pane. The other pane will change as InternetWorks begins loading the selected document into that window. Then hold **Ctrl** and click on another link—again, in the top or left pane. InternetWorks will begin transferring that document, too.

You've got the home
page in one window...

...and a linked document
in the other window.

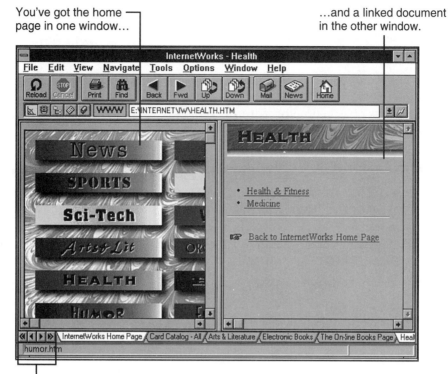

Use these buttons to move among the window tabs.

Multiple connections in InternetWorks.

When you go to the third document,
the first document isn't visible anymore,
but you'll be able to get to it using the tabs
at the bottom of the window. Use the little
right and left arrow buttons at the bottom
left corner of the InternetWorks window to
move through the list of tabs, and then
click on the tab of the window you want to
view. (We'll look closer at these tabs later
when we discuss *caching* in Chapter 18.)

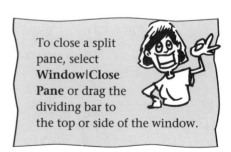

To close a split
pane, select
**Window|Close
Pane** or drag the
dividing bar to
the top or side of the window.

Been There, Done That

Some browsers have a way of showing you which links you've used.
This is very handy because it keeps you from going to the same document twice without meaning to. Most browsers that mark links do so

by changing their color. InternetWorks, Netscape, and Enhanced NCSA Mosaic use this method. (In InternetWorks, the text appears as dark blue.)

For instance, you click on a link in document A to go to B. Then you click on the Back button, to return to A. You'll notice that the B link has changed color. InternetWorks is so smart that it marks documents you have been to even if you haven't used that particular link to get there.

These links will remain in the indicator color for some time, depending on how the browser is set up. InternetWorks only keeps the marker for the current session—come back tomorrow and the markers have gone. Netscape, though, keeps them for, by default, 30 days; you can use the Preferences dialog box to change the limit, or to turn it off or clear all indicators immediately.

OS/2 Warp's WebExplorer has an unusual way of showing the links you've used. It actually shows the used link as an open-file icon, and it even adds links "downstream." For instance, you are in A, you go to B, then to C, then to D, and then return to A. In A, you will see the link to document B as an open file, but you'll also see the links to C and D below that link! WebExplorer actually adds lines (and shows them on-screen) to document A.

Getting Around the Document

Web documents are often quite large—you usually won't be able to see all of a document on the screen at once. That means you need some ways to move around in the document.

How? Well, most browsers have scroll bars on the right side and across the bottom. These will help you get around, though there are probably keyboard shortcuts, too. These will work with most browsers:

Move down a line:	Down arrow
Move up a line:	Up arrow
Move down a page:	PgDn
Move up a page:	PgUp
Go to the bottom of the document:	Home
Go to the top of the document:	End

If a document is more than a page or two, somewhere near the beginning you may find hyperlinks to the various headings within itself. That way, you can jump quickly to the section that you're interested in reading.

Why are Web documents so large, when other forms of hypertext use such small documents? Well, the Web is quite different from Windows Help, Multimedia Viewer, and other such hypertext and hypermedia programs. In some ways, it is actually *less* capable than other systems.

Windows Help, for instance, has small windows that pop up over the window you are viewing. Multimedia Viewer can have several documents displayed in one window, each one in its own "pane." These systems make it easier to break information down into small documents, yet link them closely to each other.

But the Web doesn't have these advantages. So for these, and for "cultural" reasons (the people writing Web documents have very different ideas about hypertext than the authors of many Windows Help and Multimedia Viewer systems), Web documents are often quite long.

Finding Stuff

There's another way to move around in a document; use the Find command. Most browsers have this. In most browsers, you'll select **Edit|Find**, or click on the **Find** button. You'll get a simple dialog box where you can type the text you're searching for. If you've ever used a word processor's Find feature, you'll be at home with this.

Depending on the program you're using, you may also be able to click on a Match Case or Whole Word check box. (Select **Match Case** if you want to search only for the word you typed in the case you typed, and select **Whole Word** if you don't want to find partial matches.)

Back, Forward, Take Me Home

Virtually all browsers have **Back** and **Forward** commands; many even have toolbar buttons for these functions. Look for buttons labeled Back and Forward, or buttons with little left- and right-pointing arrows. Look in the Navigate menu, too.

InternetWorks also lets you use **Ctrl-left arrow** and **Ctrl-right arrow**. You can click with the right mouse button inside the window (but *not* on a link) to see a popup menu, and then select the **Back To** command—the menu option also shows you the URL of the one you will return to.

The Back command is probably quite clear even to complete beginners—it takes you back to the last document you were viewing. The Forward command may not be quite as clear, especially for folks who are used to moving around in the Windows Help system.

What do I mean by that? Well, let me give you an example. Windows Help has something called browse sequences. These are series of documents created by the system's author. The Windows Help window has two buttons, a << button and a >> button. These move the user through the series of documents. The >> button, then, is a sort of forward button, taking you to the next document in the series.

But in the Web, a Forward command or button doesn't do this. The Forward button takes you to the document you were viewing and then came back from. For instance, you view document A, then B, then C, and then D. From D, you click on the Back button to go back to C. In C, if you click on your browser's Forward button, you'll go forward to D. In other words, you can only go forward to a document you've already visited.

Another useful navigation command is the Home command. This returns you to your home page. Most browsers have a Home toolbar button and often have a menu option, too. Even if your browser is set up so that when it opens it doesn't display a home page, using the Home command will display the home page.

Let's Speed This Up—Inline Images

If you are working across a phone line, you'll find a major problem with graphical browsers; they can be very slow. Even if you are working on a network, speed can sometimes be a problem.

The very things that make graphical browsers so neat (the pictures and colors) are also their greatest drawbacks. Transferring all those inline pictures can take a lot of time. Sometimes, you need the pictures, though; that's the point of the Web "journey" you are taking. (Say you are visiting a museum; it would be pretty meaningless without the pictures.) Other times, though, you can do without the pictures, so you can speed things up greatly by turning them off.

Mosaic has a hidden feature that lets you retrieve a single image, rather than an entire document. Very handy if you are navigating with inline images turned off but want to view a single picture. Simply point at the icon that represents the image and click the right mouse button.

In InternetWorks, use the **Options|Load Images** command. In Mosaic, use **Options|Display Inline Images** (or in the very latest Windows version, change the setting in the Preferences dialog box), and in Netscape, use **Options|Auto Load Images**. You'll find that transferring documents is much quicker. What displays in place of the images? Usually some kind of icon. InternetWorks uses its wave icon in place of the inline image. Also, some Web authors may have defined special text that will be displayed if the browser doesn't or can't display inline images.

What if you decide you need the pictures in a document you are viewing? Turn inline images back on, and then use the Reload command. (We'll look at reload more closely in Chapter 18.)

The Least You Need to Know

➤ Click on a link to see the associated document.

➤ InternetWorks, Netscape, and some other browsers use new techniques to speed up data transfers.

➤ Most browsers let you stop the data transfer—click on the **Cancel** button.

➤ InternetWorks, Netscape, and a few other browsers let you run multiple "sessions" (you can have two or more Web pages open at once).

➤ Some browsers indicate links you've used by changing their color.

➤ Use the keyboard, scroll bars, or **Edit|Find** to move through a document.

➤ Use **Back** to return to the last document, **Forward** to go to the next one (one you've seen before), or Home to see the home page.

➤ Turn off inline images (**Options|Load Images**) to speed up your work.

## Chapter 18

Advanced Moves

In This Chapter

➤ Using the cache

➤ Problems with the cache—and solutions

➤ Going directly to a Web page with the URL

➤ Opening files on your hard disk

➤ The history list

➤ Bookmarks, hotlists, and card files

➤ Using kiosk mode

What could be easier than traveling around on the Web? Just point and click, right? No doubt that's all most Web users will use or understand, but you're here to learn about power Webbing, I hope. To get the most out of your browser, you need to understand a little more. It's nothing complicated, but there are definitely one or two little things that confuse most Web users. What's this Reload thing about, for instance? And how about kiosk mode, a hidden feature in some browsers?

Carry on, dear reader, and by the end of this chapter you'll have the advanced moves down, and you'll be ready to move on and find out how to extract and save the treasures of the Web.

A Place to Store Pages: The Cache

What happens when you view a Web page and then move to another? Where does the original page go? Well, in a very simple browser, that data is thrown away. The browser stores only what it displays, but more advanced browsers have a document *cache*. This is used to store documents you've seen. For instance, you are viewing document A, and click on a link to go to B. Document B is displayed, and A is placed into the cache.

Now, the cache may be in computer memory or on the hard disk (InternetWorks, for instance, has a "smart" cache that uses both memory and disk space; Mosaic uses memory; Cello 1.0 uses the hard disk). It's nice to have the data stored in memory, because you can retrieve it very quickly. On the other hand, your hard disk quite likely has a lot more space to store documents, and although it's slower to retrieve from the hard disk than from memory, it's still much quicker than retrieving from the Web itself.

And that's the point of a cache: to save the browser from retrieving data from the Web. If you've been to a document once, there's a good chance you'll want to return. For example, from A you go to B. You read B, then go back to A. Then you go to C, read that, return to A, go to D, read that, return, and so on.

If you had to retrieve document A each time you wanted to view it, you'd spend a lot of time waiting for a document you had on your computer just a few moments before! This is especially a problem if you are working with a dial-in line, sending all the data across a phone line. Even on a network, it's a nuisance. It also slows down the entire Internet, becoming a problem for other Internet users who are not even on the Web. Web caches reduce these problems, to some degree.

The new version of Windows Mosaic (V2.0 alpha 8) lets you change the cache in the Preferences dialog box.

If your browser has a cache, it probably also lets you modify the cache, determining how much data you can store (in bytes), or how many documents it can store. In Netscape, the Directories and Images section of the Preferences dialog box lets you do so; in Mosaic, you have to modify it in the MOSAIC.INI file.

By default, InternetWorks' cache will store *everything*, assuming you have enough disk space available.

InternetWorks' Turbocharged Cache

InternetWorks has a very unusual cache. First, it stores lots of documents, as much as your hard disk can handle. Second, it provides an unusual way to view cached documents. Most Web browsers don't have any special features for retrieving cached documents. Instead, they use the same commands that would be used even if they weren't caching documents. The Back and Forward commands get documents from the cache, as does the history list (which we'll look at later in this chapter).

InternetWorks, though, keeps the cached document in the main window. It works like this.

When you open a new document, it appears within a document window. Now, when you click on a link—or use another navigation technique—to view another document, another document window opens to display that document. However, the first document remains in the InternetWorks window. How can you see it? Sure, you can use the Back or Forward commands, or the Card Catalog (InternetWork's *history* list). However, you'll also notice the small tabs at the bottom of the window. There's one for each document window, and you'll see that the tabs have the names of the documents you've seen before. Click on one of these tabs and that document window will appear. You can use the buttons to the left of the tabs to move through the tabs: one page to the left, one tab

> A *document window* is, in Windows-talk, a small window within a program's main window. For instance, many word processors let you open several documents at once. Each one is stored in a document window.

203

to the left, one page to the right, or one tab to the right. (The tab with a white background is for the document that you are currently viewing.)

You can even view the cached document at the same time you view the current document. First, use the **Window|Split Horizontally** or **Window|Split Vertically** command to split the window into two pages. Then click on the tab of the cached document that you want to view.

Reload button

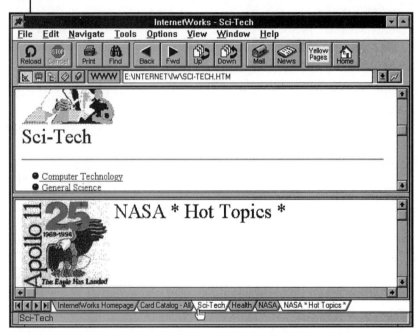

InternetWorks lets you view the current document and a cached document at the same time.

The Problem: The Cache
The Solution: Reload

The cache is a great system, speeding up your work and saving Internet resources for everyone, but it also creates problems. Consider this: each time you retrieve a document from the cache, you get the document that is stored on your computer, not the one from the Web. Aren't they the same thing? Not necessarily.

First, you may have turned off inline images. Now you decide you want to view inline images. You return to a document with inline images turned on—but still, the document has no images displayed. Why? Because the document's coming from the cache, not the Web, and the first time you transferred it, you didn't get the pictures.

The solution is to use the Reload command. Many browsers have a Reload button in the toolbar. It usually looks like a black line almost making a circle, with an arrow on one end. Also, there's usually a menu option and perhaps a keyboard shortcut. In Netscape, you'd use **View|Reload** or **Ctrl+R**, for instance. In InternetWorks, you can use the Reload toolbar button, **File|Reload**, or right-click on the document (not on a link) and select **Reload** from the pop-up menu that appears.

There are other good reasons to reload a document:

➤ If you display a document from the cache in Mosaic and some other browsers, and now want to view the source HTML document, you'll find it's not there. (It's thrown away when the document is placed in the cache.) Reload to get the source file.

➤ If you display a document from the cache in Mosaic and want to save the HTML file to disk (which we'll look at Chapter 19), you'll find you can't use the Save As command—again, because the source file has been thrown away.

➤ You are viewing a document that is constantly updated, such as the Dow Jones Industrial Average document at **http:// www.secapl.com/secapl/quoteserver/djia.html**. Each time you return to the document, you see the cached document—with the old data. To get the update, you must Reload.

∩ Direct Line—Using the URL

You'll find you often want to go directly to a document on the Web, rather than work your way there from the home page. For instance, in Chapters 25 and 26 (and scattered around the book in other chapters), you'll find URLs to interesting sites. Remember, the URL (Universal Resource Locator) is a Web address. It tells your Web browser where a document is.

Most Web browsers have an Open URL command, or something similar. (In InternetWorks and Mosaic, it's **File|Open URL**; in Netscape, use **File|Open Location**.) When you select this command, a dialog box pops up; type the URL, and click on the **OK** button.

Be careful when typing URLs to make sure you use the correct extension (the characters in the filename after the period). Perhaps most use the .HTML extension, but some use the .HTM extension, because they were created on a DOS computer (these only allow three-character extensions).

There's often another way to use a URL; many browsers have a text box at the top of the window into which you can type the URL and press **Enter**. In InternetWorks, there's also a lighting-strike button; this lets you click instead of pressing Enter. (No big deal if you are typing, but as we'll see a little later in this chapter, you can also select from the drop-down list box of Web documents you've already visited, and then click on the button.)

Notice also the small buttons to the left of the URL box. Click on the first, the **Web** button, to clear the URL box and enter **http://**. Then all you have to do is type the stuff that comes after. The next three buttons are for different types of resources: Gopher (gopher://), FTP (ftp://), and News (News:no//). You'll learn about these in Chapter 20. The last button enters **mailto:** into the URL box; type an e-mail address and press **Enter** to open the Send Mail box, from which you can send an e-mail message.

You can usually paste a URL into these text boxes, or into the URL dialog box. So you can copy a URL from an e-mail message or text file and quickly paste it and use it, saving retyping and the risk of typing incorrectly.

Whichever method you use, the browser will run out and find the document for you. Well, it probably will, anyway. As with the problems that occur when clicking on links (the ones I mentioned in Chapter 17), you'll find that sometimes the URL won't work. You may have mistyped it, it may simply be incorrect, the host may not be running or may be too busy, or the document may not be there.

There's a little trick you can use, though. Watch the status messages. If you find that you can connect to the Web server but that the document simply isn't there, you may be able to look for it. For example, look at this URL:

```
http://usa.net/cipa/cip.htm
```

This is actually incorrect. The document name has a typo in it, so if you use it, you'll get an error message (in InternetWorks you'd see **Cannot find this file**). So let's try this. Remove the document name and then try again. (In other words, use this URL: **http://usa.net/cipa/.**)

Assuming the host name and directory path is correct, you'll see one of two things. You may see a Web document. If the Web-site administrator has placed a file called DEFAULT.HTML in the directory, the Web server will automatically display that document. If there is no DEFAULT.HTML document, you'll see something like this figure, a list of the files in the directory:

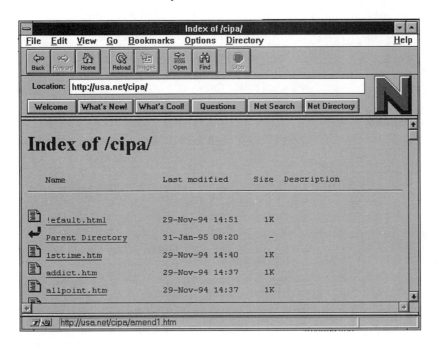

Your Web browser can view the directory.

One of the entries in this list, you'll find, is **cipa.htm**, the one we were looking for (but for which we had an incorrect spelling).

Actually, what you see here will depend on how the Web server at that site has been set up. You may see a list of documents and directories in a bulleted list, or you may see little icons to represent each item: icons for images, text files, directories, and so on. If the icons aren't available, your browser may substitute something: its own icon or perhaps a text label.

Closer to Home: Files on Your Hard Disk

Sometimes, you'll want to open a file that is on your hard disk. You may have created some of your own HTML files (see Chapter 21) or transferred an HTML file from the Web to your hard disk (see Chapter 20).

 If your browser displays error messages when it comes into a directory listing, telling you it can't find the .XBM or .GIF files (that act as the icons in the directory listing), it's because the server hasn't been set up correctly, and the browser is unable to find the necessary icons.

Most browsers make it fairly easy to open such a file. In both InternetWorks and Mosaic, you'll select **File|Open Local File**. In Netscape, you would use **File|Open File**. You'll see a typical Windows File Open dialog box that lets you select the file you want to see.

What if your browser *doesn't* have such a command, Cello 1.0 doesn't, for instance. Well, the File|Open Local File command is simply a shortcut. There is a way to define a URL that points to your hard disk, so you can use the **File|Open URL** command (or equivalent), instead. (In Cello 1.0, you'd use **Jump|Launch via URL**). Now, enter the URL in this format:

```
file:///n¦/directory/directory/filename
```

For instance, if I wanted to open the file named CIPA.HTM, on my drive E:, in directory INTERNET/CIPAWWW, I would enter this:

```
file:///e¦/internet/cipawww/cipa.htm
```

Notice that there are *three* forward slashes after `file:`, followed by the disk-drive letter. The drive letter is followed by a "pipe" symbol (|), not a semicolon. And even though I'm working on an IBM-compatible PC, I still use the URL convention of placing forward slashes between directory names and before the filename. In DOS, these would normally be backslashes, of course.

Now Where Was I?—The history list

Virtually all browsers have a history list of some kind, though its name varies (InternetWorks uses the *Card Catalog*; in the Pipeline's browser, it's a *document trail*, and in OS/2 Warp's WebExplorer, it's a *Web Map*). This is a list of the Web documents you've seen during the current session. Some browsers will even show you the documents you saw in the previous session. (SlipKnot, the Windows dial-in terminal browser will do this, for instance.)

These history lists not only let you see where you've been, but they let you return to one of these earlier documents, too. Some do a better job than others. The current version of Mosaic has a problem with its history list, for instance. It displays document URLs, not document titles, so it can be a little difficult to use. Enhanced NCSA Mosaic uses titles, as does Netscape (and perhaps later versions of Mosaic will, too).

InternetWorks' Card Catalogs

InternetWorks uses a Card Catalog system for its "history list." (In fact, it uses the same system for bookmarks, as you'll see in a few pages.) After you've cruised the Web for a few minutes, click on the tab at the bottom of the window labeled **Card Catalog – All**. You'll see the ALL.HTX card catalog, the one that was created during your current session. As you can see from the following illustration, each document you've visited has its own "card" in the catalog, and when you click on the top of the card, it expands, showing you information about the document.

OS/2 Warp's WebExplorer has a great history list (though it's actually called a *Web Map* in this program). It's not simply a list of documents you've visited, but it's an actual Web document showing you how you got to each document; you see a hierarchical listing of documents and the path through various documents that you took.

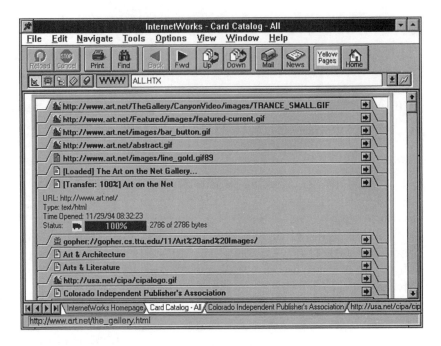

InternetWorks' Card Catalog is a fancy history list.

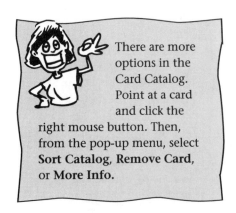

There are more options in the Card Catalog. Point at a card and click the right mouse button. Then, from the pop-up menu, select **Sort Catalog, Remove Card,** or **More Info.**

Notice also the arrow at the end of the card label; this is a button. Click on it, and you'll go to that document.

Some browsers, such as Cello and InterAp's Web Navigator, let you convert history lists and bookmark lists to HTML documents, so you can use them as Web documents. InternetWorks lets you save your card catalogs, too. Select **File|Save As,** or right-click on the white space around the card catalog and then click on the **Save As** option that appears in the pop-up menu. Then save the file as an .HTX file. You may give the file a name in the form of a date: **02-14-95.HTX,** for instance. You can open this catalog in a later session, using the **File|Open Local File** command.

Another Way—The URL Box

There's another form of history list that some browsers have. Near the top of the window is a URL text box. This is where you enter the URL you want to go to. In many cases, this box is actually a drop-down list box. In InternetWorks, for instance, you'll notice that there's a small down arrow at the end of the box. Click on this and a list opens up, showing you where you've been. Click on the document you'd like to return to, and then press **Enter** or click on the small lightning bolt button next to the down arrow and away you go. (AIR Mosaic also has this feature, though Netscape and Mosaic don't.)

You'll notice that InternetWorks does something unusual here. Unlike other browsers, it also lists the inline graphics in the drop-down list box, not just the documents containing these graphics. As you'll see in Chapter 20, this provides a quick and easy way to grab and save the inline images.

My Favorite Places—Bookmarks, Hotlists, and Card Files

The Web's a complicated place, and you can't expect to dig your way through it each time you want to return to somewhere you've been before. Most browsers let you save URLs and retrieve them later, so you can go directly to a site you visited before. In most cases, these lists are called *hotlists* or *bookmark* lists.

Generally they are fairly simple lists of document titles and URLs, though there are some variations. Mosaic lets you place bookmarks on a drop-down menu. Some browsers, such as AIR Mosaic, have hierarchical systems in which a hotlist can contain folders which contain individual bookmarks. In Netscape, you'll use the **Bookmarks|Add Bookmark** command to add the document you are viewing as a bookmark. You can administer the list using the **Bookmarks|View Bookmarks** command, which opens the Bookmark List dialog box. Click on the **Edit** button and this box expands, providing all sorts of options:

Creating a card catalog may not work well if you have loads of Windows applications open, because of memory problems. Close them and try again.

➤ Add bookmarks by typing **Copy existing bookmarks**.

➤ Import and Export HTML bookmark files.

➤ Add cascading menus to the Bookmark menu and place bookmarks within these new menus.

➤ Copy a bookmark, so you can modify it slightly.

➤ Delete bookmarks.

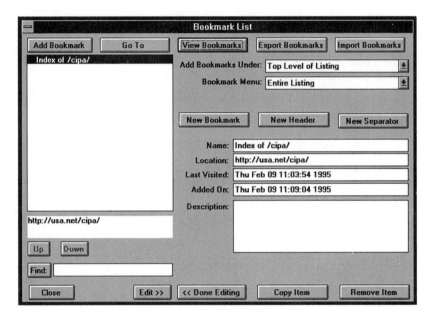

Netscape's bookmark system is easy to use and flexible.

InternetWorks uses the same Card Catalog system that it uses for its "history." This system lets you create different catalogs for different purposes; one for music sites, one for business, one for shopping, and so on. Here's how to create a list.

First, select **Tools|Card Catalogs|Empty**. An empty card catalog opens. Split the window, using the **Window** menu or the right-mouse button pop-up menu. Then click on the **Card Catalog** tab at the bottom of the window to display the "history" catalog that we looked at before.

Now, hold the **Ctrl** key down while you point at the first entry you want to place in the catalog. Hold the mouse button and **Ctrl** key down for a second or so. The mouse pointer will change to show a little rectangle next to it. Now drag the document over to the card catalog and release it. (Make sure you drop it onto the catalog itself, not the white space.)

Pointer shows a rectangle when dragging a document.

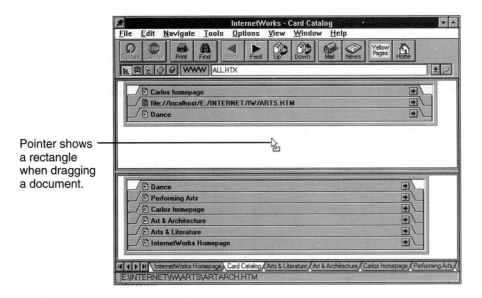

Creating "hotlist" catalogs using drag and drop in InternetWorks.

You can add as many documents as you want using this method (you can also drag from an actual document window rather than the catalog window). When you've finished, use the **File|Save As** command to save the catalog as an .HTX file. You can open the file at a later date using the **File|Open Local File** command.

Let's Make Some Room—Kiosk Mode

A few—very few—browsers have a *kiosk mode* or something similar. This started with Mosaic (though it's a "hidden feature" in that product). The idea is that when in kiosk mode all the important controls are removed from the browser. In some cases, the toolbar buttons, menu bar, and status bar are removed, so all the user can do is click on links. In Mosaic's kiosk mode, most menu options and buttons are removed, though a few remain. The user can use the Help and Starting Points menus, view the history list, search a document, and, strangely, go to another Web site by entering the URL. In AIR Mosaic and OS/2 Warp's WebExplorer, the mode takes *everything* away but the document.

213

Kiosk mode is handy in a situation in which you want to control where the user can go. For instance, a library or company lobby could have a web browser set up, with links among a small group of documents. Once in kiosk mode, users could only travel through that limited group of documents (assuming that some smart aleck who knows about browsers doesn't turn off kiosk mode). Mosaic's kiosk mode is less useful, because it provides routes out of the limited group, via an entered URL or the Help and Starting Points menus.

There's another great reason to have a kiosk mode, even for individual users. Because it removes all the extraneous stuff, it leaves lots of room for the document you are reading. Web browsers often seem very cluttered, with a title bar, toolbar, menu bar, status bar, URL text box, tab bar, directory-button bar, and whatever else a designer thinks would be neat. Jumping into kiosk mode removes all this so you can view the document with as much room as possible.

Problem is, Mosaic's kiosk mode won't let you do this. You have to turn it on *before* you start the browser. In the Command Line text box of Mosaic for Windows' Program Item Properties dialog box, for instance, you must add /k after the MOSAIC.EXE entry. Other systems are more convenient, though. In AIR Mosaic, you can select **Options|Kiosk Mode** to start kiosk mode, or click on the **Kiosk** button on the toolbar, and press **Ctrl+K** to end it. In OS/2 Warp's WebExplorer, you press **Ctrl+P** to go into *presentation mode* (same thing, different name) and **Ctrl+P** to come out of it again.

The Least You Need to Know

➤ The cache stores pages so you don't have to transfer them each time you want to see them.

➤ Use **Reload** if you want a fresh copy of a page, rather than the cached page.

➤ Type a URL into the URL text box or dialog box to go directly to a Web site.

➤ This history list shows where you've been.

➤ Bookmarks and hotlists store URLs of Web sites you want to come back to.

➤ Browsers with *kiosk* or *presentation mode* let you remove most or all controls from the screen.

## Chapter 19

Treasure! Saving What You Find

In This Chapter

➤ Saving files as text and HTML

➤ Printing Web documents

➤ Saving "hypermedia" documents

➤ Grabbing inline graphics from documents

➤ Saving linked files

➤ Using OLE to put documents in your word processor

If you find something useful out on the Web, you can save it to your hard disk. How? There are actually nine different ways to save something from the Web—though no browser I've come across so far will let you do all nine. Here's what you can do:

➤ Save the HTML source file for the document you are viewing.

➤ Save the text—without the HTML tags—from the document you are viewing.

➤ Place the text in the Clipboard.

Just because you can save it doesn't mean it's yours! Remember, there are copyright issues. A document on the Web is owned by its author, or someone to whom the author has assigned rights. It's generally not in the public domain, so you can't just copy it and reuse it however you want. Private use—saving it so you can read it later, for instance—is okay, though.

➤ Print the document.

➤ Save the complete document you are viewing, so you can open it later and it will look exactly the same.

➤ Save the inline graphics.

➤ Save computer files linked to documents through HTML links.

➤ Save URLs in links within a document.

➤ Use Windows OLE to save a Web document in another Windows application, such as a word processor.

It's not always apparent how to save things from the Web, so let's take a look at each of these methods in turn.

Saving, the HTML Way

Virtually all browsers will let you save the current document in an HTML file. This is an ASCII text file and contains all the HTML tags used by the browser to format the document.

For instance, in most browsers you'll have a **File|Save As** command that lets you save in HTML format. Some browsers vary, though; Cello makes you use **Edit|View source** and then save the document from the word processor you defined as the viewer.

Once you've saved a document, what can you do with it? Well, most browsers have a command that lets you open an HTML file that is on your hard disk, as we saw in Chapter 18. So once you've saved a document in its original HTML format, you can open it at a later date in your browser.

There are a couple of problems with this, though. First, if the graphic had any inline images, they'll be gone. You've saved the HTML document, including the link to the inline graphics, but inline graphics themselves are actually stored as separate files (.GIF or .XBM files—see Chapter 22). Saving an HTML file doesn't automatically save the graphic with it. (For that, you'll need a more sophisticated feature—not available in most browsers—that lets you save the entire "hypermedia file." We'll get to that in a moment.)

The other problem is that some links in HTML files that you save won't be any good. In Chapter 22, you'll learn about relative and absolute links. If a link in an HTML document is an absolute link, it will always work, regardless of where the HTML file is stored (on the original computer, on your computer, on someone else's computer) because the link contains the full "address" to the document being referenced. (Of course, you still need to be connected to the Web, and the document must still be available.) If the link is a relative link, though, it will only work when the document is in its original position.

If a document is part of a set of interlinked documents at the same Web site, the links are likely to be relative links. If the document contains links to other parts of the Web, though—a document containing a list of resources, for instance—the links are absolute links. To be sure, look at the URL for a particular link. If the URL contains a hostname (**http://*hostname*/ *directoryname*/ *filename*.html**), then it's an absolute reference.

Still, there are a number of good reasons for saving HTML files. Many files do use absolute links, so they will work on your hard disk. You may be more interested in the text within the document than the links to other documents—you've found a large document you want to read at leisure, for instance. You may want to save HTML documents that are similar to ones you want to create; save them and examine their formatting to pick up tips.

What else can you do with HTML files? You can give them to friends; they are just plain ASCII files, so you can e-mail them to other people quite easily. You can use them to navigate around the Web. If you do a search in Yahoo, for instance, or any of the other Web directories (see Chapter 25), you can save the search result on your hard disk, and then use it later to check out what you've found. You can also take bits and pieces out of the file and insert it into your own home page—one you've created for yourself (see Chapter 21).

Saving Plain Old Text

Some browsers also let you save just plain old text, without the HTML tags. Surprisingly, though, while Macintosh browsers generally let you do this, most Windows browsers won't. At the time of writing, InternetWorks, Mosaic, Netscape, and WinWeb won't. Which will? Cello, InterAp's WebExplorer, and Enhanced NCSA Mosaic and its "derivatives" (Super Mosaic and Luckman Interactive Enhanced Mosaic).

Why would you want to save just the text? Well, if you are interested in the document itself, not the links it contains, then it's nice to be able to save it without the tags. You can then view it in a word processor or text editor quite easily. Reading HTML files in anything but a Web browser is pretty difficult, because all those tags clutter it up.

If your browser can't save text files, but you want to do so, what can you do? Well, you can save the file as an HTML file, and then open it in a browser that can save text files. For instance, if your favorite browser is InternetWorks, you can use that program to save the HTML file, then, later, open the file in Cello and use Cello to save it as text or a Windows Write file. (Use the **File|Save As** or **Edit|View as clean text** commands.)

The Clipboard (in both Windows and the Macintosh) is a common area used to store information from one application so it can be copied to another. This information may be text or graphics.

There are also filters you can use to convert HTML files from one format to another (see Chapter 24). Right now, these don't appear to be for PCs or Macs. That may have changed by the time you read this, though. Microsoft's Internet Assistant for Word will be able to open an HTML file in Word for Windows, as will Quarterdeck's HTML authoring tools for WordPerfect and Word for Windows.

Copying Text to the Clipboard

Very few browsers let you copy text that is displayed in the browser to the Clipboard. It's a very handy feature! Once the text is in the Clipboard, you can copy it to some other application, such as your e-mail application, to include it in a message; or your word processor, database, or any other application that takes text. (Right now, browsers only transfer text—no graphics.)

The latest version of Netscape lets you highlight the text you want and copy it to the Clipboard.

So, which browsers let you do this? Some, though not all, of the Macintosh browsers do; Samba and Netscape do. Currently, MacWeb and Mosaic don't. And, in the Windows world, Enhanced NCSA Mosaic and its derivations will let you do this. The only problem with Windows browsers is that you get the entire Web document; the Macintosh browsers let you select the text you want, though.

Printing What You Find

Many browsers let you print documents, another way of storing what you find. InternetWorks has several commands on the File menu:

➤ **Print**   The normal Windows Print command.

➤ **Print Preview**   Displays a window in which you can see what the printout will look like.

➤ **Print Setup**   The normal Windows Print Setup command, where you select the printer you want to use.

➤ **Page Layout**   Lets you set margins, headers, and so on.

As you can see in the following figure, the **File|Print Preview** command shows you exactly what the printout will look like. You can click on the picture to zoom in and out on it, and you can use the buttons at the top of the window to display one or two pages, move through long printouts, and start the print job.

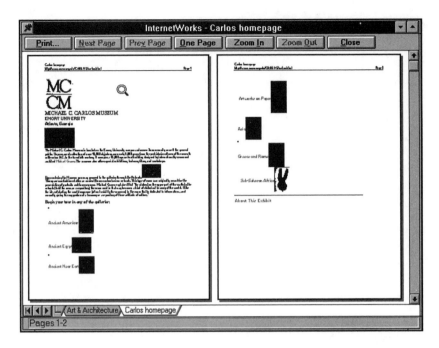

InternetWorks' Print Preview page lets you see what the finished job will look like.

It's Text, It's Graphic... It's Hypermedia

Now here's a handy feature, but one that few browsers have: the ability to save a "hypermedia" file. Documents you view in a browser have two components: the text and inline graphics. As you've seen, most browsers let you save the text in an HTML file. However, doing so doesn't save the inline graphics, because they are stored in separate files.

For instance, in Chapters 21 through 23, you'll see how I created the CIPA (Colorado Independent Publisher's Association) Web site. The main page, when viewed in a browser, contains an inline graphic, but the actual HTML file only contains this line:

```
<IMG SRC = "cipalogo.gif" ALT="CIPA_Logo">
```

When a browser views the document, it sees this line and knows what it's supposed to do: grab the cipalogo.gif file and display it "inline;" that is, in the document at the point that this tag appears. Now, if someone comes along and saves this CIPA main page as an HTML file, they'll get the tag, not the actual graphic.

So some browsers—well, only three that I'm aware of right now—have another way to save information, as a "hypermedia" file. That is, a document's text and graphics will be included.

Which browsers can do this? InternetWorks, WebSurfer, and, perhaps surprisingly, SlipKnot, the terminal-based Windows graphical browser. To save a file like this in InternetWorks, use the **File|Save As** command. When the File Save As dialog box appears, select **Hypertext Files (*.htx)** from the **Save File as Type** drop-down list box. Change the filename if you want, and then click on **OK**. To reopen the file later, use the **File|Open Local File** command. You'll see the original file, in all its glory—inline graphics included.

Saving Inline Graphics

How can you save an inline graphic? Well, there are a few ways. The best way is only available with InternetWorks. When InternetWorks transfers a Web document, it places the URL of the document in the URL text bar, near the top of the window. But it also places the URL of each inline graphic that it transfers, too. That means you can select the .GIF file from the drop-down list box, and then click on the lightning-bolt button. InternetWorks will display that image—very quickly—in its own window. Then you can use the **File|Save As** command to save it to your hard disk as a .GIF file.

In other browsers, the process is a little more complicated, and you may have to figure it all out for yourself. You can use the following method for Netscape.

You have to know the URL of the image. You can find this by viewing the source of the document. For instance, select **View|Source** in Netscape or **File|Document Source** in Mosaic. You'll have to dig your way through the HTML tags (read Chapters 21 to 23 to understand them better) looking for the **<IMG SRC=** tag for the picture you want. Then enter that URL as if you were jumping to a Web document rather than an image. In Netscape, for example, you would enter the URL into the text box near the top of the window and then press **Enter**. Netscape will transfer the .GIF image and display it. You can then use the **File|Save As** command to save it.

In Mosaic, it's still more complicated. You need to see a directory listing. Try removing the filename from the URL in the text box and then pressing **Enter**. If you see another document, try removing the last directory name in the URL and pressing **Enter**. With luck, you'll get to a directory listing (as we looked at earlier, in Chapter 18, when we discussed using the URL to travel to Web documents). You can then travel around until you find the .GIF you want; then select **Options|Load to Disk** and click on that filename. You'll see a dialog box into which you can enter a name. When you click on **OK**, Mosaic will save the file.

There's another quick way; take a snapshot of the document containing the picture. In Windows, this is done by pressing the **Print Screen** button—a picture of the entire screen is saved in the Clipboard. (If you want to save just a picture of the browser, use Alt+Print Screen.) This picture can then be pasted into a paint program. For instance, open Paintbrush, maximize the window, select **View|Zoom Out**, select **Edit|Paste**, click on the toolbar to "fix" the image, and then select **View|Zoom In**. You can now save the picture as a .PCX or .BMP file. In the Macintosh, press **Apple-Shift-3**. This creates a picture and saves it in the Hard Disk folder.

Saving Referenced Files

Web documents often have links referencing computer files. For instance, if you go to the

```
http://www.ncsa.uiuc.edu/SDG/Software/WinMosaic/General.html
```

Web document, you'll find several links pointing to installation files, which you would want to download if you wanted to install Mosaic. For instance, if you want to download the Windows version, you'll use the Win3.1, WfW or NT for the Intel iX86 processor. This link points to this URL:

```
ftp://ftp.ncsa.uiuc.edu/Mosaic/Windows/wmos20a7.zip
```

As you can see, this is a .zip file (a compressed file), not an HTML document. How, then, do you get this to your hard disk?

Well, there are two ways, depending on the browser. With some browsers, such as InternetWorks, Cello, and Netscape, you simply click on the link and let the browser figure it out. InternetWorks will transfer the file; then, if it has a built-in viewer, it displays the image. For instance, if the file is a .GIF or .JPG, it will display the image. If it's a .WAV or .AU sound file, it will play it.

If InternetWorks doesn't recognize the file, though, it will display the message **BINARY File, size = nnnn bytes** in the window. It still has it for you; it just doesn't know what to with it. Either way, you now need to use the **File|Save As** command to save the file to your hard disk (it's in a temporary file right now).

Netscape does something similar. It tries to place the file in a viewer, from which you can normally save the file. If it can't recognize the file, it displays a message box asking you what to do. You can click on **Cancel Transfer**, **Configure a Viewer**, or **Save to Disk**.

Other browsers make *you* make the decision. In Mosaic, you must select **Options|Load to Disk** and then click on the link; or press the **Shift** key while you click on the link. (If you use the first method, remember to select the command again when you've finished, or the next link you click on will be transferred as a file, too.) Either way, you'll see a Save As dialog box into which you can enter a filename and select a directory.

Netscape has this feature, too. Although Netscape can figure out if it should save a file, there may be times when you want to save an HTML to disk rather than display it. Press **Shift** and then click on the link to do so; or on the Mac version, select **File|Save Next Link as**.

Saving URLs

A few browsers have a rather useful capability; they can save a URL directly from a link in a document. This can be very handy, letting you copy a URL to an e-mail message, database, word-processing document, and so on.

In InternetWorks, simply point at the link and press the right mouse button. A menu will pop up. Select the **Copy URL to clipboard** and the URL is placed in the Clipboard.

Cello and InterAp's Web Navigator use a similar method. Point at the link and click the right mouse button; a small dialog box pops up. The box shows the URL. Click on the **Copy** button, and the link goes into the Clipboard.

If your browser doesn't have this method of copying URLs, there's another one you can use in some cases (if the browser has a text box that displays the current document's URL). Click on the link as usual to go to the referenced document. (Of course, if it's not a document, this won't work!) When you get to the document, you'll see the URL displayed in the text box near the top of the window; Netscape, Mosaic, and Mosaic derivations have this bar.

You can now highlight the URL in the text box and press **Ctrl+C** to copy it to the Clipboard, or on the Macintosh, press **Apple-C**. If this method won't work, there's one last one; take it from the HTML file. Either save the file as HTML and open in a word processor, or if your browser has a command that lets you view the document source, do so and then grab the URL from the source document.

Now This Is Fancy!—OLE and the Web

Here's a really neat trick: using OLE to place Web documents in Windows applications. OLE means Object Linking and Embedding. It's something that's only available on Windows computers, not on the Mac. (There's a similar system coming out for the Mac, OpenDocs, but the development software won't be available until early 1995, so OpenDocs won't be in wide use until *much* later.)

OLE lets you link files from one application into files from another application. For instance, a word processing file may contain spreadsheet data; when you want to edit the spreadsheet data, you can do so in the word processor, without reopening the spreadsheet. (There are different ways to use OLE and different versions; OLE 2.0, the latest version, allows editing within the host application.)

Well, OLE has reached the Web, and the first browser to work with OLE is InternetWorks (though it will be followed soon by InterAp's Web Navigator). Here's how it works. Let's say you want to place a Web document into your word processor. (I'm assuming you have a word processor that can act as an OLE client; Word for Windows, Ami Pro, or WordPerfect will do.)

Open your browser, and cruise around on the Web for a while. When you find a document you'd like to use, open your word processor and open the document you want to place the Web document into. Position both windows (the word processor and InternetWorks) so they are both visible on your screen. Now, point at the Web document and hold down the **Ctrl** key while you press the mouse button; keep both held down a few seconds, and eventually you will see the pointer change to include a rectangle icon. Now you can drag the icon over to your word processor and "drop" it into the document.

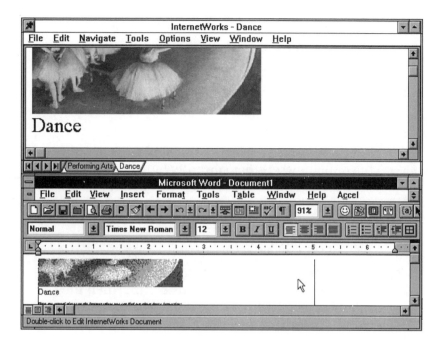

InternetWorks lets you place Web documents into OLE client applications such as Word for Windows.

The document will appear in your application window, along with any other text or graphics you've entered in a more conventional way. You can print the Web page, of course, but you can also use it at a later date. For instance, let's say you've saved the Dance page (**http://www.cs.fsu.edu/projects/group4/dance.html**) in a word processing document you've written. You come back to the document a week later, click once on the Web document embedded inside it, then select **Edit|InternetWorks Document Object|Open** and InternetWorks will open and load the document. Click on a link and away you go! (The actual command you use may vary; this is the command from Word for Windows.)

Early in 1995, Microsoft released Internet Assistant for Word for Windows, which lets you actually browse from within Microsoft Word. The Web documents, links and all, are shown and used within the word processor.

The Least You Need to Know

- ➤ Most Windows browsers won't let you save text without the HTML tags (Macintosh browsers generally do).

- ➤ You can quickly convert HTML documents to text; use Cello, a freeware browser to open the HTML and save it as text.

- ➤ InternetWorks, WebSurfer, and SlipKnot are probably the only browsers that currently let you save a "hypermedia" file on your hard disk—text and inline graphics.

- ➤ InternetWorks makes it very easy to save inline graphics. Select the .GIF from the URL drop-down list, and then select **File|Save As**.

- ➤ Some browsers make you turn on their "save to disk mode." Others automatically recognize when they should save a file to disk, or don't care; they transfer it and display it if they can.

- ➤ To save a file from InternetWorks, transfer it and then use **File|Save As**.

- ➤ InternetWorks and InterAp's Web Navigator let you place Web documents inside other applications using OLE.

## Chapter 20

Not by Web Alone—Other Stuff on the Web

In This Chapter

➤ Using your Web browser as an FTP program

➤ Gophering with your Web

➤ Searching gopherspace—Veronica and Jughead

➤ WAIS searches on the Web

➤ Using finger

➤ Reading the news

➤ Telnetting from the Web

➤ Working with forms and e-mail

In Chapter 2, I quickly ran through most of the services available on the Internet—FTP, telnet, WAIS, Gopher, and so on. Well, one of the nice things about Web browsers is that they can often work with these non-Web resources; Web browsers are becoming true Internet browsers, able to use many, though currently not all, Internet tools. It's becoming common for Web authors to create links from their HTML documents to not only other HTML documents, but to other sorts of Internet sites.

In this chapter, I'm going to explain how your Web browser will work with these systems and what you can expect to see. If you need more information about these services, take a look at *The Complete Idiot's Guide to the Internet*.

Getting from Here to There

First, how do you get to these resources? In many cases, you'll simply click on a link that an author has "pointed" at an FTP or Gopher site, for instance. You can also use the resource's URL in the same way

For a list of Internet resources available to Web servers, see Chapter 25.

that you'd use an http:// URL to go to a Web document. In Netscape and Mosaic, for example, type the URL into the text box near the top of the screen and press **Enter**.

InternetWorks has five little buttons next to its URL text box to simplify this: click on the first to enter **http://** into the URL box, the second for **gopher://**, the third for **ftp://**, and the fourth for **news:** (the **news:** URL doesn't end with //). Then type the rest of the URL, and press **Enter** or click on the **lightning-bolt** button.

Grabbing Files—FTP

The most common non-Web use to which browsers are put is to browse through FTP sites. Let's say that you want to go to Microsoft's

Don't forget Archie! Archie is a system that lets you search an index of FTP sites throughout the world, for just the file you need. Go to **http://web.nexor.co.uk/archie.html** to find a list of Archie "gateways" that you can access through the Web.

FTP site, ftp.microsoft.com. You would enter **ftp://ftp.microsoft.com** into your browser's URL dialog box or text box and press **Enter**. When you connect, you'll see something like the figure on the next page.

This is a whole lot easier than UNIX FTP! Each file and directory is a link; you can tell which is which by looking at the little icon to the left of the name. Click on a directory link to see the contents of that directory.

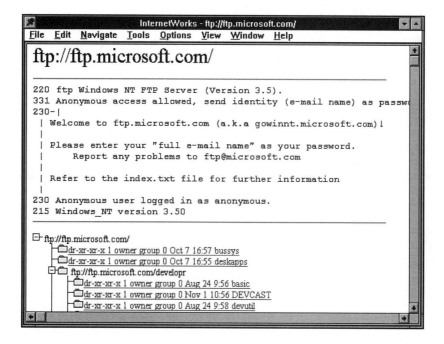

Browsing at an FTP site.

In InternetWorks, when you open a directory, it appears indented below the parent directory, rather like viewing a tree in a Windows file-management program. Other browsers will work differently; most will simply display the contents of the selected directory, not including the previous one. There will also be a way to go back to the previous directory, though—in Mosaic, for instance, you'll see an **Up to parent directory** link. (InternetWorks has small + and - icons, instead—click on these to display or remove the next level directory.)

You can work with files in the same way as I described in the "Saving Referenced Files" section in Chapter 19. If you are working with InternetWorks, the file is automatically transferred. If it's a text "readme" file, you'll see the text; if it's another format that the program recognizes, you'll see that file inside InternetWorks or in a viewer. You can then use the **File|Save As** command to save it. Netscape also automatically transfers and displays if it can. Mosaic will also display text files, but if you click on a file it can't display, it gets confused. So, to transfer a file, press **Shift** and then click on the file.

Digging Around—Gopher

Gopher servers are systems that provide a menu interface. Users can select options from a list; each option may lead to another list of options, or directly to some kind of data, such as a text file or picture. In one sense, Gophers are like Web sites; they can have connections across the world to Gopher servers elsewhere. So selecting one menu option may take you to a Gopher server in Australia, while selecting another might land you in Zimbabwe.

 **Most browsers only let you use anonymous FTP.** That is, you can't use them to access private FTP sites or areas, even if you have the password. InternetWorks *does* let you do so, though; use the **File|Open URL** command, enter the FTP URL, and then enter your username and password and click on **OK**.

For a while, it looked like Gopher servers might take over the Internet. They were really easy to use, after all. But along came the Web and Mosaic, and the superhypeway shot off in another direction. Still, there are many Gopher servers around, and they are connected to the Web! In fact, if an organization already has a Gopher server, a quick way to create a "Web" site is to write a couple of top-level Web pages with pointers down into the Gopher menus. It's not ideal, and it doesn't really take advantage of the Web, but it's quick and easy.

You can get to a Gopher server in two ways: by clicking on a link that some author has provided or by using the **gopher://** URL. For instance, **gopher://earth.usa.net** will take you to Internet Express' Gopher server. You can also include "directories" in the URL. For instance, if you use:

 So you don't want to type these huge, complicated Gopher URLs, eh? Well, if you visit a Gopher site and find a useful Gopher menu, add it to a card catalog or hotlist. See Chapter 18 for information.

```
gopher://earth.usa.net/00/
News%20and%20Information/Ski%20Information/
A%20List%20of%20Today%27s%20SKI%20CONDITIONS
```

you'll go to the Internet Express Gopher server, then automatically select the **Colorado Ski Information** menu option and the **Ski Conditions** menu option.

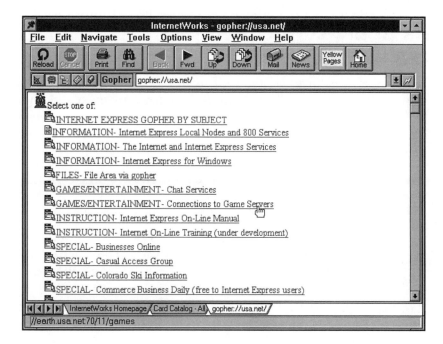

Use your Web browser as a graphical Gopher program.

How, then, do you use a Gopher server with Web browsers? Well, all of a sudden your Web browser becomes a graphical Gopher "client," similar to programs that were created specifically for Gophering (such as the commercial WinGopher, and the shareware HGopher, WSGopher, and BCGopher—see *The Complete Idiot's Next Step with the Internet* for information about these Gopher clients).

The Gopher menu options are represented by links; click on the link to select that option. If the option leads to another menu, that's what you'll see in the window. If it leads to a file of some kind, the file is transferred in the normal way, and, if your browser has a viewer (see Chapter 12 for information about viewers), the file is displayed in that viewer.

Back to the Cartoon World— Veronica and Jughead

Gopher servers have two types of search tools; Veronica (*Very Easy Rodent-Oriented Net-wide Index to Computerized Archives*) and, more recently, Jughead (*Jonzy's Universal Gopher Hierarchy Excavation and Display*). Do these acronyms mean much? No, but *you* try to create an acronym from a cartoon character's name!

Veronica lets you search Gopher servers all over the world. Jughead lets you search the Gopher server you are currently working with (but many Gopher servers don't yet have Jugheads).

If you want to search gopherspace, find an appropriate menu option somewhere. For instance, at the **gopher://gopher.cc.utah.edu/** Gopher site, you'll find menu options that say **Search titles in Gopherspace using veronica** and **Search menu titles using jughead**. (You may have to dig around to find menus on some sites—sometimes they are one or two levels down.) Many sites don't have Jughead, but most will have a link to Veronica.

Jughead

When you select the Jughead option, you'll see a few more links. You'll find links to other Jughead servers at other sites, and probably a link to information telling you how to work with Jughead. (Read this information, it will explain how to put together more complicated search statements than I'm going to describe.)

Veronica and Jughead let you do *boolean* searches. That means you can narrow the search based on criteria such as NOT, AND, OR, and so forth. Read the online instructions.

Of course, there's also a link to the actual search itself. Now, when you click on this link, you'll go to an index server. What you'll see will depend on the browser you are working with. In InternetWorks, a special dialog box pops up, as you can see in the following illustration. Cello uses a similar system—you'll see a dialog box. In Mosaic and Netscape, you'll see a form instead, with a text box into which you can type something.

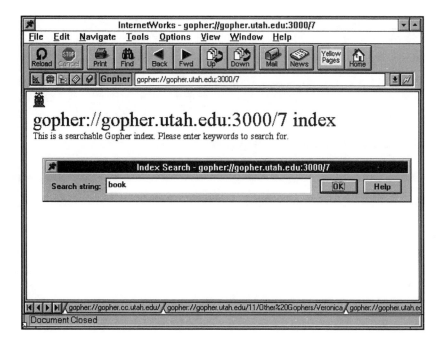

InternetWorks' Index Search dialog box appears when you start a Gopher or Veronica search.

Type a word into the dialog box or form, and click on the **OK** button. For example, you may type the word **book**.The Gopher system will search for all menu options containing that word.

Veronica

Working with Veronica is very similar to working with Jughead, with a couple of important differences. First, when you select a Veronica menu option, you'll then get the choice of servers. Veronica searches *all* of gopherspace—gopher servers all over the world. Something called a Veronica server stores an index of menu options at all of these Gopher servers, so you are actually searching one of these indexes; you get to pick which one.

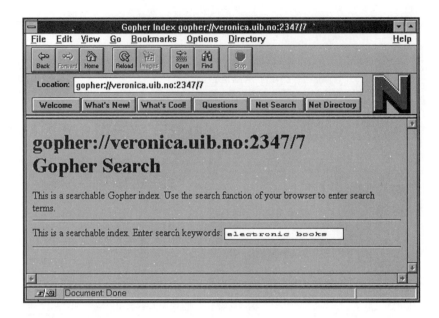

Searching with Veronica.

At the same time, you have to decide whether you want to limit your search. You can search all menu options or only menu options that lead to other menus.

So, for instance, if you select the **Find ONLY DIRECTORIES by Title word(s) (via U of Manitoba)** you will be looking for menu options that lead to other menus (often called *directories* in gopher-speak), using the University of Manitoba Veronica server. If you select the **Search GopherSpace by Title word(s) (via University of Pisa)** you will be searching all menu options, both "directories" and options lead-0ing to files and documents, at the University of Pisa Veronica server.

When you make your selection, you'll see the same Index Search dialog box that you see when doing a Jughead search; type the word and click on **OK**.

Data's a Terrible Thing to WAIS

The Wide Area Information Servers (WAIS) are one of the most infrequently used tools on the Internet, partly because the WAIS interface is rather confusing. A WAIS server lets you search databases, hundreds of them, for information about many different subjects.

You can get to these in several ways, in theory anyway. Many Gopher servers have links to WAIS servers—use Jughead or Veronica to find them. This is the easiest way to use a WAIS server, and in many cases, the *only* way. Most browsers, InternetWorks included, don't have direct WAIS support, or they need a special *proxy server* set up.

When you find a WAIS entry at a Gopher site, you'll use it in a similar way to using Jughead or Veronica. Simply click on the link and enter the search string into the dialog box or form that appears.

You'll find other WAIS-related links; links to information about how to work with WAIS, to lists of WAIS servers, and so on. The **gopher://gopher-gw.micro.umn.edu/11/WAISes/Everything** URL, for instance, will display a list of WAIS servers. Click on a link to search that server.

If you are using Cello, the search dialog box will appear automatically if the **Configure|Automatic search dialogs** option is selected. Otherwise, select **Search|Index document** to make it appear.

There's also a WAIS "gateway" program available—free of charge—that lets you search WAIS sites. You can find more information in the **http://www.eit.com/software/wwwwais/wwwwais.html** document.

When browsers have better WAIS support, you'll also be able to get to WAIS servers other ways. For instance, go to **http://info.cern.ch/hypertext/Products/WAIS/Overview.html**. From here, you can get to lists of WAIS servers, as well as a searchable index. Also, there is a **wais://** URL. For instance, using **wais://cheops.anu.edu.au:210/ANU-SSDA-Australian-Census** would take you to the Australian Census WAIS.

Digital Digits—Finger

The UNIX *finger* command lets you find information about someone's Internet account. When you type **finger** *username@hostname*, you'll see information about that person's real name, whether they are logged on, and so on. More importantly, you'll see the contents of their **.plan** file.

So finger is used to distribute information, and you can use finger from the Web with a finger "gateway." The document at **http://www.mps.ohio-state.edu/cgi-bin/finger.pl** contains a form into which you can type anyone's e-mail address and finger them. If you are lucky (it doesn't work with all addresses), you'll get back a document containing the finger information.

If you go to **http://www.jou.ufl.edu/commres/jlist.htm#Finger**, you'll go to the Finger list in the Journalism List Web document. This contains links that will get finger information from a variety of sources, on a variety of subjects: auroral activity, NASA's daily news, a hurricane forecast, earthquake information, NFL scores, and all sorts of other, wonderful information.

If It's Fit to Print—Newsgroups

You can read newsgroups through your Web browser, but it's by no means the best way to do so. A dedicated newsreader program will have many more features than your browser. Still, you may want to try it, especially if you want to use your browser as a one-program-does-it-all Internet program (it still won't do it all, of course—no e-mail, for instance).

The first thing you'll need to do is define the *news server*. This is the program that provides news messages to Internet users. Most systems have a news server; ask your service provider for the host name.

In InternetWorks, you'll use the **Options|User** command to see the User Information dialog box. Type the news server hostname into the **News Hostname** text box. For instance, I use **earth.usa.net**.

The latest Windows Mosaic (V2.0 alpha 8) lets you enter the news server in the Preferences dialog box.

With Netscape, you'll have to use **Options|Preferences**, then select **Directories, Applications, and News** from the drop-down list box, and enter the news server into the **News (NNTP) Server** box. You can also define where the newsrc file should be saved. This is the file that lists the newsgroups you have subscribed to. (It looks like Netscape plans more sophisticated newsgroup support than other browsers, though at the time of writing, it wasn't working properly.)

Other browsers, such as Mosaic, require that you edit the program's .INI file. (In Mosaic on the Mac, you'll enter the information into the Preferences box.)

To view a newsgroup's messages, use the **news:*name*** URL. Enter this into the URL text box or dialog box. For instance, **news:alt.alien.visitors**. When you press **Enter**, the browser will run out and grab a list of messages—this may take a while, though, as some of these groups are *very* large. Eventually, though, you'll see a list of messages in the newsgroup, each one shown as a link. Click on the one you want to read and the browser will get the message for you.

What if you don't know which newsgroup you want, you don't remember the name, or you just want to see a list? Well, try **news:***. This will get a list of newsgroups for you—just click on a link to go to that particular newsgroup. This works reasonably well in Netscape, but not so well in Mosaic (it may not transfer the entire list).

As for InternetWorks, newsgroups are handled completely differently. In the early betas, they worked in the same way I've just described—type a news:*name* URL to view a newsgroup in the browser window. But by beta 6, BookLink had added a complete newsgroup program; when you use the news:*name* URL or click on the Newsgroup toolbar button, the InternetWorks Messaging system program opens. This is a full-featured newsgroup program, and unfortunately I can't explain it all here.

InternetWorks Lite doesn't have extensive newsgroup support built-in (though it has as much as most browsers), because BookLink has a full-featured newsreader that is part of the InternetWorks product. Select **Tools|News** for more information.

Stop the Presses! New Netscape Features

As we went to print, Netscape added new newsgroup features. When you go to a newsgroup, you will see a toolbar at the top of the document. The bar lets you post a message to the group, "catch up" with the articles (which means mark them all as read), view all the messages (even ones you've already read), subscribe to a group, and view a list of the newsgroups you've subscribed to.

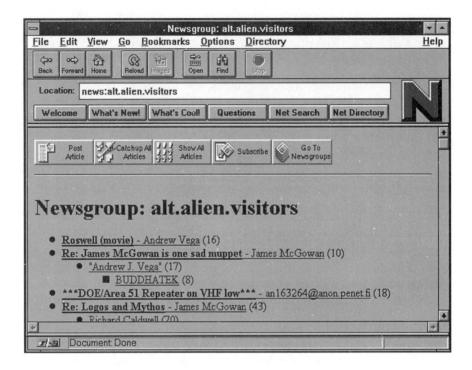

Netscape's new newsgroup features turns the Web browser into a newsreader.

Logging On Over There—Telnet

Telnet is a system that lets you log onto other computers that are connected to the Internet. You can play games, search library catalogs, dig through databases, and so on. You'll occasionally find links from Web documents to telnet sites (using the **telnet://** URL).

What happens when you click on one of these links? That depends on the browser you are using and whether you have set it up correctly. In some cases, such as AIR Mosaic, when you click on the link, the associated telnet application starts, and you are automatically connected to the telnet site. You may still have to login by typing a login name and, perhaps, password. AIR Mosaic is part of the AIR Series of applications and comes with AIR Telnet already configured.

In other cases, you'll have to make sure your Web browser is properly configured. For instance, if you wanted to use a telnet application with Cello, you'd select **Configure|Use your own|Telnet client**.

Then you'd type the path and filename of the telnet program you are using (there are a number of shareware telnet programs around— I looked at a few in *The Complete Idiot's Next Step with the Internet*).

If the telnet program you are using lets you tell it the hostname of the telnet site when you launch it, you would include **#h** after the filename. For instance, **c:\ibox\bin\airtel.exe #h** tells Cello to launch the AIR Telnet program, and to tell the program the telnet site address. Now, when you click on a link that uses a **telnet://** URL, Cello launches the program and connects for you.

Exactly how you configure a browser for telnet varies, of course. Netscape, for instance, lets you set it up in the Preferences dialog box, while Mosaic makes you do so in the MOSAIC.INI file, in the [Viewers] section.

Some browsers don't have telnet support, though—InternetWorks among them. If you click on a **telnet://** link, you'll get an error message. Close the document that appeared (the one that now says **Document not accessible**), then point at the link and click with the **right mouse button**. Select **Copy URL to Clipboard**, then open your telnet program and paste the URL into the program's connection dialog box; remove the **telnet://** part, and away you go.

Here's a good place to start if you want to find some interesting telnet sites: **http://www.cc.ukans.edu/ hytelnet_html/ START.TXT.html**. This will take you to the hypertext version of HYTELNET, a telnet directory.

Lots, Lots More

These are only the most common resources linked to the Web—it's by no means an exhaustive list. Go to **http://akebono.stanford.edu/ yahoo/Computers/World_Wide_Web/Gateways/** to find links to other things you can play with, such as links to IRC (Internet Relay Chat), X.500, whois, even TeleText and Sybase, and other strange and obscure stuff.

There's more to come, too. Go to the **Data Sources not yet online** document at **http://info.cern.ch/hypertext/DataSources/ Overview.html** to get an idea of what's happening on the Web.

Working with Forms

Many Web documents these days contain forms. These let you type information in and click on buttons. For example, let's say you want to search for a file at an FTP site. You could go to this "ArchiePlex" site: **http://www.lerc.nasa.gov/Doc/archieplex.html**.

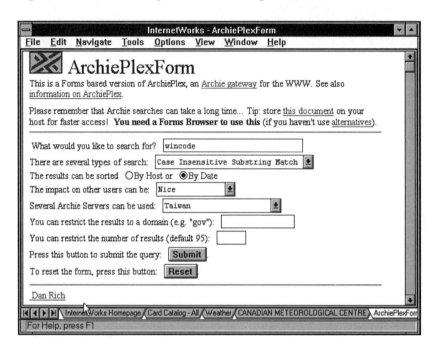

InternetWorks, at the NASA ArchiePlex site.

This document contains several forms elements:

➤ Text box—type in here.

➤ Drop-down list box—select an option here.

➤ Option (or radio) button—click on one of the options.

➤ Command button—click to carry out the command.

Anyone who's familiar with today's graphical user interfaces (Windows, the Macintosh, X Window, OS/2, and so on) will understand all this.

We'd start by typing the name of the file we are looking for—in this case, I'm looking for Wincode, a Windows UUENCODE program. Then we select the type of search. (Note that you can't Tab between these boxes in most browsers; you have to move the highlight with the mouse.) Click on the down arrow to open the list, and then click on the item you want to select (in most cases, you'll use **Case Insensitive Substring Match**). Next, we decide how to sort the result—I want it sorted **By Date**, not host.

Then we select the "impact" on other users: how much of the system resources we want to hog; the Archie server we want to use; the type of host we want to restrict the search to, if any; and the number of results we want to set as the maximum. (Read the online documentation to get more information about these options.)

Not all browsers have forms support. Most form documents, however, have a link to a non-forms alternative. Notice the **alternatives** link in the ArchiePlex illustration.

Finally, we click on the **Submit** button to start the search.

Using E-Mail

Many browsers these days have e-mail support (sometimes called *mailto* support). This means that when you click on a **mailto:** link, the browser's e-mail window pops up. The To and From boxes will already be filled in. All you need to do is write a message and click on **Send**.

Browsers that have e-mail support require that you enter some basic configuration information. (In InternetWorks, select **Options|User**. In Netscape, select **Options|Preferences**, and then select **Mail and Proxies**.) You'll need to enter your e-mail address (so the program knows what to enter into the From line); your full name, perhaps (so it adds your name, in parentheses, to the From line); and, sometimes, your mail server—the host that handles your e-mail (so it knows where to send your e-mail).

If a browser has e-mail support, it probably lets you open the e-mail window from a menu, too. In InternetWorks, select **File|Send Mail**. In Netscape, it's **File|Mail Document**. (Mosaic only lets you send mail to technical support.) You'll have to enter the To address, although the From address will be there.

Getting More Info

Browsers sometimes let you get to more information about the document you are viewing. Most let you view the source. In Netscape, for instance, you'd select **View|Source**; in Mosaic, **File|Document Source**. In Internet Works, you'll see a window with the document's source HTML displayed, tags and all. (If the source doesn't appear, you may be viewing a cached document—close the source window, reload the document, then try again.)

You may be able to view other information, too. In InternetWorks, you can select **Window|Document Info**. You'll see a dialog box showing the document's title, URL, and transfer-information properties (when the file was transferred, the Web server type, and so on). There's also a Comments box, though this is not currently in use.

The Least You Need to Know

➤ Use the **ftp://** URL to go to an anonymous FTP site. *Much* easier than UNIX FTP!

➤ Use an ArchiePlex server to find the files you want.

➤ Use the **gopher://** URL to go to a Gopher site.

➤ Find a Veronica or Jughead link at a Gopher site to search gopherspace.

➤ WAIS is not supported very well from Web browsers; the best way to use it is by pointing your browser to a Gopher server and then finding a gateway to a WAIS server.

➤ There are a couple of finger servers around the Web.

➤ Most browsers let you read newsgroup messages; but they are not very convenient.

➤ Telnet support isn't built into a browser, but many will automatically start a telnet program for you.

➤ If a Web browser has *mailto* support, you can click on e-mail links or open a mail window from a menu.

Part 6
Web-Preneurship

Until now, you may have been thinking, "How can I add my information to the Web?" What information? Anything. A chapter from a novel you've just finished, photos from your trip to Lhasa, information about your company, or the latest jai alai scores.

Well, creating Web documents is pretty easy, with a little effort spent. (No wait, not much effort, really—you'll create your own home page by the time you finish Chapter 21!)

I'll tell you all you need to set up a simple Web site. I'll explain how to link documents together, add inline images, make links within documents, format your text, and more. I'll even tell you how to find somewhere to put your Web site. (It may be free, too!)

Creating Your Own Home Page

Publishing on the Web is surprisingly easy, and the first step to publishing should probably be creating your own home page. It's a great way to get a feel for how HTML works, and you'll produce something you can use, too.

What is a home page? Here's a quick refresher:

➤ It's the page that appears when you open your browser.

➤ It's the page that appears when you click on the Home toolbar button or select some kind of Home command (virtually all browsers have a Home command somewhere).

Home Page: What's It Good For?

Why bother creating your own home page? There are a few reasons. First, telling your browser to view a home page on your hard drive will speed up loading the program; it's much quicker to load from a "local" drive than to transfer it from across the Internet. However, if that were the only reason, you could just copy an HTML document from the Web somewhere and put it on your hard drive. (And anyway, plenty of Web browsers come with default home pages loaded on the hard drive.) Why create your own?

Well, on the Internet, one size doesn't fit all. Everyone uses the Internet in a different way. The home page someone else has created won't have all the links you want and will contain plenty that you don't want.

Why not customize your home page with links across the Internet to where you want to go? Or have a home page, plus a series of documents on your hard drive linked to that home page: one document for work, one for music, one for newsgroups, one for whatever else. Then you can have links from the home page to those separate documents. Hey, let's try that!

First, the Basics

You're about to learn about HTML, so we're going to get into some highly complicated stuff... *Not!* HTML is remarkably simple. Sure, turn off *Melrose Place*, put down *The Enquirer*, and pay attention, but don't expect to be blinded by science.

Remember that HTML files are simple ASCII text files, right? ASCII means *American Standard Code for Information Interchange*. This is a standard system used by computers to recognize text. An ASCII text file comprises the letters of the alphabet, the punctuation characters, the numbers, and a few special characters. The nice thing about ASCII is that it's widely recognizable by thousands of programs and many different types of computers.

HTML files are ASCII files that have been specially designed to be read by Web browsers. These files use the same characters as any other ASCII file, but they use a special convention that all Web browsers "know" about. That convention is this: "if you see anything in brackets like these < >, you know that it's a special code." So Web browsers, when they are rendering the HTML document into normal text, look for these brackets and examine the text inside them to look for instructions.

Rendering is the term used to describe the action of looking at the HTML codes, formatting the text in the ASCII file according to the instructions held in the codes, stripping the codes out of the text, and displaying the resulting text in the browser.

Well, let's create an HTML file—you'll see how easy it really is. Start by opening Notepad (okay, any word processor that you like working with). Now, enter this text; you can replace the text with other stuff, but don't change the tags between the brackets (< >):

```
<TITLE>My Home Page</TITLE>
<H1>My Very Own Home Page</H1>

<H2>Really Important Stuff</H2>
These are WWW pages I use a lot. <P>

<H2>Not So Important Stuff</H2>
These are WWW pages I use now and again. <P>

<H3>Not Important At All Stuff</H3>
These are WWW pages I use to waste time. <P>
```

What are these codes?

The correct term for the HTML codes is *tags*, so I guess I'd better start using it.

<TITLE> </TITLE> The text between these tags is the title of the document. You won't see the text in the document itself. Rather, it's an identifier used by browsers. For instance, Netscape and Mosaic would put the text in the title bar. The title is often used in bookmark and history lists, too.

<H1> </H> The heading level. You can have up to six different levels. We've used levels 1, 2, and 3.

247

Don't worry about the *case* of the tags. You can type *title* or *TITLE*, or *Title*, or *TItlE*, or *TiTlE* or whatever takes your fancy.

<P> This denotes the end of a paragraph. Simply typing a carriage return in your HTML file will not create a new paragraph in the final document as it's displayed in the browser. You must put in the <P> tag. Without the tag, you will find that lines run into each other.

 If you are using Notepad, you don't have to close, just save. If you are using a word processor, though, you may have to close, because many word processors won't let other programs use a file while it's open. And remember, save in ASCII (plain text) format!

Notice that, in most cases, tags are paired. There's an opening and a closing tag, and the closing tag is the same as the opening tag with the exception of the forward slash after the left angle bracket, <H> and </H>, for instance. The <P> tag is an exception; there's only one, and it appears after the paragraph.

Now, save the file as a text-only file and close it. Save it using the .HTM extension rather than .TXT, even though it's still plain text. For example, don't call it HOME.TXT; call it HOME.HTM. Put it in the directory that your other HTM files are stored in, if any, or the directory your browser is saved in.

Now, go to your browser and open the document, using whatever command is appropriate for that particular browser. In Netscape, use the **File|Open File** command; in Mosaic or InternetWorks use the **File|Open Local File**.

What do you see? A formatted WWW document. It's rubbish, of course, but you can see how easy it was to create.

Now we're going to get fancy. Let's add an *anchor*, a link to another document. Let's say you are "studying" erotic art. You've just discovered an archive of art by the well-known Olivia de Berardinis (well known to the readers of *Playboy*, anyway) and found that its address is

```
http://www.mgainc.com/Art/jsd/olivia/od_list.html.
```

You can add this line to your document, (under the Really Important Stuff heading, of course), in this manner:

```
<A HREF="http://www.mgainc.com/Art/jsd/olivia/od_list.html">Olivia</A>
```

You'll want to add all sorts of other stuff, of course, such as the Alberto Varga and Ted Kimer Web documents, too. Save the file again. Add any other links you think would be useful.

When you've finished, you need to set this up as your home page. Again, the procedure varies depending on which browser you're using. For InternetWorks, you should use File Manager to view the IW directory (or wherever you stored the program) and rename the file DEFAULT.HTM to DEFAULT2.HTM. Then rename your new home page file DEFAULT.HTM. (You'll probably want to add a link from your home page to the DEFAULT2.HTM file—you'll see how in a moment.)

Using Mosaic and you can't open the file? Some early versions of Mosaic had a bug that stopped you from opening a local file. *Get the latest version of Mosaic!* See Chapter 27 to learn where to get it.

To change the home page in Version 2 alpha 8 of Mosaic for Windows, select **Options|Preferences** and type the path and filename into the **Home Page** text box. If you have an earlier version of Mosaic, though, you'll have to change the MOSAIC.INI file. Open your MOSAIC.INI file in Notepad (it's probably in the WINDOWS directory, or maybe in the same directory as the program), and find this line:

```
Home Page=
```

Change whatever comes after the = sign. You need to end up with this (or something similar):

```
Home Page=file://c:\mosaic\homepage.htm
```

Your "path" to the HOMEPAGE.HTM may be different, or course. Enter the correct drive and directories after **file://**. Save and close the file.

No home page when you start your browser? Although you've defined a home page, you may also need to "turn it on." In Netscape, you'd need to select the Home Page Location option button in the Preferences dialog box. In Mosaic, you'd need to make sure that the MOSAIC.INI file has a line that says `Autoload Home Page=yes`.

Other Web browsers vary. In Cello, you'll select **Configure|Files and directories|Home page** and type the URL into a dialog box. In Netscape, you'll select **Options|Preferences**, select styles in the Preferences dialog box's drop-down list box, and then type the URL into the Home Page Location text box. Check your browser's documentation if you can't figure out how to change the home page.

Now, the next time you start your browser, you'll see your very own home page. Simple, eh?

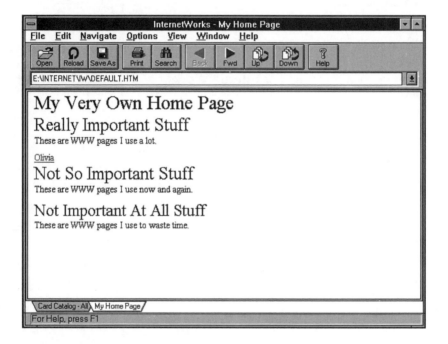

Creating a simple home page is… simple.

Go Forth and Create More!

You can use this method to create a hierarchy of documents. Have a document that appears when you open, with a table of contents linked to several other documents. In each of those documents, you could then have links related to a particular subject.

Let's say you want to set up a document for the music sites you are interested in. We'll call it RNR.HTM. Create that document in the same way as the first one and put it in the same directory. We can then create a link from your home page to the Rock n' Roll document; but first, we'd better talk a little about the types of links that you can create.

Linking Documents

First, let's look at that Olivia link again:

```
<A HREF="http://www.mgainc.com/Art/jsd/olivia/od_list.html">Olivia </A>
```

Notice that the URL is included *within* the angle brackets and within quotation marks. A link tag (a tag that is used to create a hypertext link in your document) starts with <A followed by a space, followed by **HREF="**. Then you enter the URL. We've looked at URLs before. This is the same URL that you can use to tell a browser to go to a particular Web site. At the end of the URL, you have ">, followed by some kind of text, anything you want. This is the text that will appear as the link in the browser. In InternetWorks, Mosaic, and Netscape, for example, it's the text that is underlined (in this case, you would click on the word **Olivia**). Following the text, you have the closing tag </A>.

The <A HREF="*url*"> tags are often known as *anchors*; for this reason, many people refer to the links themselves in the Web documents as anchors.

So, let's create a link to the RNR.HTM file, like this:

```
<A HREF="RNR.HTM">Rock n' Roll</A>
```

Is **RNR.HTM** a URL? Well, yes. It's a *relative* URL. In Chapter 22 we're going to get more complicated and explain *relative* and *absolute* URLs. But for now, all you need to know is that this link means "look for the RNR.HTM file." Where? Well, it doesn't say, so the only place the browser can look is in the same directory as the original file. (Which is fine, because you are going to place the RNR.HTM file in the same directory, right?)

This is really simple, isn't it? You create a home page (called HOME.HTM) with links to any number of other documents in the same directory. One for Rock n' Roll, one for art, one for music, one for conspiracy theories, one for... whatever sort of information you are interested in and can find on the Web. Then, you fill those documents up with more links to all those interesting sites. Whad'ya know, you're a Web publisher!

A Word About Paragraphs

Web browsers don't deal with paragraphs in the same way that word processors do. If the browser finds several spaces, including blank lines, it will compress all the space into a single paragraph, unless it sees the <P> tag somewhere. When it finds the <P>, it ends the paragraph and starts a new one on the next line. (Actually, browsers vary; some will end the paragraph, leave a blank line, and then start a new paragraph.)

There's a new form of HTML on the way, though; HTML+. In this system, <P> is actually a tag denoting the *beginning* of a paragraph, and there *is* an ending </P>. However, you can omit the </P> because each time the browser sees the <P>, it starts a new paragraph—so it has to end the previous one, right?

In InternetWorks, you may want to add a link like this:

```
<A HREF="DEFAULT2.HTM">InternetWorks' Default Home Page</A>
```

This link points to the DEFAULT2.HTM file you created earlier in this chapter, so you can quickly use InternetWorks' directory system whenever you need it.

Do you need to worry about this? No. HTML+ isn't in use yet, so you can forget it for now. And HTML+ will be able to figure out the meaning of the current HTML <P> tags, anyway.

Want a Shortcut?

There are shortcuts to creating home pages. Who wants to type all those URLs, after all?

Well, one way to grab the URLs, for instance, is to visit the Web page you are interested in, and then copy the text from the Location text box above the document in InternetWorks or Netscape, or the URL box in Mosaic. You can highlight this text; then press **Ctrl+C** or select **Edit|Copy**. (Most browsers have some method to copy the URL.) You can then just paste it into your home page. You can also grab URLs from links on a document—first, view the source. For example, in Netscape, you would select **View|Source**; in Mosaic, you would select **File|Document Source**. (In InternetWorks, you have to save the document using **File|Save As**; then open it in a word processor.) Find the link you want (it's a little tricky with all those codes in there), and highlight the URL you want—in fact, highlight everything from the <A to the </A>. Press **Ctrl+C**, and you've copied it to the Clipboard.

> InternetWorks, Cello, and InterAp's Web Navigator have another way to grab links; in all of these, point to the link and press the **right mouse button**. In InternetWorks, you will see a pop-up menu; select **Copy URL to Clipboard**. In the other two, you'll see a dialog box; click on the **Copy** button.

Feeling *really* lazy? Then "borrow" a Web document. Copy this Web document to your hard disk: http://www.ncsa.uiuc.edu/SDG/Software/Mosaic/StartingPoints/NetworkStartingPoints.html. (You can view this from Mosaic by selecting **Starting Points|Starting Points Document**). The document provides access to many different types of WWW resources.

Some browsers also let you copy the bookmark list (the *hotlist*) or the history list to an HTML file. You can then use that file as your home page, or simply copy the pieces you want into your home page. Cello, Web Navigator, and Netscape let you do this, for instance, and Mosaic lets you copy individual links from the Menu Editor.

The Least You Need to Know

➤ Creating a home page is very simple—a five minute job.

➤ HTML *tags* are enclosed within brackets < >.

➤ In most cases, you need an opening tag and a closing tag—`<TITLE>My Home Page</TITLE>`, for instance.

➤ These tags are used to create titles, headings, links, and much more.

➤ A link is created thus: `<A HREF="url">Your Link Text</A>`.

➤ If you use a filename in place of the *url* in the link, the browser will look in the same directory as the current document.

➤ You can replace your browser's default home page with your new one.

The Word on the Web: Web Publishing

Just before I started work on this book, a small publisher's organization asked me to set up a Web site for them, on the cheap. Sure, there are companies asking for several thousand bucks to set up a Web site, and another thou or two a year to maintain it. But hey, why pay that when you can set up a Web site for *free*! (Well, almost.) Anyway, the Colorado Independent Publishers Association (CIPA) wanted a site, and in this chapter, we're going to use their site as a simple example of how to create the HTML files you need if you want to publish on the Web (you can visit this site at **http://usa.net/cipa**).

In Chapter 23, we'll talk a little about actually setting up the site: finding a service provider's system on which you can place your HTML files. In this chapter, we're going to get a bit deeper into Web publishing and learn a few more HTML tags (oh joy!) and see how to fit all sorts of neat things into your documents.

WYSIWTBWYTS

Okay, I made this up. In Chapter 24, we'll talk a little about *WYSIWYG*, computer jargon for *What You See Is What You Get*. But *WYSIWTBWYTS* refers to what your Web documents will look like; it means *What You See Is Whatever The Browser Wants You To See*.

We're going to learn how to define parts of your document as different styles: headers, addresses, lists, and so on. You may have an idea of what each style is (based on what your browser does, or perhaps, how you have configured your browser), but remember that other people's browsers will do different things.

For instance, here's an interesting tag pair, the <BLOCKQUOTE> and </BLOCKQUOTE> tags. The text between these tags is defined as a *quote*. What does that mean? Whatever the browser wants it to mean. Most browsers will automatically indent the text a few spaces, and they generally don't let users modify the indentation. However, browsers often let the user change the text. For example, using InternetWorks, I could change the <BLOCKQUOTE> text to be any font on my system; I could pick bold, italic, or bold italic; and I could change the color and size. I could even add an underline and strikethrough. Take a look at the following quote:

```
blah, blahdey blah, blahblah blah blah blah, blahdey blah, blah<P>

<BLOCKQUOTE>The English have "the best constitution and the best
King any nation was ever blessed with."</BLOCKQUOTE>
<B>Benjamin Franklin</B><P>

blah blah blah blah, blahdey blah, blahblah blah blah blah.<P>
```

(The text between the <BLOCKQUOTE> and </BLOCKQUOTE> is the quote; the text between the <B> and </B> is an ordinary paragraph using bold text.)

This quote may end up looking like either of these two examples, or like something different entirely.

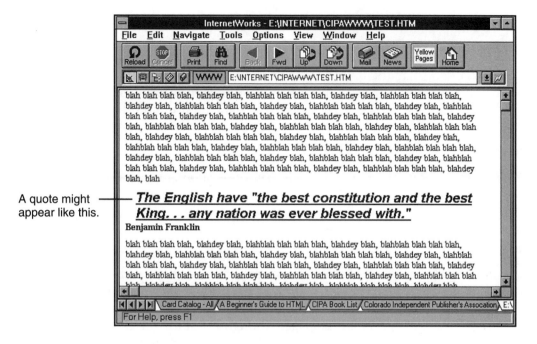

A quote might appear like this.

Here's one way to show a quote...

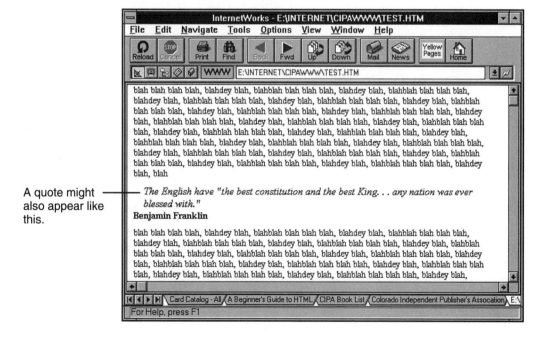

A quote might also appear like this.

...and here's another.

So remember, in many cases, you are providing text with a style name, but the way it will actually appear depends on the browser.

Here's another problem: bugs in browsers. Many have bugs, so they don't display the text the way they are supposed to. The next time you view a Web document and see some strange formatting, don't be quick to blame it on the author—it may be the fault of your browser!

Step One—Where Do We Start?

Publishing on the Web is simply an extension of what we learned in the last chapter. If you haven't read that chapter (naughty!), then go back. You'll need that knowledge in this chapter.

It's a good idea to use two or more browsers to check your documents before putting them on the Web. That way, you'll get a better idea of what the documents will look like in different situations.

Now, we first need to create some kind of main document, the page that most Web browsers will see when they visit your site (all right, all right, what most people are calling the "home page," though I don't think that makes much sense!). That is the document in which you will channel people where you want them to go. You'll publicize the URL for that document (we'll see how in Chapter 23) and get other documents around the Web to link to that main document.

Here's what I have at the top of my document (remember, the final version of the HTML file is an ASCII text file):

```
<TITLE>Colorado Independent Publisher's Association</TITLE>
<H1>Colorado Independent Publisher's Association</H1>
<IMG SRC = "cipalogo.gif" ><P>
<HR>
```

I start with the <TITLE> and </TITLE> tags. The text between these is the document title. It's not seen in the document when viewing it in a browser—it's a reference, the name of the document. Mosaic, for instance, displays it in the program's title bar, and many browsers display the name in their history list and hotlist. InternetWorks, for instance, displays it in the Card Catalog.

Next, we have the <H1> and </H1> tags. These are Heading 1 tags, and I generally use the same text as the TITLE text, so the heading at the top of the document is the same as the heading that will appear in the history list or hotlist. Next we have the <IMG SRC = "cipalogo.gif" > line, followed by a <P>. This line puts the CIPA logo just below the heading—we'll come back to this in a moment. Finally, I end with <HR>. This is a divider line (a horizontal rule) across the screen, a good way to break up portions of the document. Below this line, I've added some introductory text about the CIPA site. So, here's what you'll actually see when viewing the document.

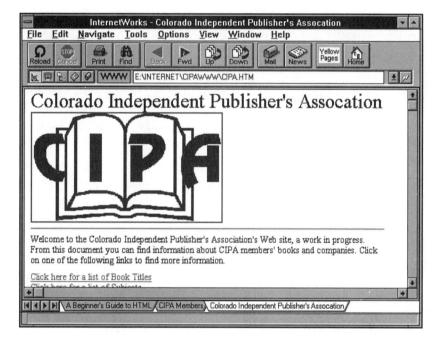

The top of the CIPA main document.

Pretty Pictures

What's the first thing you notice at Web sites these days? Some kind of picture. A logo, someone's face, a landscape, or whatever. These pictures are *inline images*, and they can be one of two kinds: .GIF files

259

(Graphics Interchange Format) or .XBM files (an X Window System graphics format). Where are you going to get these? Lots of Windows graphics programs can create .GIF files, these days, and if you are working on UNIX, you can find programs to create .XBM files easily enough.

The easiest way to deal with an inline image is to put it in the same directory as the document, and then use a *relative* URL to point to it, like this:

```
<IMG SRC="url">
```

(What's IMG SRC? Nothing technical—just *Image Source*.) Here's what I actually put in the document:

```
<IMG SRC = "cipalogo.gif" ><P>
```

The text `cipalogo.gif` is the picture I'm using, and I've added a <P> tag to break the paragraph up, so this will sit on a line by itself. You must use the correct extension for the image filenames, by the way— .GIF or .XBM.

Now, what about turning a graphic into a link so that when the user clicks on the graphic, it takes him somewhere? Easy; place the entire graphic entry, tags and all, inside a link:

```
<A HREF = "contact.htm"><IMG SRC = "cipalogo.gif"></A><P>
```

Notice that the `<IMG SRC = "cipalogo.gif">` appears where a link's text would; the picture *is* the link. When the reader clicks on this picture, the CONTACT.HTM file appears.

Move It Over Here—Image Positioning

You can place an image on a line with text and then determine the position of the text relative to the picture. For instance, if you have a tag like this:

```
<IMG ALIGN=TOP SRC = "filename" ><P>
```

you'll get the text aligned with the top of the image. If you use `ALIGN=BOTTOM`, the text is at the bottom of the image, and if you use `ALIGN=MIDDLE` the text is in the middle of the image. This doesn't work well with very large images, such as the CIPA logo, but can work well for images that are relatively small that you want to be inside a sentence or paragraph. (With large images, you end up with loads of space above or below the text that's on the same line.)

Want to find some icons you can use in your documents? Go to an *icon server*: a Web site from which you can download icons or even link your documents across the Web to a particular icon. Try these:

```
http://www.bsdi.com/icons
http://www-ns.rutgers.edu/doc-images
http://www.di.unipi.it/iconbrowser/icons.html
http://www.cit.gu.edu.au/~anthony/icons/
```

For Graphic-less Users

What does a user see if he doesn't have a graphics browser, or if he has turned inline images off? Well, he'll see one of two things. He'll either see what the browser automatically displays when it can't display an image, or he'll see the text *you* want him to see. Browsers often display a small logo (for example, InternetWorks displays its "wave" icon), or some text, such as [IMAGE] for instance, if it's not displaying inline images. But you can use the ALT= parameter to display something else. For instance, if I use this:

```
<IMG SRC = "cipalogo.gif" ALT="CIPA_Logo"><P>
```

the user will see the word "CIPA_Logo" in place of the actual logo. (Put the text in quotation marks, and don't put any spaces inside; you can use an underscore character in place of the space.)

Now Where? Linking to Other Places

We've already looked at linking to other documents in Chapter 21. Here's what I added to the main CIPA page:

```
<A HREF = "book.htm">Click here for a list of Book Titles</A><BR>
<A HREF = "subject.htm">Click here for a list of Subjects</A><BR>
<A HREF = "publish.htm">Click here for a list of Publishers</
A><BR><P>
<A HREF = "contact.htm">Click here for information about joining or
contacting CIPA</A><BR><P>
<A HREF = "members.htm">Click here for information for CIPA
members</A><BR><P>
If you are interested in joining an organization for small
```

261

```
publishers, but don't live in Colorado, <A HREF = "pma.htm">click
here</A><BR><P>
<A HREF = "1sttime.htm">For the First Time Publisher...</A><P>

<HR>
```

As you can see, I have several links to other documents. In fact, this site (like most Web sites) is a series of interlinked documents. For example:

```
<A HREF = "book.htm">Click here for a list of Book Titles</A><P>
```

This line will appear as the text **Click here for a list of Book Titles**. That text is a link to the BOOK.HTM document. This is a relative URL, meaning "look for BOOK.HTM in the same directory as the current document." Within that document are a series of links to other documents, each about a particular book, and *those* documents have links to other documents containing information about publishers and ordering.

At the bottom of this list of links is another <HR> tag; again, this puts a line across the screen. (By the way, I later turned this list into a *bulleted* list—we'll look at this later.)

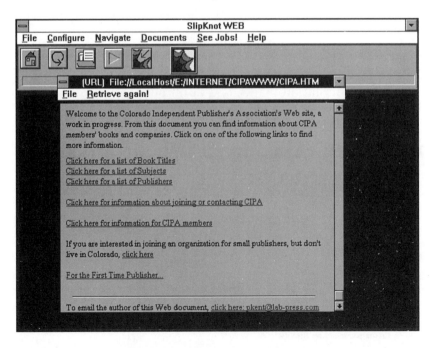

The list of links at the CIPA site, shown in the SlipKnot browser.

You'll also notice that some of the lines have <P>, some have <BR>, and some have both. We'll cover that in a moment. But first, let's take a closer look at addresses and URLs.

It's a Family Affair—Relative Versus Absolute Links

Let's come back to this issue of relative and absolute links. I'm using relative links here. I can do so safely because all these documents are going to be grouped together—in the same directory—so the links will always work. In fact, it's better that I do so because I don't know the name of the directory the files will be placed in when I've finished; I'm creating these files at home on my PC, but eventually they'll sit on my service provider's system somewhere. If I used absolute addresses, I'd have to know for sure where the files would be when I finally place them on that system.

Sometimes, of course, you *have* to use absolute addresses. If I want to create a link from this document to a document elsewhere in the world (perhaps to a Web site created by another small-publisher's association), I'd have to give the absolute URL. I'd use `http://this.web.site.com/this_directory/thisfile.htm` or whatever.

If you are creating Web documents that are probably going to be copied by people back to their computers, then you'll have to use absolute addresses. If you copy the CIPA main page back to your hard disk, the URLs will no longer make sense because they refer to files on a different computer. If I'd used an absolute address, this wouldn't be a problem—wherever the file is, the links make sense.

A URL for Every Purpose

Now, about those URLs. A URL is, you'll remember, a *Uniform Resource Locator*. It's an address to a file somewhere else on the Web. We've looked at the http:// URLs so far. These are pointers to files on a Web server, but the Web lets you link to much more than just Web documents. You can also link to Gophers, FTP sites, newsgroups, and more. So there are other forms of URLs, ones that tell the browser the sort of resource it's going to. There's `gopher://host.name/`, for instance. This points to a Gopher server. There's `file://host.name/directory/filename`, which points to a particular file on a particular machine, perhaps an FTP site. And there's `ftp://host.name/directory/filename`, which also points to an FTP site.

URLs are not alone. There are also URIs (*Uniform Resource Identifier*), URNs (*Uniform Resource Name*), and URCs (*Uniform Resource Citation*).

URI is the name for an address in which objects are defined using short text strings. (URLs are a form of URI.) URNs and URCs are still in development. URNs are another form of address, more advanced than URLs. And URCs are object descriptions that may include the URL but also may contain information about the author, copyright, date, and any other relevant information. (Now forget all this—you may never need to know it again.)

Links Within Documents

What happens if you want to create a link that jumps from one part of a document to another? That is, when your reader clicks on the link, you want to take the reader to a point further down (or maybe higher up) in the same document, not a different document.

No problem. First, you have to set a <A NAME= > tag. For instance, let's look at the Travel and Learn document at the CIPA site, which contains a sample book chapter. In that chapter is a list of companies that have archaeology, history, and dinosaur programs. In the actual paper book, the list sits on a page preceding the information about each company, and you have to flip through the pages to find the one you want. In the Web document, why not let the user click on the one he wants to find out about and go directly there?

One of those companies is called Archaeological Tours. I set this tag on the line immediately preceding the heading for that company:

```
<A NAME = ARC>
```

This acts as a sort of bookmark. Then, I created the link earlier in the document:

```
<A HREF = "#Arc">Archaeological Tours</A> <P>
```

This is just like a normal, document-to-document link, *except* that instead of placing a filename into the link, I use the # sign followed by the name of the <A NAME = > tag. Easy. Now, when my readers click on the words **Archaeological Tours**, they go straight to that section.

Gimme Room—Adding Blank Lines

As you've already seen, you can end a paragraph using the <P> tag. Wherever a Web browser sees a paragraph, it will assume the paragraph has ended, and start subsequent text on the next line.

Now, some browsers simply start the next paragraph immediately below the end of the last paragraph. Others leave a space and *then* start a new paragraph. For instance, here's your HTML:

```
Item 1<P>
Item 2<P>
Item 3<P>
Item 4<P>
Item 5<P>
```

Web browsers may display this in two different ways. Many will display it like this:

```
Item 1
Item 2
Item 3
Item 4
Item 5
```

But others, such as Cello Version 1.0, will display it like this:

```
Item 1

Item 2

Item 3

Item 4

Item 5
```

How can you make sure that there's no space left between the lines? Use a line break, rather than a paragraph break: the <BR> tag:

```
Item 1<BR>
Item 2<BR>
Item 3<BR>
Item 4<BR>
Item 5<BR>
```

Now, even Cello will display the text like this:

```
Item 1
Item 2
Item 3
Item 4
Item 5
```

Give Me More Control!

As you've seen, browsers ignore spaces and line breaks. They are only interested in the tags. Take a look at this example:

```
Blah blah blah, blahdey blah, blah blah blah. Blah blah blah,
blahdey blah, blah blah blah. Blah blah blah, blahdey blah, blah
blah blah. Blah blah blah, blahdey blah, blah blah blah.
```

And now this example:

```
Blah blah blah, blahdey blah,        blah blah blah. Blah blah
blah, blahdey blah, blah blah blah.        Blah blah blah, blahdey
blah, blah blah blah.

Blah blah blah, blahdey blah, blah blah blah.
```

Want several blank lines? Just run several <P> or <BR> tags together (as in <P><P><P>); there's no need to put them on separate lines.

These actually display exactly the same thing, because your Web browser won't use the extra spaces and blank lines—it moves everything together. There *is* a way to force browsers to use the extra spaces and lines (and other items, such as indents). Use the <PRE> and </PRE> tags (the *preform* tags). The following figure shows what the second example looks like in a browser, first without the <PRE> and </PRE> tags, and then with them.

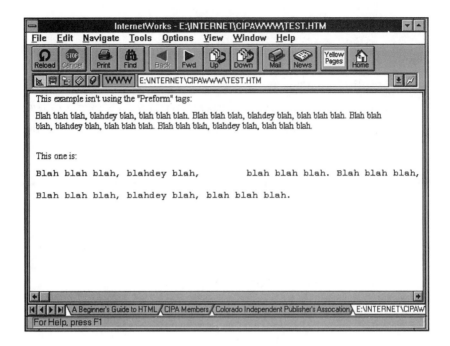

The <PRE> and </PRE> tags force the browser to display text as originally formatted.

You'll notice also that the text has run off the screen (it's not being "wrapped" onto the next line); the browser is only starting a new line when a new line begins in the HTML document. Also, notice that the text, in this case, is Courier. InternetWorks, by default, uses Courier for <PRE> text, though it can be modified. However, these tags are often used to show program listings, and sans serif fonts are commonly used in documentation for such listings.

That's a drawback, of course, that will limit the use you can put these tags to. You can't just create your HTML files in a word processor; format them anyway you want, use the preform tags, and expect them to look good!

The Least You Need to Know

➤ Web browsers all display Web documents differently. You only have a general idea of what your documents will look like.

➤ Use the <HR> tag to place a horizontal rule across the page.

➤ Use the <IMG SRC = *"filename*.gif" > tag to place an inline image.

➤ Use **ALIGN=*TOP/BOTTOM/MIDDLE*** and **ALT="*text*"** within the image tag to position the text relative to the image, and to provide text for browsers that are not displaying inline images.

➤ Use the <A NAME = *targetname*> and <A HREF = "#*targetname*">*link text*</A> tags to link one part of a document to another.

➤ Use the <P> tag to end a paragraph; use the <BR> tag to move text to the next line, ensuring that the browser doesn't leave a blank line.

➤ Use the <PRE> and </PRE> tags to make browsers use the original text format, line breaks, indents, and all.

It's Not Finished Yet—More Web Publishing

In the last chapter, you learned to create a basic Web document, but there's a lot more to learn before you're ready to go out bragging that you have your own Web site. In this chapter, we'll take a look at some more advanced HTML techniques, find out where to go for more information, and learn about placing the HTML documents on a system with a Web server.

Meet the Author!—Web E-mail

Some Web browsers let you send e-mail. InternetWorks, for instance, displays a dialog box where you can type a message. You can either select **File|Send Mail**, then enter the address of the person you want to write to, or you can click on a *mailto* link in the document.

Flip back a few pages to the picture of the SlipKnot Web browser in Chapter 22. At the bottom, you'll see this line:

```
To email the author of this Web document, click here:
    pkent@lab-press.com
```

The words **click here: pkent@lab-press.com** are a link, and when you click on them (in a browser with e-mail functions), you'll see the e-mail box, with the correct e-mail address already filled in.

How is this created? Using this line in the HTML document:

```
To email the author of this Web document, <a href =
"mailto:pkent@lab-press.com">click here: pkent@lab-press.com</a>
```

Simply replace **pkent@lab-press.com** after **mailto:** with the address you want to use, replace the link text, and presto! You've created your own mailto link.

There Must Be More...

Yes, there is. Let's look at a few other things I did at the CIPA site, plus a few things that I *didn't* do but that you may want to. You may want to place addresses into documents, use italic and bold text, put information in lists, and more.

Formatting Addresses

In the Travel and Learn document, I had several addresses I wanted to set on the left side of the page in italics, without blank lines between each line of the address. Here's how I did it:

```
<H5><A NAME = Arc></A>ARCHAEOLOGICAL TOURS</H5>
<I>271 Madison Avenue/Suite 904<br>
New York NY 10016<br>
Phone: (212)986-3054<br>
Contact: Linda Feinstone</I><P>
```

The first line is the heading (the name of the company). Then I just placed each line of the address on a separate line, with a <BR> tag to force a line break. That way, browsers that leave blank lines after <P> tags wouldn't break up this address (I ended with a <P> tag, though).

To make the text italic, I placed it between <I> and </I> tags. A browser will display everything between those tags as italic.

Why didn't I use the <ADDRESS> and </ADDRESS> tags for this address? Well, these are not really for street addresses. Rather, they are intended for a single line of information about a document's author, such as the e-mail address. Cello 1.0 even pushes the address text way over to the right, where I don't want it. I figured it was safer to set it using italics and a line break, so I could be sure how it would look.

> Be careful when embedding tags. That is, don't mix tags together. For example, don't try to make text both bold and italic like this: <I><B>this text</I></B>. It may work on some browsers but won't on many others. Don't try to embed other types of elements, such as headings, within character formatting tags.

More Text Formats

There are other text formatting tags, such as <B> and </B> (bold); <U> and </U> (underlined); <TT> and </TT> ("typewriter-style" font); and <STRONG> and </STRONG> (emphasis). There are *loads* of these, but you'll find that some browsers simply don't use them. Both InternetWorks and Cello 1.0, for instance, ignore <CODE> and </CODE>. In other cases, the browsers simply won't do what you think they should. Should the <STRONG> and </STRONG> tags display the text as bold or italic? It's probably bold. What about <EM> and </EM> tags (more emphasis tags)? Probably italics, but who knows for sure? If you want to make sure the text is bold or italics, don't use these tags; use the <B></B> and <I></I> sets, instead.

Lists of Stuff

There are several tags you can use if you'd like to like to place lists of items:

> **Unnumbered (Bulleted) Lists** Place a <UL> tag before the first item in the list, and </UL> after the last. Place <LI> before each

item in the list. When a browser displays the list, each item will be preceded by a bullet.

Numbered (or Ordered) Lists   Use the <OL> and </OL> to add numbers to the items (the numbers are added automatically for you). Place <LI> before each item in the list.

Definition Lists   Start the list with <DL>, and end it with </DL>. Place <DT> before each definition term and <DD> before each definition. This creates a list of terms followed by their definitions.

The <LI>, <DT>, and <DD> tags are single tags; they have no corresponding </> tag and are placed *before* the text they are formatting.

Don't Get Your Readers Lost!

One of the major problems with hypertext is that readers often get lost. They have trouble finding their way back to where they've been or forward to where they need to go.

You can never be sure how long a line will be in a hypertext system (it depends on how the reader sizes the browser window). Sometimes it's difficult to tell if a word at the beginning of a line is the start of an item in the list or part of the previous line that's wrapped down to the next line. Using bullets or numbers helps readers differentiate each entry in the list.

Part of the problem is that you don't know for sure how your readers are going to get to a particular document. They may have the URL of a document and go directly to that document, bypassing the "main" page. Or there may be several ways into a document—which did they take? For instance, at the CIPA site, there's a list of publishers, a list of books, and a list of subjects. Plus, there are individual documents for each book discussed at the site.

So, a reader could go to the publisher's list, go to a particular publisher's page, and then go to a book. Or the reader could go to the subject list and then directly to a book, or to the book list and then to a book.

It's a good idea to help the reader out by proving lots of links. For instance, in each book document, I've provided a link to the publisher's page, where the reader can find ordering information. Of course, the reader *may* have come from the publisher's page in the first place, in which case he could simply click on his browser's **Back** button to go back. If he *didn't* come from that page, he'd have no quick and easy way to find the publisher and shipping information without the link I provide.

I also provide links back to the main CIPA page, just in case a reader came directly to a page using the URL, bypassing the CIPA page. So think about the ways people can work in your site, and do them a favor: provide links to important places!

A Sneaky (and Smart) Trick—Steal It!

Here's a quick way to create HTML pages and page components: steal them! Many browsers let you take a look at the source document for the page you are viewing (and copy text from it), or save the HTML document.

If you find a page that looks very much like the one you want to create, view the source document, highlight the pieces you want, and then copy them. Paste the text into your text editor or HTML editor. Then edit the pieces you want to change, or simply save the entire document and work with it offline later.

Now, if you plan to use the page for personal use, there's no problem. If you are going to put the page up on the Web, however, you'd better change stuff. There are copyright issues here; you can't just steal someone's words and claim they are yours. What I'm suggesting is that you steal (...oops, borrow) the *structure* of the document and insert your own text between the HTML tags, as a way to quickly learn how Web documents are created.

Want to put notes into the HTML file that nobody can read? In DOS batch files, you start a line with **rem**, and in Windows .INI files, you start the line with the ; symbol. People often use these indicators so they can add reminders about important information. Well, in HTML files you can use the <!-- --> tag. None of the text that appears in the middle will be seen by the Web document reader, for example, **<!--Created 1/14/95-->**.

Also, if you find a link to a place that you'd like to use in your own documents, you can copy just the link, paste it into your document, and modify the text between the tags. In InternetWorks, for example, point at the link you want to copy, press the mouse button, and then select **Copy URL** from the pop-up menu. Cello and InterAp have a similar feature, too.

So What's All This, Then?

If you dig around in other people's HTML files, viewing the source to see what you can find, you will run across *loads* of stuff I haven't mentioned here (I'll explain how to find more HTML information in a moment).

You'll also find three tag sets that raise a couple of important questions: "What are these and why aren't I using them?" These are the tags:

<html></html>   This means, "everything between these tags is part of the HTML document."

<head></head>   This means "everything between these tags is part of the HTML document's header—the title and notes, and so on."

<body></body>   This means "everything between these tags is part of the HTML document's body—the actual text that the reader will see."

Why aren't we using these? Well, you really don't need them. They are actually ignored. The idea is that these tags identify the three main portions of the HTML document: all the text that is intended to be part of the HTML document and not just extraneous notes (**<html></html>**); all the text that is part of the document header— information such as the document title that is not seen by the reader (**<head></head>**); and everything that is part of the Web document that will be seen by the reader (**<body></body>**). But they are more for the author's use, or for use, perhaps, by an HTML editing program, which we'll look at in Chapter 24. In fact, some HTML editors will automatically place these tags for you. But they are ignored by Web browsers.

This Is Great! Gimme More!

I've told you about just a few HTML features. It's enough for you to start creating a pretty good little Web site, but as you get further into things, you may find that you want to try something more, such as creating forms.

If you want *more* information, you'll have to go elsewhere—no room left in *this* book! And there's enough information about HTML to fill a book larger than this, anyway. (But don't worry, there will be plenty of HTML books at your local bookstore very soon!) You can find loads of information online, too. Try these Web documents:

➤ **A Beginner's Guide to HTML:**

http://www.ncsa.uiuc.edu/SDG/Software/Mosaic/Docs/d2-htmlinfo.html

➤ **HTML Quick Reference:**

http://kuhttp.cc.ukans.edu/lynx_help/HTML_quick.html

➤ **How to Write HTML Files:**

http://www.ucc.ie/info/net/htmldoc.html

➤ **Introduction to HTML:**

http://melmac.harris-atd.com/about_html.html

➤ **The Official HTML Specification:**

http://info.cern.ch/hypertext/WWW/MarkUp/MarkUp.html

➤ **Composing Good HTML:**

http://www.williamette.edu/html-composition/strict-html.html

➤ **CERN's Style Guide for Online Hypertext:**

http://info.cern.ch/hypertext/WWW/Provider/Style/Introduction.html

➤ **Fill-out Forms Overview:**

http://www.ncsa.uiuc.edu/SDG/Software/Mosaic/Docs/fill-out-forms/overview.html

➤ **The HTML Design Notebook:**

http://www.hal.com/~connolly/drafts/html-design.html

➤ **The Cello Help File:**

If you have the Cello browser, take a look in its help file. It has a lot of useful information about HTML, including lists of the codes used to create special characters.

Finally, We're Ready to Publish!

Creating your HTML documents is one thing, but now you have to figure out how to make them available to people on the Web. A little while ago, I suggested to a small publisher that he set up a Web site. "I can't do that; I don't have $50,000!" For some reason, many people have the idea that setting up a Web site is very costly—it doesn't have to be. How does $10 or $20 a month sound to you? Or if you already have an Internet account (and if you are this far, you probably do), how does $1 a month sound? Or perhaps, 10 cents a month? Or *zilch*? Okay? Then read on.

Where Do You Store It?

The first question is, "Where are you going to put your Web documents?" The first thing you should do is ask your current service provider.

You may find that your service provider is quite happy to set up a site for you; that is, he may let you place your HTML documents and associated .GIFs and whatever on their system, and make sure that their Web server knows where to find them—maybe even at no cost to you. When I set up the CIPA site, my service provider told me all I'd have to pay is the normal hard-disk-storage charge. That is, the first megabyte of data they store for me is free, but every megabyte after that is $2.50 a month.

Remember that HTML files are simple text files—they don't take up much room. The largest one I created for the CIPA site was 12 kilobytes, around 1/85th of a megabyte. It's really the graphics that can take up room, but even then, it doesn't have to take too much; .GIF files are relatively small (compared to other graphics formats). The CIPA logo I used in the main CIPA document takes up less than 3 Kbytes.

What Does It Cost?

So, all in all, what did the first "go around" of the CIPA site take up? Only 54 Kbytes. Because I wasn't using a full megabyte of storage space, that means the site was costing me nothing. Let's say I *was* using a megabyte and was being charged for excess storage. Then the Web site would cost me around 13 cents a month. That won't break the bank, I don't think!

But perhaps I don't have an Internet account already and only want one so I can set up and maintain a Web site. What will it cost me? Depending on the billing plan I choose, the site may cost me as little as $10 a month. (I'm using Internet Express. Your mileage may vary.)

Be clear about what you want when talking with your service provider. There are three basic services they can provide. They can set you up so their Web server knows which directory your HTML files are stored in, so the rest of the world can use your main page's URL to get to you. (That may cost little or nothing.) They can also add a link from their "home page" to your documents. To do that, they are likely to charge you—perhaps a $75 setup fee and $75/month. (Some service providers may only provide the *second* of these services and prices vary widely.) Also, they may want to sell you their services for *creating* the HTML documents, which you can do yourself with this book!

My Provider Doesn't Have a Web Server!

What if your service provider doesn't have a Web server? That means you can't set up a Web site on their system. Or rather, you can, but nobody will be able to use it! Plenty of people will be in this position. At the time of writing, there are around 8,000 Web servers, which means the vast majority of Internet hosts *don't* have servers. If you have an account through a Free-Net, your local college, or your company, there's a good chance that you won't have an available server.

In many cases, the real cost of a Web site won't be placing the files on a service provider's system—it will be the time involved in *maintaining* the site. Remember, time is money!

So what do you do if you can't simply place the Web files on the existing system? Well, perhaps you could change the existing system. Convince the system administrator to set up a Web server, or set up a Web server yourself.

Setting up Web servers is *way* beyond the scope of this book! But if you'd like to at least investigate the subject, take a look at the **http://info.cern.ch/hypertext/WWW/Provider/Overview.html** document. This will lead you to all sorts of useful information you'll need. You'll find software for UNIX, VAX, VMS, the Macintosh, Windows NT, Windows 3.1, and more. Whatever your host machine, you'll probably find a server.

Finding Another Provider

Setting up a server will be too much effort for most people. So another option is to find a service provider that *will* let you place your Web documents on their system and link them to their server.

Check with all the local service providers in your area. You may also want to use a service out of town. Many services these days have local access numbers in major cities other than the one they're based in. Even if you have to dial long distance, it may not be a substantial cost. If you set up an account to be used for the Web site and nothing more, you may not spend much time actually online—just now and again when you upload new and modified documents from your computer to the Web site.

To find a list of service providers, send e-mail to **info-deli-server@netcom.com**. In the body of the message, type **Send PDIAL**. You'll get a listing returned to you.

Today, most commercial service providers are setting up Web sites. If you'd like to find a list of service providers with information about their Web services, send e-mail to **listproc@einet.net**. In the body of the message, enter this command: **get inet-marketing www-svc-providers**. (Then wait. I found it took about 24 hours to get a response; you may be luckier. Of course, it helps if you spell the command right the first time.)

You'll get five e-mail messages back containing all sorts of information. Unfortunately, most of the companies in these documents are in the business of selling Web consulting services and sites, *not* in the business of giving people dirt-cheap Web sites! You may have to do some more digging, calling up service providers and asking what their policy about Web sites is. You can also check the **comp.infosystems. www.providers** and **alt.internet.services** newsgroups for more information.

A Free Web Site—The Home Page Publisher

There's a system provided by the Byrd Polar Research Center at Ohio State University called the *Home Page Publisher.* (No, I don't know why they are doing this, or what a polar research center is doing so far from the poles.) It's a neat little system that lets you publish a small Web site *on their computer!* This is a very simple system, though— no substitute for a site of your own.

You can't upload graphics for use in your Web site; though you can link to graphics at other Web sites (at icon servers, for instance—see Chapter 22). Also, creating the page is not so easy here. You create your pages online using Web forms that let you type the HTML text into a large text box. So you'd better know all the tags you need and get them just right! No HTML editor to help you here (see Chapter 24 for information about HTML editors).

Here's an example of how to display a graphic in a Web document, when the graphic is at another site: **<img src=http:// www.ncsu.edu/images/ under_const2.gif>**. As you can see, the image referenced in this tag contains an absolute URL—the exact position, host, directory, and all.

You will get a login name and a password so only you can modify or delete the documents. If you don't change the document at least every 30 days, it will be removed. If you'd like to check this system out, go to the **http://www.mps.ohio-state.edu/HomePage/** document.

Getting from Here to Theirs— Uploading Your Pages

Once you've found a service provider to take your Web documents, you'll have to put them into the correct directory. Talk to the system administrator about where to put them. He'll have to configure the Web server so it knows where your documents are and can get to them when a Web browser wants to see them.

If you are creating your documents on a PC, you'll have to transfer the files over to your service provider's system. You can use your FTP program if you have a dial-in direct account. That's probably the easiest way to do it; use WS_FTP (on the PC) or Fetch (on the Mac), or whatever. If you have a dial-in terminal account, you'll have to use a transfer protocol such as Xmodem or Zmodem (Zmodem's easier, especially when you are transferring several files). It all depends on what your communications program and your service provider have available. Log into your account, change to the directory you've been told to place the files into, and then transfer them. For more information about FTP, see *The Complete Idiot's Guide to the Internet*.

DOS-to-UNIX Pitfalls

Once you have your files onto your service provider's system, check out the site with several browsers. If some treat your .HTM files as text (you see all the tags), then the server hasn't been set up correctly. Ask your service provider to change the AddType "directive" in the configuration file.

UNIX and DOS files are a little different, and if you transfer text files from one to the other, they may not be formatted correctly. You might find ^M at the end of each line, for instance. If this happens, you need to convert files from DOS to UNIX format.

First, make sure you are transmitting them as text files, not binary files. That way, the end-of-line markers will be translated correctly. If you are using WS_FTP, for instance, make sure you select the ASCII option button at the bottom of the screen before sending your files.

(Of course, this only applies to the HTML files you are transmitting, not your .GIF files or any other format you are uploading!)

If you are using Zmodem or Xmodem, send the files as ASCII, also. Check your communications program's transfer-setup parameters. You may find something like an **End of line conversion** option, which automatically converts the end-of-line characters when the files are transmitted to the UNIX machine. If you are using Xmodem, you may need to use the **rt** command at the service provider's computer (the *receive text* command), though this varies between systems. Ask your service provider for more information.

You can also convert files from DOS to UNIX format once they've already been transferred. Perhaps your service provider has set up a menu system to help you do this. Or you may have to do it at the command line. If so, you'll have some kind of utility, such as **dos2unix** (this is a SunOS program that will convert the text files from DOS format to a format that the SunOS recognizes). Type **man dos2unix** at the shell and press **Enter** to find information about this command.

Getting the Word Out

Now that you have your Web site up and running, you need to let people know about it. Here are a few ideas:

➤ Tell all your Internet friends.

➤ Add the URL and some information to your e-mail signature so everyone who gets your e-mail will find out about it.

➤ If the site is for a company or organization, ask other employees and members to tell their friends and modify their signatures.

➤ Post messages in newsgroups and mailing lists related to the subject matter covered at your Web site. Announce the site and provide the URL.

➤ If you have access to other online services (CompuServe, America Online, GEnie, and so on), post information there, too.

➤ Go to the *San Francisco Examiner* Web site for information about how to add a link from there to your Web site (**http://sfgate.com/ examiner/freehomepage.html**). They'll even let you put a page on their site.

➤ Find other Web sites with similar subjects; ask the authors if they will add a link to your site. This will channel people to you and also help to get you into the various Web directories.

➤ Go to the What's New on the Web site, (**http://www.ncsa.uiuc.edu/SDG/Software/Mosaic/Docs/whats-new.html**) and submit information about your site.

➤ Spend some time traveling around in the directories listed in Chapter 25. Some will let you submit information about your site. All will help you find related Web documents.

We'll Help!

If you use the information in the book to get started in Web publishing, let us know and we'll add a link from the Macmillan Web site to yours. Send e-mail to **pkent@lab-press.com**. Include the URL of your site and its title. Also include a short (one sentence) description of it. (I'm not promising next-day service, but I'll add links to my Web document at the Macmillan site now and again.)

Good luck!

The Least You Need to Know

➤ Use this tag to create an e-mail link:
`<a href = "mailto:emailaddress">link text</a>`.

➤ Use <I></I> for italics and <B></B> for bold text.

➤ Create bulleted lists with <UL></UL>. Each item in the list must start with <LI>.

➤ Numbered lists are like bulleted lists, but they use <OL></OL>.

➤ Use plenty of links between your documents so readers don't get lost.

➤ Web sites can cost from many thousands of dollars... to nothing. Shop around.

➤ The Home Page Publisher provides a free Web site for virtually anyone.

## Chapter 24

Just a Little Help—HTML Authoring Tools

In This Chapter

➤ Two types of HTML editors: programs and templates

➤ HTML converters and filters

➤ Using HTML Assistant, HoTMetaL, and CU_HTML.DOT

➤ Using Easy HTML Writer

➤ Working with filters

If you've read the previous few chapters and are a little flustered (Imagine typing all those stupid tags!), don't worry, there's help at hand. There are special tools available (for the PC, Macintosh, UNIX, and more) that will help you create HTML files. In some cases, you won't even *see* the tags; the program will enter the tags for you.

What Are My Options?

Well, there are *editors* and *converters*. Editors help you create an HTML file from scratch or modify an existing one. Converters take a file that has been saved in one format and convert it into another—either from a non-HTML format to HTML, or from HTML to some other kind of format.

All About Editors

There are two basic types of HTML editors: *programs* and *templates*.

Programs are, well... you know, programs: computer applications that are used to create HTML documents (you may call them *stand-alone editors*, as you can create an HTML document with the program alone; you don't need a word processor).

Templates require a particular word processor. A word processor template is a set of tools designed to be used to create a particular type of document, within a particular word processor. For instance, I use Word for Windows. When I create a new document, I can choose which template to use. I may use my LETTERHD.DOT template (for writing letters) or my IDIOT.DOT template (for writing *Complete Idiot's Guides*). There are templates specially designed to be used for creating HTML documents, too.

When you use a template, you have to work with the word processor it's designed for. There are a number for Word for Windows, as well as for WordPerfect for DOS, FrameMaker, and so on.

Some editors are hybrids. SGML TagWizard, for example, works inside Word for Windows. Rather than being a simple document template, it actually runs as a Word for Windows *wizard*, a sort of document template on steroids.

A *wizard* is actually a program that runs within another program, in this case, within a word processor, such as Word for Windows. When you open the wizard, in the same way you open a document template, the program runs and "holds your hand" while it helps you set up the document.

How Does It Work?

Some editors simply help you enter the tags; click on a button and the tag is placed. Currently, most of the program-type editors work that way. The WYSIWYG editors, though, work like word processors. You enter your text and select particular styles to modify the text. You would create a Heading 1 line, for example, by selecting the Heading 1 style. The program applies all the appropriate tags for you. You don't get to touch the tags at all; it's all left up to the program. This is how templates generally work.

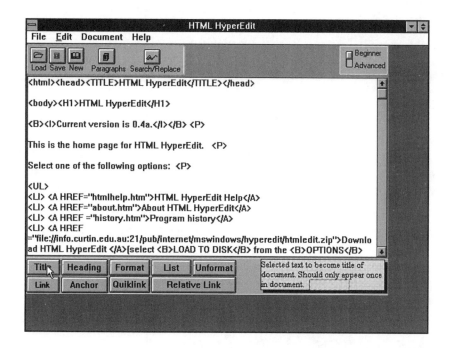

HTML HyperEdit, a stand-alone, non-WYSIWYG HTML editor.

By the way, when we're talking about HTML editors, WYSIWYG really means WYSMBWYG: **What You See Might Be What You Get**. Remember, the way the text in a Web document is formatted is determined by how the browser viewing the document is set up. So the way your WYSIWYG editor displays the text is not the same as every Web user's browser will see it. Still, it's a good indication of what they may be seeing, more or less, showing different types of text in different fonts—and most importantly, showing the document without the tags.

WYSIWYG is computer-geek talk for **What You See Is What You Get**. That is, when you are working in a WYSIWYG program, you see pretty much what the end product will look like. (In the olden days, you saw all sorts of codes and garbage even in good word processors, so you had to guess what the final product would look like.)

285

Working with a WYSIWYG editor is, in some ways, easier. You don't have to worry about the tags. You just have to worry about making the text look the way you want it, the way you would do so for any other kind of document by applying paragraph styles. Creating an HTML document by entering codes is okay but primitive. Kind of like typesetting books by placing metal type!

How many times do I need to tell you? Look in Chapter 27 for the source of the products mentioned in this chapter.

If your editor is not WYSIWYG and lets you modify tags directly, it's possible to accidentally mess them up. On the other hand, some HTML authors may feel that the non-WYSIWYG editors give them more flexibility and that they let them "see what is going on." I'd suggest you try a couple of editors to see which you are most comfortable with, and then experiment with other types later when you've completely mastered your original choice.

For a list of HTML editors, take a look at the **http://akebono.stanford.edu/yahoo/Computers/World_Wide_Web/HTML_Editors/** document. The **http://www.uth.tmc.edu/mac_info/machttp/doc/** document lists Macintosh tools. You may also find a list of word-processor templates in the **http://werple.apana.org.au/~gabriel/information/html/html-templates.html** document.

Windows-Based HTML Editors

There are *loads* of Windows editors for HTML. (It's clear that the Internet is no longer a UNIX dominated world—Bill Gates is running it!) Here's a list of most of the editors available; undoubtedly, more will appear soon.

ANT_HTML.DOT   A Word for Windows 6.0 template with macros that help you create HTML documents using WYSIWYG editing.

CU_HTML.DOT   Another Word for Windows document template, this time for both Word 2.0 and 6.0.

GT_HTML.DOT   *Another* Word for Windows document template with macros. This one has been described as providing "pseudo" WYSIWYG.

HoTMetaL Probably one of the best WYSIWYG editors around (it's a stand-alone program), though perhaps complicated to learn. It also has a non-WYSIWYG mode. There are both shareware and commercial versions available (around $150). It's from SoftQuad.

Cyberleaf This is a rather pricey product from Interleaf that lets you take an existing document and convert it to HTML. You can use any word processor (you don't have to have the Interleaf desktop-publishing system). It will convert files from Interleaf, FrameMaker, Word for Windows, and WordPerfect, or files in the ASCII format. It should be available early in 1995.

HTML Assistant A non-WYSIWYG editor for simple documents. There are both freeware and commercial versions available (around $100).

HTML HyperEdit A freeware non-WYSIWYG editor with some very good features but lacking other important ones.

HTML Writer A *donationware* (pay what you want!) non-WYSIWYG editor that provides some important tools for creating more complicated HTML features, such as forms and images.

HTMLed A shareware non-WYSIWYG editor that covers the basics well but doesn't cover forms.

Want more detailed information about these Windows editors? I found product reviews at the **http://werple.apana.org.au/~gabriel/information/html/html-editors.html** document.

SGML TagWizard Another template editor for Word for Windows 6.0. (Actually this one's a *wizard*, not a simple template.)

WebAuthor At the time of writing, Quarterdeck, the people who sell the QEMM memory manager for IBM-compatible PCs, were about to release a suite of Web tools, including an HTML template for both Word for Windows and WordPerfect. It looked pretty good, too.

Internet Assistant for MS Word This is a Microsoft product that's a free HTML template for Word for Windows.

Editors for the Macintosh

Windows isn't the only operating system getting in on the HTML act, of course. There are also plenty of Macintosh editors:

BBEdit HTML extensions   Freeware add-ons for the Macintosh BBEdit text editor. BBEdit is available in both shareware and commercial versions; the extensions will work with either one.

BBEdit HTML Tools   More tools based on the BBEdit text editor.

HTML Editor for the Macintosh   A "semi-WYSIWYG" editor.

HTML Grinder   This is more than just a simple HTML editor. It also helps you with "intelligent link building." Contains all sorts of utilities for automating the task or creating linked Web documents—creating indexes and *Stretch Lists*, for instance (clicking on links expands the list, adding entries).

HTML SuperText   A freeware HTML editor.

HTML.edit   Another freeware editor, this one created by a systems analyst at NASA.

HTML Writer   An HTML editor based on SuperCard, although saved as a stand-alone product—you don't need SuperCard. (This program is often known as Jon's HTML Editor.)

Simple HTML Editor (SHE)   The "grandmother" of all Macintosh-based HTML editors, this is in the form of a HyperCard stack, so it requires HyperCard or HyperCard Player.

WYSIWY(N)G   *What You See Is What You (Nearly) Get*. A "near" WYSIWYG editor.

Alpha   A simple HTML editor.

SGML TagWizard   This program should be available for the Macintosh soon; it requires Word for Windows 6.0.

Bits n' Pieces for Other Systems

There are a few editors available for other computers:

FrameMaker WebMaker is an HTML tool for the FrameMaker desktop-publishing program.

NeXT Step   There are a couple of HTML editors available for the NeXT Step computers: the **eText Text Engine** and **HTML-Editor**.

UNIX   There are several editors available for UNIX: **City University HTML Editor** (if that's its name; it doesn't appear to have one!); **Cyberleaf** (a system from Interleaf; the UNIX versions will be available late in 1995); a UNIX version of **HoTMetaL**; **Phoenix**; **tkHTML** (an editor created using the Tcl script language and the Tk toolkit, so you'll need both on your system); and **tkWWW**, another Tk toolkit editor.

Emacs   There's an HTML editor for Emacs systems: **hm-html-menus**.

Just a Quick Look—A Few Examples

Let's take a quick peek at some of these tools. First, take a look at the following illustration. This is HTML Assistant, a fairly simple stand-alone, non-WYSIWYG editor for Windows. (I used this to create the CIPA site we looked at in Chapters 22 and 23.)

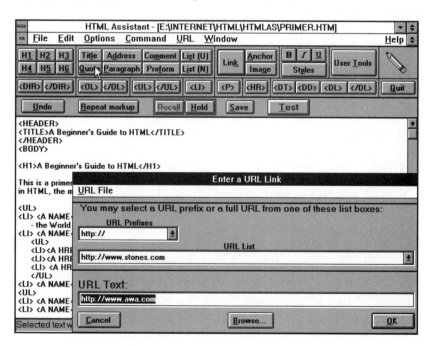

HTML Assistant—a simple click places a tag.

If you are using a non-WYSIWYG editor like HTML Assistant, open your Web browser while you work. You can quickly save the HTML file you're working on and then view it in the browser. When you make a change and want to see the results, use the browser's **Reload** command to reload the file. This way, you can quickly check not just what it looks like, but whether the links work. (This won't work in all editors. Word for Windows, for example, locks files that it opens, so other applications can't use them.)

Much of the window is taken up with a toolbar. You can place the cursor in your text, click on a button in the toolbar to place the tag you want to use, and then type the text between the <> and <> tags. You can even highlight text and then click on a button; HTML Assistant will place a tag on each side of the selected text.

Most of HTML Assistant's tools are fairly simple; a button enters the appropriate tag. Click on **H1** to place <H1></H1>, **Address** to place <address></address>, and **Quote** to place <blockquote></blockquote>, for example. Other tools are more sophisticated. The **Link** button displays a dialog box into which you can enter information about the link you want to create. You can even select a link from a list of links you've used in the document so far, or select a filename from a Browse dialog box. There's even a User Tools box that lets you create your own buttons.

There's also a nice, simple test mode. Click on the **Test** button and HTML Assistant loads the document into a Web browser that you've defined, so you can see what it looks like.

HoTMetaL

HoTMetaL is another well-known editor. (Have you figured out HoTMetaL yet? Take away the lowercase letters and what's left?) This can be used as both a WYSIWYG and a non-WYSIWYG editor; use the **View|Hide/Show Tags** menu option to remove or replace the tags. HoTMetaL differs from HTML Assistant, though, in that it doesn't place ordinary text tags. That is, in HTML Assistant, you can get in and edit the tags because the program places the actual tags. In HoTMetaL, though, it places small icons to take the place of the tags. You can't modify the tags, except to remove or move them.

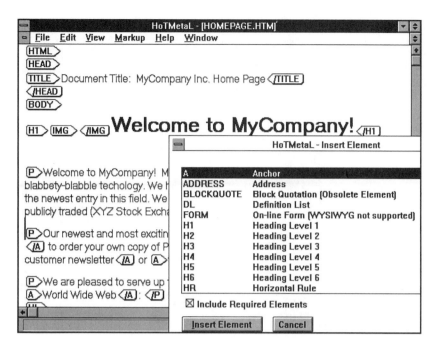

HoTMetaL, a popular editor with both WYSIWYG and non-WYSIWYG modes.

As with HTML Assistant, HoTMetaL lets you place tags and then type your text, or highlight existing text and then place the tags. Instead of using a toolbar, though, there's a dialog box from which you select the type of tag you want to use.

The Template Route: CU_HTML.DOT

Using a document template is one of the easiest ways to create an HTML file. The following figure shows a simple document with the Select Linkage File dialog box open. This lets you place a link on the selected text; you can select an existing file or enter the name of a file you plan to create later. The CU_HTML.DOT template adds the link tags as Word for Windows fields, which are normally invisible. Very nice and easy.

291

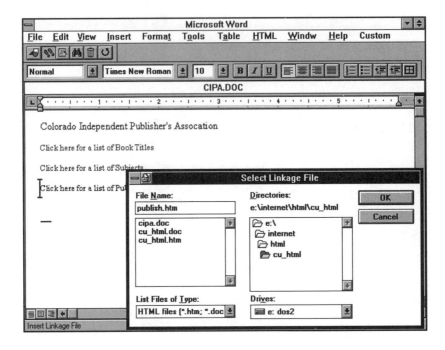

Placing a link using Word for Windows and the CU_HTML.DOT document template.

To assign a particular tag to a block of text, you simply place the cursor in the text and then assign the appropriate style: Title, Heading 1, Address, or whatever. Later, when you use the **HTML|Write HTML** command, the template creates the final HTML file, placing tags and links in the appropriate positions and saving the file as a text file.

There are several advantages to using a template like this. If you can find one for the word processor you work with, you'll find learning the HTML editor very easy—you already know how to use the word processor, after all. Most of what you will do is simply assign styles to text. Also, word processors are stacked full of useful features that most HTML editors don't have, such as spell checkers, sophisticated search and replace commands, keyboard shortcuts for placing styles, and so on. Finally, these are WYSIWYG editors, so you can see the text clearly, not in a jumble of HTML tags.

Remember, though, that a template may not let you enter all the available tags. CU_HTML.DOT, for example, only allows you to work with about 17 different tags. You can't, for instance, enter a separator line (<HR>), because the template doesn't have a command for this. In fact, I wouldn't be able to use CU_HTML.DOT for the CIPA site. (You can, however, go into the finished HTML file and add the separator tags "by hand.")

A Little Bit Different—Converters

There are dozens of other systems, called *converters*. These take a file from another file format (ASCII text, RTF, e-mail messages, WordPerfect for DOS files, and so on) and convert it to an HTML file. There are even utilities that take the hotlist from the MOSAIC.INI file or the Mosaic for Macintosh hotlist and convert it to an HTML file or, in the case of the Macintosh, into a HyperCard stack.

These are not the same as editors, as they are not designed to help you create HTML files, adding all the tags. They simply take an existing file and then convert it to HTML using a few simple rules. You can take that HTML file and open it in one of the editors to continue modifying it. If you'd like to see what's available, check out the **http://akebono.stanford.edu/yahoo/Computers/World_Wide_Web/HTML_Converters/** document.

There's a tool on the Web that will take a Web document, convert it to a PostScript document, and then send the PostScript document back to you. Point your Web browser to **http://info.cern.ch/hypertext/WWW/Tools/www-print.html** for information, or directly to the *World Wide Web Wonder Widget* (at **http://home.mcom.com/people/mtoy/cgi/www-print.cgi**).

This Is Weird—The Easy HTML Writer

There's a strange little site—the Easy HTML Writer site—that lets you create Web documents and save them to your hard disk. Point your Web browser to the **http://peachpit.ncsa.uiuc.edu/easyhtml/easy.html** document (you'll need a Web browser with full forms-support for this). When you get there, you'll see a form into which you will type your name and the document title. Click on the button at the bottom, and you are presented with another form, as you can see in the following figure.

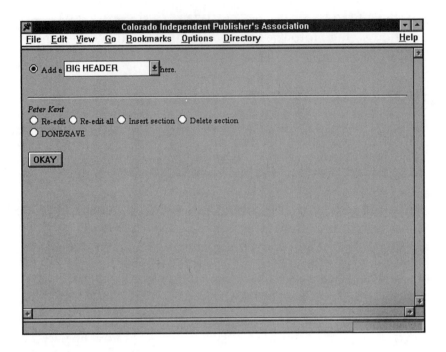

Starting an Easy HTML Writer document.

All you need to do is decide which element you want to begin the document with—probably the Big Header, but you could also try the Medium Header, Little Header, Paragraph, and so on. Click on the **OKAY** button and you'll continue. You'll see another form, this time with a text box into which you'll type the text you want to use as the big header.

Click on the **Done** button to move to the next screen where you'll see what you've just entered and be asked what you want to enter next. Again, select the document element you want to use from the drop-down list box, and then click on **OKAY**.

You'll see another form, in which you'll type the next information—the next header or paragraph text—and click on the **Done** button.

You'll continue like this, adding various HTML elements, until you are finished, or until you make a mistake that you want to fix. Then you'll use one of the option buttons near the bottom of the window and click on the **OKAY** button:

Re-edit This displays a form with a check box before each element. Check the one you want to modify and then click on the **OKAY** button to see a form in which you can modify that element.

Re-edit all This displays the entire document as a form, with all your text in text boxes. You can go in and modify pieces.

Insert section This displays a form with a check box before each element. Check the one before which you want to insert a new element, and then click on **OKAY**.

Delete section This displays a form with a check box before each element. Check the one you want to delete and then click on **OKAY**.

DONE/SAVE Lets you save your work. You can save it as an HTML file that you can use right away, or in a format that Easy HTML Writer can use later. (The next time you want to modify the file, open it from your hard disk using the browser's **File|Open File** command or equivalent, and then click on the **Continue editing** button that you'll see.)

If You Don't Want HTML, Filter It Out!

How about going the other way? Taking an HTML file and converting it to plain old text? As you've seen, many browsers won't do it for you. Mosaic for Windows and InternetWorks won't, for instance. (This is particularly a problem with Windows browsers for some reason, not for Macintosh or UNIX browsers.)

There are other tools, sometimes called *filters*, that will do the job for you. These are a type of converter, like the ones I mentioned earlier, though instead of going from one format to HTML, you go from HTML back to another format. For a list of filters, see the **http://info.cern.ch/hypertext/**

When you know you will want to grab plain text from a Web document, use a browser, such as Cello, that can do the job. Or use your favorite browser to save a document in HTML format on your hard disk, and then open the file using another browser later and resave the file as plain text.

WWW/Tools/Filters.html document. You'll find filters for all sorts of systems: programs for converting from HTML to PostScript, FrameMaker, LaTeX, RTF (Microsoft's Rich Text Format file format), TeX, and so on. Most of these are *not* for Windows and Macintosh computers. (Microsoft's Internet Assistant for MS Word lets you filter HTML files, though.)

You can find more information about filters at the **http://union.ncsa.uiuc.edu/HyperNews/get/www/html/converters.html** document. If you can't find a suitable filter, find a Web browser to use as a filter.

The Least You Need to Know

➤ There are *loads* of HTML editors available.

➤ There are two basic flavors: stand-alone programs, and templates or wizards, designed for use with a particular word processor.

➤ Some editors are WYSIWYG; you don't see the tags while you are working. Others are not; you can see the tags. And others let you work in both modes.

➤ HTML Assistant and HoTMetaL are good stand-alone editors for Windows. The first is not WYSIWYG, the second has both WYSIWYG and non-WYSIWYG modes.

➤ CU_HTML.DOT is a pretty good template editor for Word for Windows.

➤ Easy HTML Writer is a program running on the Web that makes it very easy to create an HTML file—give it a try.

Part 7
The Atlas:
Traveling on the Web

If you've gotten this far, you know more about the Web than 99% of all Web users. You're ready to take on the world. So, in this Part of the book, I'll give you the world—the world of the World Wide Web.

I'll show you where to go to find just the Web page you need. I'll give you examples of neat and weird and interesting Web sites, so you can check on the Dow Jones Industrial average, listen to Socks the cat, read loads of online newspapers and magazines, check out Dr. Fun's daily cartoon, and lots more.

Plus, you get a chapter telling you where to find all the software I mention in the book, plus my copyrighted Webossary—a list of words you'll run across on the Web. What a deal!

Web Central

The Web is a large and confusing place. It's all very well knowing how to use your browser, but where do you go? You need some kind of list of Web sites. There's not much point in me providing one, for several reasons. First, it would be huge; there are thousands of different Web sites. It would also be out of date; dozens of new sites are added every day, and you really need several lists, categorized in several different ways. Anyway, the ideal list is one that is interactive. Search for something you need; then, when the list shows you what's available, go directly to that Web site.

Interactive Maps

These Web lists are like interactive maps. Imagine a journey sometime in the future. You are visiting Aunt Edna on Mars, who has been begging you to make the trip for some time. You are out on a little hike and have stopped for a snack. Looking at your map, you notice a strange topological structure in the shape of a human face. It's miles away, too far to walk. So you press on that spot on the map with your finger, and a few seconds later, there you are walking along the nose.

That's how these lists work. They are not simply lists that tell you where you can go on the Internet, not simply road maps to the Information Superhypeway. They are interactive maps; they show you what's available, and then they take you there. If you find you don't like where you are, then use your browser's **Back** button or command to go return to the directory.

There are actually many different ways to find what you are looking for, lots of different Web sites that help you on your way. This chapter includes a few useful sites. As you travel around the Web, you'll probably find more; add them to this list.

Note that these directories all have their strengths and weaknesses. They don't all work the same, and they won't all give you the same results. Spend a few days goofing with them (you don't have to work, do you?) and find the ones you like best.

If you'd like to get an electronic copy of this chapter and Chapter 26, go to my Web page at the Macmillan Web site and download them. You need the files called CHAPT25.HTM and CHAPT26.HTM. These are plain text files, so you can use them on any computer. Load them to your hard disk, and then open them in your Web browser. That way, you'll be able to click on links to go directly to the sites I mention.

Here's my URL:

```
http://www.mcp.com/authors/pkent/
```

So, let's get started. With the following tools, you'll be able to find just about anything you want on the Web—assuming it's there. With the Web growing as fast as it is, just about anything you want *is* there *somewhere.*

Directories of Directories

We'll start with a general category: a list of Web documents that will help you find more specific directories.

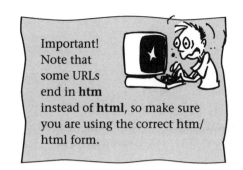

Important! Note that some URLs end in **htm** instead of **html**, so make sure you are using the correct htm/html form.

The World Wide Web Initiative

"Everything there is to know about the World Wide Web is linked directly or indirectly to this document." This statement is from the W3 Organization, the people planning the future of the Web.

```
http://info.cern.ch/hypertext/WWW/TheProject.html
```

The Mosaic Communications Internet Directory

This is a "directory of directories," leading you to other useful listings (most of which are mentioned in this chapter).

```
http://home.mcom.com/home/internet-directory.html
```

Mosaic Communications also have a document that points you to other Web search tools:

```
http://home.mcom.com/home/internet-search.html
```

Both of these documents are accessible to all browsers, but Netscape users can get to them quickly by clicking on a button in the button bar.

ANANSE—Internet Resource Locators

I found this one when I let Yahoo (see *Yahoo*, next section) pick a "random" Web document for me; it must have known that I was looking for Web directories! Wow, WebESP. Links to lots of other directories.

```
http://ananse.irv.uit.no/law/nav/find.html
```

List of Robots

This is a directory of programs that dig around on the Web, creating indexes and measuring its size.

```
http://web.nexor.co.uk/mak/doc/robots/active.html
```

General Directories

The following lists are directories of Web documents. You can search or browse for just about any subject.

Yahoo

Yahoo means *Yet Another Hierarchy* and also refers to the database's authors (who claim to be yahoos). It's a neat directory that lets you select a category and view a list of related Web sites, search the entire database, or select other lists, such as the What's Cool, What's New, and What's Popular lists. You also can view the statistics or let Yahoo pick a site for you.

```
http://akebono.stanford.edu/yahoo/
```

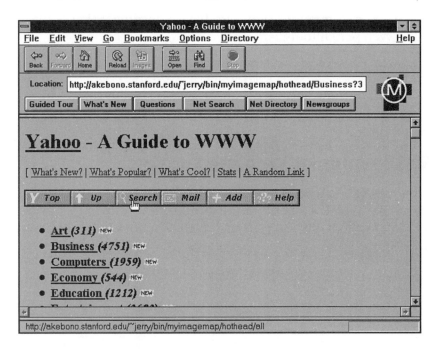

Yahoo—definitely the coolest directory on the Web.

The World Wide Web Worm (WWWW)

The World Wide Web Worm is a system that digs around on the Web looking for documents. It follows links through the Web and builds an index of Titles and URLs. You can enter keywords to search for any subject; you'll find detailed instructions on how to search. (Important: there are *four* W's in the following filename, not three.)

```
http://www.cs.colorado.edu/home/mcbryan/WWWW.html
```

Web Crawler

This system crawls around on the Web, creating an index. You can search that index.

```
http://www.biotech.washington.edu/WebCrawler/Home.html
```

The WebCrawler Top 25

The Web Crawler also publishes a document that lists the 25 most-referenced documents on the Web. That is, the documents that are referenced by other document links more than any others.

```
http://www.biotech.washington.edu/WebCrawler/Top25.html
```

The JumpStation

Another simple index that you can search.

```
http://www.stir.ac.uk/jsbin/js
```

Wandex

Wandex, the World Wide Web Wanderer Index, lets you search an index of thousands of documents.

```
http://www.mit.edu:8001/afs/sipb/user/mkgray/ht/compre.bydomain.html
```

The Spider's Web

Over 1,000 links to "cool places."

```
http://gagme.wwa.com/~boba/spider.html
```

Zorba (Formerly Nomad)

This is an index created by Rockwell Network Systems and Cal Poly, San Luis Obispo. Type the keyword you are looking for.

```
http://www.rns.com/cgi-bin/nomad
```

RBSE's URL Database

Finally, a *spider*! I've been waiting for someone to name a tool "spider." After all, this is the *Web*. Anyway, the RBSE (Repository Based Software Engineering) spider "walks the web" grabbing URLs. You can search the resulting database.

```
http://rbse.jsc.nasa.gov/eichmann/urlsearch.html
```

Best of the Web '94

This is a list of the "best" Web documents, chosen in an online contest and announced at the International W3 Conference in Geneva: from the NCSA (Best Overall Site) to the Sports Information Service (Best Entertainment Service), Travels With Samantha (Best Document Design) to the Xerox Map Server (Best Use of Interaction).

```
http://wings.buffalo.edu/contest/
```

The Web of Wonder

Another simple directory; select the category, select the subcategory, select the Web document.

```
http://www.digimark.net/wow/index.html
```

ALIWEB

ALIWEB stands for *Archie-Like Indexing for the Web*. It lets you search for Web sites in the same way you can use Archie to search for FTP files. There are several different interfaces: a form-based search, a multiple-keyword form-based search, and a simple index search.

```
http://web.nexor.co.uk/aliweb/doc/search.html
```

The Mother-of-All BBS

Search this giant database of Web sites, or select a category first: from Agriculture to Writing on the Net, and subjects as diverse as Underwear and the Sheffield Ski Village.

```
http://www.cs.colorado.edu/homes/mcbryan/public_html/bb/summary.html
```

NCSA's What's New on the Web

A list of new Web pages where you can view the current month's crop of new stuff or go back and view previous months. This is a great way to get a feel for just how much new information is being added to the Web.

```
http://www.ncsa.uiuc.edu/SDG/Software/Mosaic/Docs/whats-new.html
```

The same lists are also available from Mosaic Communications (Netscape users can click on the What's New button).

```
http://home.mcom.com/home/whats-new.html
```

NCSA's Starting Points

This site is handy for newcomers wanting to get an overview of what's on the Web. You'll find links to useful services and other directories.

```
http://www.ncsa.uiuc.edu/SDG/Software/Mosaic/StartingPoints
     NetworkStartingPoints.html
```

The WWW Virtual Library

This is at CERN, the home of the Web. Select a category and you'll be shown a list of related Web sites.

```
http://info.cern.ch/hypertext/DataSources/bySubject/Overview.html
```

The CUI W3 Catalog

This directory (the Centre Universitaire d'Informatique W3 Catalog in Geneva) lists over 10,000 Web pages. You type the word you are looking for, and the catalog looks for matches. It's actually an index of the WWW Virtual Library.

```
http://cui_www.unige.ch/w3catalog
```

Lycos

This Web index provides a "probabilistic ('fuzzy') search" of over 600,000 Web documents.

```
http://fuzine.mt.cs.cmu.edu/mlm/lycos-home.html
```

Virtual Libraries

This site points you to Web reference documents, such as Scott Yanoff's Internet Services List and Big Dummy's Guide to the Internet. You'll find pointers to useful directories as well as individual documents.

```
http://info.cern.ch/hypertext/DataSources/bySubject/
```

EINet Galaxy

The home of WinWeb and MacWeb. This site is another directory that can be searched by entering a keyword or by browsing through links to different subjects. There's also a What's New page.

```
http://galaxy.einet.net/
```

The Harvest WWW Home Pages Broker

Another searchable index of Web sites. This has an unusual but useful feature, though: it displays information about a Web document that it finds, even showing part of the document's text.

```
http://www.town.hall.org/brokers/www-home-pages/query.html
```

W3 Servers

This is a *very* big list. It's an almost complete list of Web servers, broken down by geographical location. This is a classic example of a Web document that you should really use Lynx to reach, or you can download it as a file and then load it from your hard disk. Even if you are using Lynx, you can expect it to take a minute or two to open. If you are using a graphical browser over a phone line... go to the following document (or go for coffee).

> http://info.cern.ch/hypertext/DataSources/WWW/Geographical.html

W3 Servers—By Area

This provides an easier way to work with the W3 Servers list. Select the continent, country, and state to see a list or sensitive map showing servers in that area.

> http://info.cern.ch/hypertext/DataSources/WWW/Servers.html

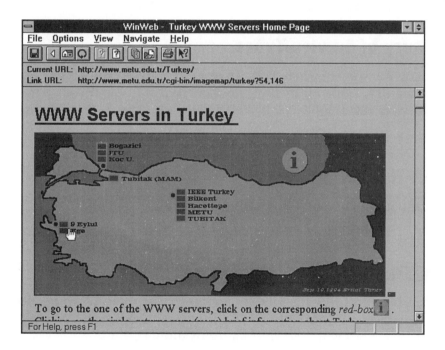

A sensitive map linked to the W3 Servers (By Area) document.

GNN NetNews

This one isn't really a directory, but it's worth mentioning because it's a great way to discover many interesting things. It's O'Reilly & Associates' online magazine about the Internet. It's a great place to find out about new programs and services, Internet news stories and controversies, and neat stuff on the Net.

```
http://nearnet.gnn.com/news/index.html
```

Finding Internet Resources

These are directories that will help you track down all sorts of Internet resources, not just Web sites.

Inter-Links

Select a category to see lists of related documents and tools.

```
http://alpha.acast.nova.edu/help/about.html
```

Directory of Service Types

If you want to see where you can use WAIS, newsgroups, Gopher, telnet, FTP, whois, and other Internet services through your Web browsers, take a look at this Web document.

```
http://info.cern.ch/hypertext/DataSources/ByAccess.html
```

Telnet Browsers List

A list of Web browsers you can access via telnet.

```
http://info.cern.ch/hypertext/WWW/FAQ/Bootstrap.html
```

ArchiePlex

This is a directory of ArchiePlex servers throughout the world—servers that let you search Archie directly from the Web. You'll find sites for browsers both with and without forms support.

```
http://web.nexor.co.uk/archie.html
```

Internet Resources—Meta-Index

This is a list of directories containing references to various Internet resources: the Web, Gopher, telnet, FTP, and more.

```
http://www.ncsa.uiuc.edu/SDG/Software/Mosaic/MetaIndex.html
```

Internet Services List

Scott Yanoff's Internet Services List has been around in text files for about three years, but it's now available on the Web—in interactive form, of course. When you find something of interest (whether a Web site, an FTP site, a chat service, or whatever), you can go right there.

```
http://slacvx.slac.stanford.edu:80/misc/internet-services.html
```

Commercial and Business Lists

These are lists of Web documents maintained by businesses.

Open Market's Commercial Sites Index

A large alphabetical listing of commercial Web documents. You can also search for a keyword or look at the What's New section.

```
http://www.directory.net/
```

Interesting Business Sites on the Web

A small list (around 50 entries) of interesting business Web pages. There's no searching, just select a category, such as Pick of the Month, Financial Services, Virtual Malls, and so on.

```
http://www.rpi.edu/~okeefe/business.html
```

Sell-it on the WWW

This is a Directory of Advertisers' Web sites. You'll find links to companies selling CD-recordings, business supplies, computer equipment, books, and general services and stuff.

```
http://xmission.com/~wwwads/index.html
```

The Business Page Yahoo

The Yahoo directory also provides a good business listing.

> http://akebono.stanford.edu/yahoo/Business/Corporations/

The Internet Business Directory

Businesses register with IBD and can then be searched for by the general Web population. You can also search newsgroup messages from here. There's even a free résumé service so you can distribute your résumé via the WWW.

> http://ibd.ar.com/

CommerceNet

A Silicon Valley based directory where you can find out about products and services, associations, news, information and events related to the participants in CommerceNet—Companies such as American Express, Amdahl, Apple, Fedex, and many more. (There are cool graphics in this directory.)

> http://www.commerce.net/

More Specific Stuff

The following are directories designed to help you find more specific information.

Web Newspaper List

This lists magazines and newspapers on the Web. It also contains links to other lists of publications.

> http://www.jou.ufl.edu/commres/webjou.htm

Campus Newsletters on the Net

This list has links to dozens of college newspapers.

> http://ednews2.asa.utk.edu/papers.html

Journalism and Communications Schools

Links to Journalism and Communications colleges.

```
http://www.jou.ufl.edu/commres/jouwww.htm
```

The Journalism List

In theory, this provides information about Internet and Web resources that may be of use to journalists, but it's a great list for *anyone* who wants to find their way around. Not only does it have Web resources, but newsgroups, finger, FTP, Gopher, WAIS, and more.

```
http://www.jou.ufl.edu/commres/jlist.htm
```

Internet Law Sites

These are good places to find information about the law. The **General Lists of Various Law Sites:**

```
http://ananse.irv.uit.no/law/nav/law_ref.html
```

and **Law related sites on the Internet:**

```
http://www2.waikato.ac.nz/law/law-related.html
```

Multimedia Information Sources

This is an index to Web sites related to multimedia. You'll find links to documents with information about current events in multimedia, various company sites, software archives, and so on.

```
http://cui_www.unige.ch/OSG/MultimediaInfo/index.html
```

Web Exhibits

This list links to dozens on Web exhibits, from art to the Dead Sea Scrolls.

```
http://155.187.10.12/fun/exhibits.html
```

U.S. Government Web

This is a Web site that lets you search for U.S. Government Web documents, such as White House press releases, the National Trade Data Bank, the President's speeches (audio files), and more.

```
http://sunsite.unc.edu/govdocs.html
```

Irena, Australia's Beauty

Irena is, apparently, named after "one of the most attractive women in Australia" (perhaps it's an inside joke understandable only to Australians). It lets you search the Web server at the Australian National University for information on the social sciences, humanities, and Asian Studies.

```
http://coombs.anu.edu.au/bin/irena.cgi/WWWVL-Aboriginal.html
```

Take a Chance!

The following two entries don't tell you where you are going until you get there!

URouLette

You've seen and done it all on the Web. You've got an hour or two to kill. Where now? Why not take a magical mystery tour, courtesy of the **URouLette** site? Click on the roulette wheel, and off you go, who knows where!

```
http://kuhttp.cc.ukans.edu/cwis/organizations/kucia/uroulette
     uroulette.html
```

Yahoo's Random Link

Yahoo also has a similar feature called Random Link.

```
http://akebono.stanford.edu/~jerry/bin/myimagemap/hothead/Art?31,9
```

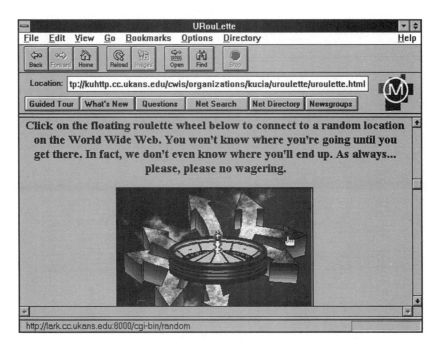

URouLette takes you to a mystery Web site.

The Least You Need to Know

➤ There are *lots* of Web documents that will help you find your way around.

➤ Some of these documents let you simply select a category and then display a list of related Web pages.

➤ Other documents let you search an index by typing a word and pressing **Enter**.

➤ There are many directories that seem to serve the same purpose, but you may get a different result from each.

## Chapter 26

Webs'ploration

In This Chapter

➤ Rock and Roll with the Stones online

➤ A $10,000 gift (?)

➤ The daily news, via the Web

➤ O.J. Simpson (if you haven't yet heard enough)

➤ And lots of other weird and wonderful Web sites

You've learned a lot about the Web, so maybe you're ready to spend some time out there (or maybe you've skipped most of the book to get here). In this chapter we're going to take a look at some of the important, neat, goofy, strange, unusual, and useful Web sites. You'll learn how to dissect a frog, rock with the Rolling Stones, check traffic report maps, keep an eye on the Dow Jones, and all sorts of other wonderful things. (No particular order; this book isn't a directory, so I don't *have* to put them in order!)

I've put this chapter (and Chapter 25, too) into an HTML file, so you can click on links to go to the places I've talked about. For more information, see Chapter 25.

Nanotechnology Site

Most people haven't even heard the term *nanotechnology* yet, but they will if the nanotechnologists are right. It's a form of engineering by which it's possible (in theory, anyway) to create things from the atom up. By sticking one atom to another we can, perhaps, build *anything* imaginable, and quickly and cheaply, too.

```
http://galaxy.einet.net/galaxy/Engineering-and-Technology/
Mechanical-Engineering/Nanotechnology/Nano.html
```

The Rolling Stones Web Site

The Stones reach the Web, and you can reach them at this site. Why? Find a schedule of tour dates, stuff for sale (mostly with large tongues on it), photos, audio, even video. Now you have a reason to install your sound card!

```
http://www.stones.com/
```

Bill & Hillary's Incredible Adventure—The White House

Want to visit the Clintons? Find out about "Family Life at the White House," take a tour, read various speeches and briefings (from foreign policy to health care), and even sign the guest book and listen to Socks meow? Then point your Web browser here.

```
http://www.whitehouse.gov
```

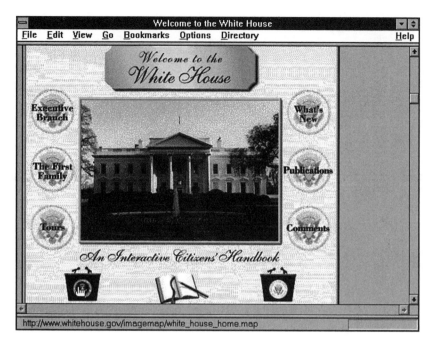

Visit Bill and Hilary at the White House.

A Great Travelogue!

The Travels With Samantha document got the Best of the Web '94 prize for Best Document Design. It's the story of a trip through North America, with a 250-picture slide show. Really neat, but very slow if you are working over phone lines.

        http://martigny.ai.mit.edu/samantha/travels-with-samantha.html

Dissecting Frogs—(But Is It Politically Correct?)

I'm not sure about this Web site. I never liked the idea of gazillions of kids having to dissect frogs just because some idiot put it in the curriculum. (How many of those students ever go into the biological sciences, anyway?) So there are two ways to look at this Web site. You can think of it as a site that explains the best way to dissect a frog, or you can think of it as a site that lets you see how a frog is dissected, without actually doing it.

        http://curry.edschool.virginia.edu/insttech/frog

Interactive Map

This is a really neat toy. You start with a picture of the globe. Click on somewhere, and you zoom in on that area. There are many options: search for your hometown, change the type of map projection, enter the coordinates you want, and so on. This is from the Xerox Palo Alto Research Center.

```
http://pubweb.parc.xerox.com/map
```

Money, Money, Money

If you want to check up on the Dow Jones Industrial Averages, this document contains a chart that is updated every five minutes. (Remember to use your **Reload** command to get a fresh shot.)

```
http://www.secapl.com/secapl/quoteserver/djia.html
```

CompuServe on the Net?

CompuServe is planning a big presence on the Internet, and it already has a Web site up and running. Right now it mainly explains what it *plans* to do on the Internet and lists the few Internet services it currently has.

```
http://www.compuserve.com/
```

Accept My Gift—$10,000!

The author of this document will give you $10,000 to help you set up a business! You know what they say, "if it sounds too good to be true... ."

```
http://xmission.com/~wwwads/creative.html
```

Wow, It's Big!

Want an idea of just how big the Web is? Take a look at this Web document created by someone who runs a Web indexing tool.

```
http://www.mit.edu:8001/afs/sipb/user/mkgray/ht/wow-its-big.html
```

The Prototypical American Family?

Here's a document that proves the value of the Internet and the power of cultural imperialism at the same time. This is a Web page in Finland, of all places, with a nice picture of the Simpsons and a few links to sounds. Listen as Homer Simpson says, "Bart can kiss my hairy yellow butt!" or "Shut up, boy!" Definitely the Internet at its best.

```
http://cc.lut.fi/~mega/simpsons.html
```

Will that site be around for long? Maybe not (is it a copyright contravention?). So here's another Simpsons page—one that provides links to all sorts of other Simpson pages:

```
http://smithers.gsfc.nasa.gov/HTML_PAGES/Simpsons.html
```

You may want to check out Dave Blanton's term paper on the Simpsons, a history of the show:

```
http://www.eden.com/users/my-html/textfiles/Simpsons-Paper.txt
```

Ziffnet

This is the Ziff-Davis Web page. Ziff-Davis publishes *PC Magazine*, *Inter@ctive Week*, and *PC Week*. You'll find recent articles and product reviews online.

```
http://www.ziff.com/
```

The World Wide Web Hall of Fame

Find out about important Web people, such as Tim Berners-Lee (the father of the World Wide Web) and Lou Montulli (famous for working on the Lynx design team and for his amazing hair).

```
http://wings.buffalo.edu/contest/awards/fame.html
```

Web Confessional

If you haven't made it to confession yet, no problem. Visit this Web page. You'll need a browser with forms support. Type in your sins, and a "priest" will tell you your penance.

```
http://anther.learning.cs.cmu.edu/priest.html
```

319

Encryption

If you want to get hold of a copy of PGP (Pretty Good Privacy), an encryption program for the Mac, Windows, DOS, Amiga, UNIX, and Atari, visit this page.

http://www.mantis.co.uk/pgp/pgp.html

The South Pole

Discover *The New South Polar Times*, a biweekly newsletter from the Amundsen-Scott South Pole Station!

http://www.deakin.edu.au/edu/MSEE/GENII/NSPT/NSPThomePage.html

Planet Earth Home Page

Check out this site with images and videos of Planet Earth.

http://white.nosc.mil/info.html

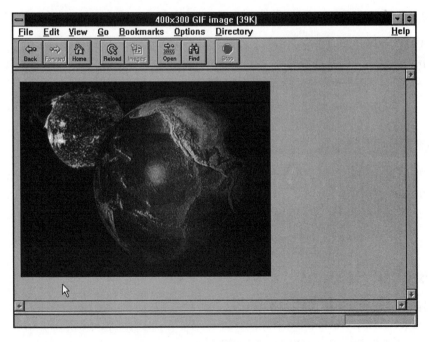

You'll find all sorts of images at the Plane Earth Home Page.

Newspapers and Magazines

Newspapers are going online at an alarming rate. Here are a few.

The Palo Alto Weekly   Palo Alto, California.

```
http://www.service.com/PAW/home.html
```

The Learned InfoNet   This is published by the British company that owns magazines such as *Information World Review, Electronic Documents,* and *CDROM Review*. The Learned InfoNext contains highlights from current issues.

```
http://info.learned.co.uk/
```

The Electronic Newsstand   Articles and information from around 200 magazines: from *AI Expert* to *Yoga Journal, American Quarterly* to *Worth Magazine*. Arranged both by subject and alphabetically.

```
http://enews.com/
```

NOS TeleText   Netherlands TeleText, in Dutch.

```
http://www.iaehv.nl/teletext/nos/index.html
```

Gazeta On-Line   A special edition of Poland's largest newspaper, the *Gazeta Wyborcza*—in Polish, of course.

```
http://info.fuw.edu.pl/gw/0/gazeta.html
```

L'Unione Sarda Online   A Sardinian newspaper online.

```
http://www.crs4.it/~ruggiero/unione.html
```

Pilot Online   From *The Virginian-Pilot* newspaper in Norfolk, Va.

```
http://www.infi.net/pilot/vpls.html
```

The San Francisco Chronicle   From the, er, *San Francisco Chronicle*, of course.

```
http://cyber.sfgate.com:80/~sfchron/
```

NandO.Net   *The News and Observer*, Raleigh, North Carolina.

```
http://www.nando.net/
```

The San Francisco Examiner   More news from San Francisco.

```
http://sfgate.com/examiner/
```

Daily News Online   From Halifax, Nova Scotia.

```
http://www.cfn.cs.dal.ca/Media/TodaysNews/TodaysNews.html
```

GT Online   *The Gazette Telegraph*, Colorado Springs. You need to subscribe to this one, though.

```
http://usa.net/gazette/today/Gazette.html
```

Teletimes   A general-interest magazine from Vancouver, Canada. Excellent—check it out.

```
http://www.wimsey.com/teletimes/teletimes_home_page.html
```

Computer Sun Times   An online computer newspaper.

```
http://usa.net/cstimes/cstimes.html
```

Really Old Stuff

For pictures of old fossils, old animals, and old stuff, go to the U.C. Berkeley Museum of Paleontology.

```
http://128.32.146.30/
```

Art Site

This is a fantastic collection of pictures and presentations related to the history of art, from the Australian National University.

```
http://rubens.anu.edu.au
```

Britannica Online

The world's best general-subject encyclopedia. You can search Britannica articles, the *Britannica Book of the Year*, *Nations of the World*, the *Propaedia*, and *Merriam Webster's Collegiate Dictionary*. This is a commercial site, though; you can use the demo for free, but making real searches will cost you. It's available to schools and colleges right now, other markets later.

```
http://www.eb.com
```

NetVet and the Electronic Zoo

Created by a Doctor of Veterinary Medicine, this document provides a list of animal-related Internet resources.

```
http://netvet.wustl.edu/00n%3a/e-zoo
```

Star Trek: The Next Generation

A multimedia/hypertext guide to all the episodes, plus more.

```
http://www.ugcs.caltech.edu/~werdna/sttng/
```

The Star Trek: The Next Generation *guide.*

Unicycling

Everything you ever wanted to know about cycling on one wheel but were afraid to ask.

```
http://nimitz.mcs.kent.edu/~bkonarsk
```

Data Sources Not Yet Online

This document will give you an idea of where the Web is going and the type of services that will be added soon (maybe already, by the time you read this). Expect to see MUDs, the NeXT Digital Librarian, UNIX "man" manual pages, and lots more.

```
http://info.cern.ch/hypertext/DataSources/Overview.html
```

WWW FAQ

Frequently asked questions about working on the Web.

```
http://sunsite.unc.edu/boutell/faq/www_faq.html
```

Browsers List

For a list of the different Web browser programs, go to

```
http://info.cern.ch/hypertext/WWW/Clients.html
```

The Dr. Fun Page

Dr. Fun puts out a new cartoon every weekday.

```
http://sunsite.unc.edu/Dave/drfun.html
```

Calvin & Hobbes

A Web document dedicated to these cartoon characters.

```
http://www.eng.hawaii.edu/Contribs/justin/Archive/Index.html
```

WebLouvre

The world-famous museum hosts Web exhibitions.

```
http://mistral.enst.fr/~pioch/louvre/louvre.html
```

Sumeria

"Files on alternative science, suppressed and neglected medical ideas, plus areas for politics, fiction, animal issues, and anything else that seems like a good idea at the time." Very interesting—sometimes weird —stuff.

```
http://werple.apana.org.au/sumeria/sumeria.html
```

Operate a Robot! The Mercury Project

"Tele-operate a robot arm moving over a terrain filled with buried artifacts. A CCD camera and pneumatic nozzle mounted on the robot allow users to select viewpoints and to direct short bursts of compressed air into the terrain, thus users can "excavate" regions... ." Everyone gets five minutes. Expect to wait!

```
http://www.usc.edu/dept/raiders/
```

O.J. Simpson!

Why should the Web be left out? Read the San Francisco Examiner's O.J. articles:

```
http://sfgate.com/examiner/simpsonhome.html
```

Find O.J. jokes:

```
http://www.cs.odu.edu/~cashman/OJ.html
```

Earthquake!

Recent earthquake reports from around the world.

```
http://www.civeng.carleton.ca/cgi-bin/quakes
```

Commuting in CA?

Real-time traffic reports from San Diego, L.A., Orange County, and more. All sorts of information, including clickable maps showing freeway speeds. Look at this before driving home.

```
http://www.scubed.com:8001/caltrans/transnet.html
```

Taglines

A collection of over 11,000 "tag lines." One-line "witty" aphorisms that you may find in e-mail signatures, car acronyms, book titles (*Breaking the Law*, by Kermit A. Krime, for instance). From *Anarchists do it revoltingly*, to *Zen Druidry: transcendental vegetation*.

```
http://www.brandonu.ca/~ennsnr/Tags/
```

Macmillan Publishing Web site

Of course, there's also the Macmillan Publishing Web site (Alpha Books is a division of Macmillan). I don't know what's going to be there right now, but come on over and check it out.

```
http://www.mcp.com
```

My Web page is

```
http://www.mcp.com/authors/pkent/
```

There's so much more. I get paid to look at this stuff—if you *don't*, realize that surfing on the Web can be as addictive as reading newsgroup discussions. Be careful out there!

The Least You Need to Know

➤ Goof around with what you find in this chapter for a while, then...

➤ Go to Chapter 25 and search for whatever interests you.

➤ If you can't find something interesting on the Web, there's something wrong with you!

➤ If you're short on time, stay away. The Web's addictive!

## Chapter 27

Finding the Goodies

In This Chapter

➤ The Macmillan Internet site

➤ Finding commercial Web software

➤ Finding shareware and freeware Web software

In this chapter, I've provided sources for all the products—commercial, public domain, and shareware—that I've mentioned in this book. Remember, though, prices and source information will change. This information was correct (pretty much; it's always difficult to know for sure on the Internet) at the time of writing.

Visit Us!—The Macmillan Site

Macmillan Computer Publishing (the big company that Alpha Books is a small part of) has its own Internet site. You can access the Macmillan Computer Publishing host by anonymous FTP, Gopher, and WWW. You can download sample chapters of books that interest you, read reference articles, and even order books online.

The Macmillan folks are going to do you a favor. They're going to make all the freeware and shareware programs I talk about in this book available there for FTP, and they'll update their stacks periodically. (We're still going to give you information about finding programs elsewhere, in case you can't get through to the Macmillan site, or you want to be *absolutely* sure you've got the latest.)

To get to the Macmillan site, point your Web browser to **http://www.mcp.com** or FTP to **ftp.mcp.com**. You can also get to the Gopher server at **gopher.mcp.com**. Or, go directly to my Web page at **http://www.mcp.com/authors/pkent**.

Your Friendly Service Provider

You should always check with your service provider if you are looking for a bit of software. Not only is it convenient to get stuff out of the file library on your host—no need to worry about FTP sites being clogged up with other people trying to grab stuff—but in some cases, your service provider or system administrator may be able to help you. Why spend an hour or two writing a login script for MacPPP, for instance, if your service provider has already created one? Use the existing one, and all you need to do is modify one or two things: the username and password, of course, and maybe the phone number.

The Rest of This Chapter May Be Wrong

Hey, I can't be responsible for changes, you know that. Prices may change. In some cases, addresses and phone numbers may change, void where prohibited, plus shipping and handling. Most importantly, though, FTP sites may change; they often do. And sometimes, the FTP site is still there, but you just can't get onto it, because there are another five zillion people trying to do so at the same time. So what do you do?

Well, remember the Macmillan Computer Publishing site. If you can get on, we'll have the software there. If you can't get onto the Macmillan site, or you really want to get to the source of the program, you'll need to go to the program's *home* site. Check to see if the FTP site you've been trying displays a list of *mirror* FTP sites when it tells you that you can't log on. If so, try a few of the mirror sites. Somewhere on those sites should be an area that stores exactly the same files as the original site.

If you *can* get on to the site, but can't find the files you are looking for, they may have been moved; try digging around. Spend some time picking likely directory names and looking inside. Remember to read the INDEX files that many directories have (sometimes they won't be called INDEX; there may be a text file with some other name). The Web browsers and graphical FTP programs make reading these files very easy.

If you still can't find what you need, try Archie, Veronica, and Jughead. These tools often grab files that seem to have disappeared off the edge of the cyberworld.

> If you're hunting down applications on the Internet, the *first thing* you should find is a Windows FTP program. It'll only take a few minutes to install and learn, and then you'll be able to grab the other applications much more quickly and easily. If you already have a graphical Web browser, though, you can use that as an FTP tool (see Chapter 20).

Windows TCP/IP & FTP Programs

There are all sorts of Windows TCP/IP programs. Windows 95 has a TCP/IP stack and dialer built in, but if you want to add TCP/IP to Windows 3.1 or Windows for Workgroups, you can use a shareware program called Trumpet Winsock.

Trumpet Winsock   To find the latest version of Trumpet Winsock, including beta versions, try the **biochemistry.bioc.cwru.edu** FTP site in the directory **/pub/trumpwsk**. You can also try the **ftp.ncsa.uiuc.edu** FTP site in the **PC/Mosaic/sockets/** directory.

WS_FTP   This free program is *the* best FTP program for windows, better than any other freeware, shareware, or commercial program— and it's free. WS_FTP's "home" site is **ftp.usma.edu**. You should be able to find it in the **/pub/msdos/winsock.files** directory.

Mac TCP and FTP Software

MacTCP   This is required for all Macintosh TCP/IP connections. You can find this bundled with some Mac Internet books, though it's probably an earlier version. You can also buy a copy of TCP/IP Connection for Macintosh (about $100) or the System 7.5 operating system (about $90).

MacPPP   Lets you setup a PPP connection (in conjunction with MacTCP). Freeware from Merit Network, Inc., you can find this at the **merit.edu** FTP site in the **/pub/ppp/mac** directory, in a file currently called macppp2.0.1.hqx. (This is a BinHex file that must be converted using one of the Macintosh conversion utilities.)

InterSLIP   Lets you set up a SLIP connection (in conjunction with MacTCP). Freeware from InterCon Systems. You can find it on the **ftp.intercon.com** FTP site in the **/InterCon/test** directory. Or try sending e-mail to **slip-help@intercon.com** for information about where it's available. There may soon be information about it available at **http://www.intercon.com/**.

Fetch   This is a shareware FTP program for Macintosh dial-in direct connections. You can find it in the **net-dist.mit.edu** FTP site, in the **/pub/mac/fetch** directory.

The Internet Adapter

If you want to try fooling your software into thinking it's running on a TCP/IP connection, you'll need to get hold of The Internet Adapter (TIA). It's $25, though you can try it for free for 30 days or so. Send e-mail to **tia-info@marketplace.com** for information on how to get started.

Browsers—Windows

Win32s   If you want to run any kind of 32-bit Windows software (such as the latest version of Mosaic) on a 16-bit version of Windows (Windows 3.1 or Windows for Workgroups), then you need to install Win32s. You can find this at the **ftp.microsoft.com** FTP site in the **d:/softlib/mslfiles** directory; get the file named PW1118.EXE.

You can also find this software at the **ftp.ncsa.uiuc.edu** FTP site (the home of Mosaic). It's in the **/PC/Mosaic/** directory (though under a different name, because NCSA added a text file to the package—at the time of writing it was called win32s.zip).

If you have problems installing the Win32s software, there's a Microsoft Knowledge Base document you may want to get. Go to the **ftp.microsoft.com** FTP site, change to the **/developr/win32dk/kb/ q106/7** directory, and then get the file called **15.txt**.

SlipKnot   This dial-in terminal-based browser's home site is **oak.oakland.edu** in the **/SimTel/win3/internet/** directory. You can also try **ftp.netcom.com** in the **/pub/pbrooks/slipknot/** directory. Look for a file called **slnot***nnn***.zip**, where *nnn* is the version number. You can get information from the **http://interport.net/~pbrooks/ slipknot.html** Web document, or by sending a blank e-mail message to **slipknot@micromind.com**.

A good general FTP site for finding Web browsers is the **ftp.w3.org** FTP site in the **/www/bin** directory.

Mosaic   You'll find Mosaic all over the place. However, its home site is **http://www.ncsa.uiuc.edu/SDG/Software/Mosaic/ NCSAMosaicHome.html**. From here, you can find out about the different versions and download what you need. To FTP it, go to the **ftp.ncsa.uiuc.edu** FTP site and look in the **PC/Mosaic** directory. If you want to use the **16-bit version**, look in the **PC/Mosaic/old** directory. You'll also find the last *released* version in that directory (currently version 1.0).

Netscape   This is freeware from Mosaic Communications. You can find it in the **ftp.mcom.com** FTP site, in the **/Netscape** directory. **http://home.mcom.com/info/how-to-get-it.html** Web document. This is a very busy site, though, so you can use a "mirror" site, such as these: **ftp.digital.com** in **/pub/net/infosys/Netscape**; **ftp.barrnet.net** in **/netscape**; and **ftp.uu.net** in **/networking/info-service/www/ netscape**.

Cello   You can find this free program in the **ftp.law.cornell.edu** FTP site in the **/pub/LII/Cello** directory.

WinWeb   WinWeb is freeware (for noncommercial use). Currently it's in its first "alpha" phase, so the software may be unstable. You can find it at the **ftp.einet.net** FTP site, in the **/einet/pc/winweb** directory, or point your Web browser to **http://galaxy.einet.net/** for information about both WinWeb and MacWeb.

Internetworks   Produced by BookLink, which was was bought by America Online just before we went to print, so right now we don't know how this program will be distributed. You can get more information from BookLink at 508-657-7000 or at **http://www.booklink.com/**.

Enhanced NCSA Mosaic This product, from a company called SpyGlass, is being sold to software and hardware manufacturers, such as DEC, and to some book publishers, such as O'Reilly. Call 217-355-6000 for more information.

Super Mosaic This is being sold through software retail channels for around $49. Call 613-729-7974 for more information.

Luckman Interactive Enhanced Mosaic This is the same as Super Mosaic, but it's not being sold directly to the public; it's being bundled with various software, hardware, and books.

GWHIS Viewer This is part of a suite of tools for companies wanting to publish on a network or the Web.

512-346-9199
ftp.quadralay.com
http://www.quadralay.com/products/products.html
info@quadralay.com

Tapestry Tapestry comes with the SuperHighway Access suite of programs from Frontier Technologies. The second edition of *The Complete Idiot's Guide to the Internet* contains the SuperHighway Access sampler, which has a TCP/IP stack, and FTP program, and a news-reader. You can use the FTP program to go to the Frontier Technologies FTP site and download a Tapestry sampler.

414-241-4555
414-241-7084 (fax)

AIRMosaic This comes with Internet in a Box (by O'Reilly, sold through bookstores) or SPRY's AIR series of products.

800-777-9638
206-447-0300
206-447-9008 (fax)
info@spry.com

Web Navigator (InterAp) This suite of programs is sold by California Software Incorporated.

415-491-4371
415-491-0402
Sales@calsoft.com
Support@calsoft.com

ftp.calsoft.com or 199.4.105.10
http://www.calsoft.com

The list price is around $295 for single users.

NetCruiser   NetCruiser is a NETCOM product and can only be used
with that service provider's system. There's a $25 registration fee
(which gets you the software). Then you'll pay $19.95 a month. For
that, you'll get 40 "peak" hours and as many hours as you want at
weekends and from midnight to 9 am during the week. If you use more
than 40 peak hours you'll pay $2/hour for those extra hours.

800-353-6600
408-345-2600
408-241-9145 (fax)
info@netcom.com

The Pipeline Internaut   The Pipeline's Internaut software is a full
suite of Internet tools, including a Web browser (in Version 2.0). You
can use this with the Pipeline Network, Inc., in New York. But The
Pipeline Network, Inc. is selling this system to other service providers,
so you may find a local provider using the software. To find out if
there's a service provider in your area using this system (there are a
number all over the country, and the list is growing quickly), you can
contact The Pipeline at staff@pipeline.com.

212-267-3636
212-267-4380 (fax)
info@pipeline.com
212-267-6432 (modem—login as *guest*)
telnet, Gopher, FTP: pipeline.com

InterNav   This Delphi interface is available from Phoenix software (it's
marketed under the name *Internet Express*—no relation to the service
provider by that name). Call 800-452-0120, contact Delphi at 800-
695-4005, or e-mail INFO@delphi.com.

Word Viewer   This free Word for Windows add-on from Microsoft
was not available at the time of writing. When it's finally released, you
may find it in the **ftp.microsoft.com** Web site, or try calling 800-
426-9400 (sales) or 206-462-9673 (technical support).

WebSurfer   This suite of programs is about $200, from NetManage.

> 408-973-7171
> 408-257-6405 (fax)
> info@netmanage.com

Quarterdeck Mosaic   This is a browser from Quarterdeck; it hadn't been released at the time of writing. You can get a free beta at their Web site, though: **http://www.qdeck.com**. Call 310-392-9851 for more information.

Browser—OS/2

The OS/2 Warp operating system is being sold with a "bonus bundle" of software, including the WebExplorer. The "street price" is around $80. For more information, call 1-800-426-7999, or try **http://www.ibm.com**.

Browsers—DOS

DosLynx   You can find DosLynx in the **ftp2.cc.ukans.edu** FTP site, in the **pub/WWW/DosLynx** directory. At the time of writing, the latest version is Version 0.7 alpha and is in a file called DLX0_7A.EXE, which is a self-extracting archive; that means you just "run" the file to extract all the necessary files. You can also get to the FTP site using your Web browser by pointing the browser to the **ftp://ftp2.cc.ukans.edu/pub/WWW/DosLynx/** URL.

UMSLIP   To use DosLynx, you'll need a DOS SLIP program. You can try UMSLIP. This is a program from the University of Minnesota that lets you set up a dial-in direct connection for your DOS computer. You can find it at the **boombox.micro.umn.edu** FTP site, in the **/pub/pc/slip** directory. Get the file named **sliparc.exe**. This program is free to students at the University of Minnesota, $50 for others.

Browsers—Macintosh

Netscape   There's also a Macintosh version of Netscape. See the Windows browsers for information.

Mosaic   This free program's home site is the **ftp.ncsa.uiuc.edu** FTP site, in the **Mosaic/Mac** directory, or go to **http://www.ncsa.uiuc.edu:80/SDG/Software/MacMosaic/**.

MacWeb   MacWeb is freeware (for noncommercial use). Currently it's in its first "alpha" phase, so the software may be unstable. You can find it at the **ftp.einet.net** FTP site in the **/einet/mac/macweb** directory, or point your Web browser to **http://galaxy.einet.net/** for information about both WinWeb and MacWeb.

Samba   You can find this at the **ftp.w3.org** FTP site in the **/pub/www/bin/mac/old** directory. I had trouble downloading this, for some reason; make sure you set your FTP program to binary transfer before transferring the file (Fetch was unable to figure it out).

GWHIS Viewer   For more information about this browser, see the Windows browsers, above.

Enhanced NCSA for the Macintosh   There's a Macintosh version of this program. See the Windows browsers, which were covered earlier.

The Pipeline   At the time of writing, The Pipeline Macintosh software did not include a Web browser, but it may by the time you read this. For information about The Pipeline, see under the *Windows Browsers*.

NetCruiser   NETCOM's Macintosh software was not available at the time of writing, though they claim they will have a version out early in 1995. See under the *Windows Browsers*.

Amiga Browsers

AMosaic   You can find this at the **max.physics.sunysb.edu** FTP site in the **/pub/amosaic** directory or at the **http://insti.physics.sunysb.edu/AMosaic/home.html** Web document.

Emacs-W3   This is available at the **moose.cs.indiana.edu** FTP site in the **/pub/elisp/w3** directory.

NeXTStep

OmniWeb   For information, view the document at **http://www.omnigroup.com/**.

The NeXT Browser-Editor   Try the **info.cern.ch** FTP site in the **/pub/www/bin/next-fat** directory.

The Lynx Browser

This browser is available for all sorts of systems. FTP to the **ftp2.cc.ukans.edu** FTP site, and look in the **/pub/lynx** directory. Get the version appropriate for your system.

UNIX and VMS—With the Neat Stuff

NCSA Mosaic for X Window   Go to the **ftp.ncsa.uiuc.edu** FTP site, and look in the **Mosaic** directory, or go to **http://info.cern.ch/ hypertext/WWW/XMosaic/Status.html**.

GWHIS Viewer   See the contact information under *Windows Browsers*.

tkWWW   Look in the **harbor.ecn.purdue.edu** FTP site.

MidasWWW   From the **info.cern.ch** FTP site in the **/pub/www/src** directory. Also, **http://info.cern.ch/hypertext/WWW/MidasWWW/ Status.html**.

Viola   Find more information in the **http://xcf.berkeley.edu/ht/ projects/viola/README** Web document.

Chimera   Try the **ftp.cs.unlv.edu** site in the **/pub/chimera** directory.

Tom Fine's perlWWW   Go to the **archive.cis.ohio-state.edu** FTP site in the **pub/w3browser** directory.

NCSA Mosaic for VMS   Look in the **ftp.w3.org** FTP site in the **/www/ bin/vms** directory, or in the **http://alephinfo.cern.ch/ @ALEWHO?nilsson** document.

FrameMaker as browser   Look at the **http://info.cern.ch/hypertext/ WWW/Frame/fminit2.0/www_and_frame.html** document.

VMS for the Rest—Text-Based Browsers

Rashty VMS Client   Try the **vms.huji.ac.il** FTP site, in the **www/ www_client** directory. Test the program by telneting to **vms.huji.ac.il**; log in as **www**, and then select **2**.

Emacs w3-mode   FTP from **moose.cs.indiana.edu** in the directory **pub/elisp/w3**.

The IBM VM/CMS Operating System

Albert Find detailed information by pointing your Web browser to **ftp://www.ufl.edu/pub/vm/www/README**. (This document explains how to get a live demonstration.) FTP to **www.ufl.edu** in the **/pub/vm/www** directory.

HTML Editors

Editors for Windows

ANT_HTML.DOT FTP to **ftp.einet.net** and look in the **/einet/pc/** directory for ANT_HTML.ZIP.

CU_HTML.DOT Go to **http://www.cuhk.hk/csc/cu_html/cu_html.htm**.

GT_HTML.DOT Go to **http://www.gatech.edu/word_html/release.htm**.

HoTMetaL Go to the **gatekeeper.dec.com** FTP site, and look in **/.3/net/infosys/NCSA/Web/html/hotmetal/Windows/**.

Cyberleaf You can find information at **http://www.ileaf.com/ip.html**.

HTML Assistant FTP to **gatekeeper.dec.com**, and look in **/.3/net/infosys/NCSA/Web/html/Windows/** for **htmlasst.zip**.

HTML HyperEdit Try the **info.curtin.edu.au** FTP site in the **/pub/internet/windows/hyperedit/** directory.

HTML Writer Look at **http://wwf.et.byu.edu/~nosackk/html-writer/get_copy.html**.

HTMLed FTP to **pringle.mta.ca** and look in **/pub/HTMLed/**.

SGML TagWizard Look at the **http://www.unige.ch/general/tagwiz/taghtm.html** or e-mail **100043.3201@compuserve.com**.

WebAuthor This product, from Ouarterdeck, hadn't been released at the time of writing. You can get a pre-release version, though. Go to **http://www.qdeck.com**.

Internet Assistant for MS Word See information about Word Viewer, under *Windows Browsers*.

Editors for the Macintosh

BBEdit HTML extensions Read the **http://www.uji.es/bbedit-html-extensions.html** document.

BBEdit HTML Tools Go to **http://www.york.ac.uk/~ld11/BBEditTools.html**.

HTML Editor for the Macintosh Read the **http://dragon.acadiau.ca:1667/~giles/HTML_Editor/Documentation.html** document.

HTML Grinder Read **http://www.nets.com/site/matterform/grinder/htmlgrinder.html**.

HTML SuperText Read **http://www.potsdam.edu/HTML_SuperText/About_HTML_S.html**.

HTML.edit Go to the **http://nctn.oact.hq.nasa.gov/tools/HTMLedit/HTMLedit.html** document.

HTML Writer Go to **http://www.uwtc.washington.edu/JonWiederspan/HTMLEditor.html**.

Simple HTML Editor (SHE) Read **http://dewey.lib.ncsu.edu/staff/morgan/simple.html**.

WYSIWY(N)G Go to the **cs.dal.ca/giles** FTP site.

Alpha Try the **cs.rice.edu** FTP site, in the **/public/Alpha/** directory.

SGML TagWizard Read **http://www.unige.ch/general/tagwiz/taghtm.html**.

Bits n' Pieces

Here are a few editors for other computers:

WebMaker (FrameMaker) Look at the **http://info.cern.ch/hypertext/WWW/Frame/fminit2.0/www_and_frame.html** document.

eText Text Engine (NeXTStep) Go to **http://etext.caltech.edu/eTextEngine.html**.

HTML-Editor (NeXTStep) FTP to **scholar.lib.vt.edu** in the **/pub/NEXT/** directory.

City University HTML Editor (UNIX) Try **http://web.cs.city.ac.uk/ homes/njw/htmltext/htmltext.html**.

Cyberleaf for UNIX Go to **http://www.ileaf.com/ip.html**.

HoTMetaL (UNIX) Look at the **http://akebono.stanford.edu/ yahoo/Computers/World_Wide_Web/HTML_Editors/X_Windows/ HoTMetal_SoftQuad_/** document.

Phoenix (UNIX) Look at **http://www.bsd.uchicago.edu/ftp/pub/ phoenix/README.html**.

tkHTML (Tcl script language and the Tk toolkit) Go to **http:// alfred1.u.washington.edu:8080/~roland/tkHTML/tkHTML.html**.

tkWWW (Tk toolkit) Go to **http://uu-gna.mit.edu:8001/tk-www/ help/overview.html**.

hm-html-menus for Emacs Look at **http://www.tnt.uni- hannover.de/data/info/www/tnt/soft/info/www/html-editors/ hm—html-menus/overview.html**.

Webossary:
Speak Like a Web Geek

.AU   A sound-file format.

.GIF   Graphics Interchange Format, a type of graphics file. The .GIF format was originally developed by CompuServe. Inline graphics in Web documents can only be .GIF or *.XBM* format.

.JPG   The extension generally used for graphics files in the JPEG format.

anchor   A techie word for an HTML tag that is used as a *link* from one document to another.

annotation   A note. There are two types of annotations on the Web: the type provided by, for instance, the Mosaic Web *browser*, in which you can link your own notes to a particular Web page; and notes that can be provided by a reader at a Web page as feedback to the Web page's author.

Archie   An index system that helps you find files in thousands of *FTP* sites.

ASCII   Remember that HTML files are simple ASCII text files, right? ASCII means *American Standard Code for Information Interchange*. This is a standard system used by computers to recognize text. An ASCII text file comprises the letters of the alphabet, the punctuation characters, and a few special characters. The nice thing about ASCII is that it's widely recognizable—by thousands of programs and many different types of computers.

attributes   HTML tags are sometimes followed by more information; these *attributes* provide further definition of the component being created by the tags.

bookmark   A *URL* that has been saved in some way so that you can quickly and easily return to a particular Web document.

browser   A program that lets you read HTML documents and *navigate* around the Web.

cache   A place that a *browser* stores Web documents that have been retrieved. The cache may be on the hard disk or in memory, or a combination of the two. Documents you "return to" are retrieved from the cache, saving transmission time.

Cello   A free Web *browser* from the Legal Information Institute at Cornell Law School.

CERN   The European Particle Physics Laboratory (CERN) in Switzerland, the home of the World Wide Web. These people develop lots of Web software and have good Web and FTP sites for people looking for information and programs.

chmod   A UNIX command used to modify who can do what to your files and directories.

client   A program that receives information or services from another (the *server*). Web *browsers* are clients, because they receive the information they need from the Web servers.

CSLIP   Compressed *SLIP*, a communications protocol for *dial-in direct* connections.

CWIS   Campus Wide Information Systems. An online system that provides information on terminals spread around a campus. The Web is a relatively easy way to set up such a system.

daemon   A program that carries out certain system management tasks in the "background;" that is, users don't usually know it's even running. A Web *server* is a type of daemon; it sits around waiting for a Web *browser* to ask it for information.

dial-in direct account   An Internet account using *SLIP*, *CSLIP*, or *PPP*.

dial-in terminal account   An Internet account using basic serial communications.

document   An *HTML* file that contains text and appears in a Web *browser* as a page of information.

DosLynx   A Web *browser* that runs on DOS computers.

download   The act of transferring data from a computer back to your computer.

e-mail   Electronic mail, a system for exchanging messages across computer networks.

Enhanced NCSA Mosaic   A Web *browser* sold by SpyGlass. This is a derivation of the original *NCSA* program.

firewall   A division between a computer system on the Internet and the Internet as a whole. This is used to limit access to outsiders for security reasons, and to limit the access of the system's users to the outside world for economic reasons!

form   A Web form is a sort of interactive document. The document can contain fields into which readers can type information. This information could be used as part of a survey, to purchase an item, to search a database, and so on.

forms support   A Web *browser* that has forms support can work with a Web *form*. Not all browsers can use forms.

FTP   File Transfer Protocol. A *protocol* defining how files are transferred from one computer to another. FTP can be used as a verb to describe the procedure of using FTP. As in, "FTP to ftp.demon.co.uk," or "I FTPed to their system and grabbed the file." Web *browsers* can be used as graphical FTP programs.

GIF   See *.GIF*.

Gopher   A system using Gopher *clients* and *servers* to provide a menu system used for navigating around the Internet. Web *browsers* can work with Gopher systems.

GUI   Graphical User Interface, a program that provides a user with tools, such as menus, buttons, dialog boxes, a mouse pointer, and so on.

GWHIS Viewer   A Web *browser* from Quadralay.

helper See *viewers*.

history list A list of Web document's that you've seen in the current session (some *browsers'* history lists also show documents from previous sessions). You can return to a document by selecting it in the history list.

home page 1. The Web document your *browser* displays when you start the program. 2. A sort of "main page" at a Web site. Personally, I don't like this second definition, but there's not much I can do about it.

host A computer connected directly to the Internet. A *service provider's* computer is a host, as are computers with *permanent connections*. Computers with *dial-in terminal* connections are not; they are terminals connected to the service provider's host. Computers with *dial-in direct* connections can be thought of as "sort of" hosts. They act like a host while connected.

hotlist A list of *bookmarks*, *URLs* of Web documents you want to save for future use. You can return to a particular document by selecting it from the list.

HTML HyperText Markup Language. The basic "coding" system used to create Web documents.

HTTP HyperText Transfer Protocol. The data-transmission *protocol* used to transfer Web documents across the Internet.

HTTPD HyperText Transfer Protocol Daemon. A *Web server* program. See also *daemon*.

hyperlink See *link*.

hypermedia Loosely used to mean a *hypertext* document that contains, or has links to, other types of media, such as pictures, sound, video, and so on.

hypertext An computerized document that contains *links* to other documents. These links may work when you type a number, select a link and press Enter, click on the link with the mouse, click on a button, select from a list of documents, and so on.

IAP Internet Access Provider, another term for *service provider*.

index documents A Web *document* that lets you search some kind of database.

index servers   A special program, accessed through an *index document,* that lets you search some kind of database.

inline images   A picture inside a Web *document.* These graphics must be *.GIF* or *.XBM* format files.

Internet   The term internet spelled with a small i refers to networks connected to one another. The Internet is not the only internet; it's simply the largest.

JPEG   A compressed graphic format often found on the Web.

kiosk mode   A special mode—present in Mosaic, AIR Mosaic, and OS/2 Warp's WebExplorer—that lets you remove most or all controls (toolbar buttons, URL bar, and menu options) from the *browser,* so the program may be run in a public place. It's also very handy for making room for a document. (In Web Navigator, it's called *presentation* mode.)

Line Mode browser   A very simple text-based *browser* available for most computer systems used by *service providers.*

link   A connection between two Web documents. Links are generally pieces of text or pictures that, when clicked on, make the *browser* request and display another Web document.

linked image   An image that is not *in* a Web document (that's an *inline image*), but is "connected" to a document by a link.

Lynx   Probably the best text-based Web *browser,* available for most systems used by *service providers.*

MacWeb   A Macintosh Web *browser,* from EINet.

mail robot   An e-mail system that automatically carries out some sort of procedure for you. The system that retrieves Web documents and e-mails them to you is a mail robot.

mailto: URL   This *URL* makes a *browser's* e-mail window appear (if that browser has mailto: support). You can type the mailto: URL into a URL text box, in the same way you'd type a normal document URL into a text box. Or you can click on a link in which a Web author has placed a mailto: URL.

main screen   Lynx refers to the first page you see when you start a Lynx session as the *main screen.* This is the equivalent of the *home page.*

MIME Multipurpose Internet Mail Extensions, a currently little-used system that lets you send computer files as e-mail. However, Web browsers often use this system to recognize files of different types.

Mosaic The best-known Web *browser*, from the *NCSA*.

MPEG A computer video format.

navigate Refers to "moving around" on the Web using a *browser*. When you jump to a Web document, you are navigating.

NCSA National Center for Supercomputing Applications, the home of *Mosaic*.

NetCruiser A suite of programs that includes a Web *browser*, from a *service provider* called NETCOM.

Netscape A new *browser*, created by some old *NCSA* programmers who started a company called Mosaic Communications.

OLE Object Linking and Embedding, a Microsoft Windows feature that lets you merge the functions of different applications. The InternetWorks Web *browser* lets you "embed" a Web document in another application—a Word for Windows document, for instance. InterAp's Web Navigator should also have OLE functions (they weren't working at the time of writing).

permanent account An Internet account with a permanent connection to the Internet. That is, you don't need to dial into the Internet to use it.

Pipeline, The A *service provider* in New York, founded by best-selling author James Gleick. The Pipeline has a good Windows and Macintosh interface for almost all Internet functions, including the Web.

PPP Point-to-Point Protocol, a communications protocol for *dial-in direct* connections.

presentation mode See *kiosk mode*.

protocol A set of rules that defines how computers transmit information to each other, allowing different types of computers and software to communicate with each other.

proxy server If your system has a *firewall*, you can get around the firewall to carry out certain operations using a proxy server defined by your system administrator.

reload   A command that tells your *browser* to retrieve a Web *document* even though you have it in the *cache*.

rendered   An HTML document that is being viewed in a Web *browser*. The browser *renders* it into a normal text document. You don't see the codes, just the text that the author wants you to see. An *unrendered* document is the source HTML document, codes and all.

server   See *Web server*.

service provider   A company that provides a connection to the Internet. Service providers sell access to the network, for greatly varying prices. Shop around for the best deal.

site   See *Web site*.

SLIP   Serial Line Interface Protocol, a communications protocol for *dial-in direct* connections.

source document   An *HTML* document, the basic *ASCII* file that is *rendered* by a *browser*.

stack   See *TCP/IP stack*.

tags   The "codes" inside an *HTML* file.

TCP/IP   Transmission Control Protocol/Internet Protocol. A set of *protocols* (communications rules) that controls how data is transferred between computers on the Internet.

TCP/IP stack   The software you must install before you can run TCP/IP programs across a dial-in direct connection. You may think of the TCP/IP stack as an Internet *driver*. In the same way you need a printer driver to send something from your word processor to your printer, you need the TCP/IP stack to send information from (and receive information) your dial-in direct programs, such as Mosaic.

Title   A Web document may have a Title. The Title does not appear in the document when you view it in a *browser*, but the browser may use the Title in some other way. Mosaic, for instance, places the Title in the window's title bar.

transparent GIF   Transparent *GIFs* appear to blend in smoothly with the user's *browser* background, even if the user has set an unusual background color.

UNIX   A computer operating system. Most hosts connected to the Internet run UNIX.

unrendered   An *HTML document* that has not been *rendered.*

URC   Uniform Resource Citation, object descriptions that may include the *URL*, but also may contain information about the author, copyright, date, and any other relevant information.

URI   Uniform Resource Identifiers, a type of address in which objects are defined using short text strings. (*URLs* are a form of URI.)

URL   Uniform Resource Locator, a Web "address."

URN   Uniform Resource Name, another form of address, more advanced than *URLs.*

Veronica   The Very Easy Rodent-Oriented Net-wide Index to Computerized Archives, a very useful program for finding things in a *Gopher* system.

viewer   A program that displays or plays computer files that you find on the Web. For instance, you need a viewer to play video files you find. These are sometimes known as *helpers.*

WAIS   Wide Area Information Server, a program that lets you search a group of databases. You can access WAIS through the Web, but generally you need to connect to a *Gopher* system first.

Web server   A program that makes Web *documents* available to *browsers.* The browser asks the server for the document, and the server transmits it to the browser.

Web site   A collection of Web *documents* about a particular subject on a *host.*

Webspace   The area of cyberspace in which you are traveling when working on the Web.

WinWeb   A Windows *browser* from EINet.

X Window System   A *GUI* (graphical user interface) "windowing" system developed at MIT. It's mostly used for UNIX computers.

XBM   X Bitmap graphics format, a bitmap from the UNIX X Window system. These are simple images, one of only two types that can be used as inline graphics; the other is *.GIF.*

Index

Symbols

< > brackets and HTML, 246
</ADDRESS> tag, 271
</B> tag, 271
</BLOCKQUOTE> tag, 256
</DL> tag, 272
</EM> tag, 271
</H> tag, 247
</H1> tag, 259
</I> tag, 271
</OL> tag, 272
</PRE> tag, 266-267
</STRONG> tag, 271
</TITLE> tag, 247
</TITLE> tag, 258
</TT> tag, 271
</U> tag, 271
</UL> tag, 271
<ADDRESS> tag, 271
<B> tag, 271
<BLOCKQUOTE> tag, 256
<body></body> tags, 274

 tag, 271
<CR> tag, 112
<DL> tag, 272
<EM> tag, 271
<H1> tag, 247, 259
<head></head> tags, 274
<HR> tag, 259
<html></html> tags, 274
<I> tag, 271
<OL> tag, 272
<P> tag, 248
<PRE> tag, 266-267
<STRONG> tag, 271
<TITLE> tag, 247, 258
<TT> tag, 271
<U> tag, 271
<UL> tag, 271
32-bit Windows, 133

A

About command (Help menu), 102
absolute links
    compared to relative links, 263-264
    saving HTML files, 217
absolute URLs, 251
Add Current to Hotlist command (Navigate menu), 144
addresses
    e-mail (Lynx), 61
    publishing, 270-271
    URLs (Universal Resource Locators), 23-24
Adobe Acrobat Reader, 126
AIR Mosaic, 42, 174-175, 332
    configuration, 174-175
    hotlists, 175
    kiosk mode, 175, 214
    Telnet, 238
    transfer cancellation, 193
Albert, 49, 337
ALIWEB, 304
Alpha, 288, 338
alpha versions (Mosaic), 132
America Online, 8
    InternetWorks, 43
American Standard Code for Information Interchange, see ASCII
Amiga
    browsers, 47, 335
    Mosaic, 131-132
AMosaic, 47, 335
ANANSE-Internet Resource Locators, 301
anchors, see links
animal-related resources, 323
Annotate command (Annotate menu), 142
Annotate menu commands, 142
Annotate Window dialog box, 142
annotations, 26-30, 341
    Mosaic, 142-143
    Mosaic for Macintosh, 149
anonymous FTP, 15
ANT_HTML.DOT, 286, 337
applications, 284
Archie, 15, 341
    ALIWEB, 304
ArchiePlex, 308
ARPANET, 12

C

355

G

357

H

Everyone's talking about

"Thanks for helping me get started."
Jim Ellars, Greenfield, IN

"It is written in plain, old English and tells me what I need to know to do what I want to do."
Craig Connolly, Lincoln, NE

"I've made friends with my computer."
Marjorie Bock, Slidell, LA

"...quite helpful in gaining familiarity and confidence in various computer topics."
Martin Bondy, New York, NY

"...most of all, the books helped build a much-needed confidence."
Bill Shepson, Sacramento, CA

"I could hardly put it down—anxious to find out a little more and more."
June Littlejohn, Irving, TX

"...covered the basics of the entire program without getting too bogged down in details."
Robert Matson, New York, NY

"...one of the best introductory computer books that I have come across in the past few years. It's refreshing to have instructional material written at the level of the beginner and not making many assumptions regarding prior computer ability."
Daniel Green, Saratoga Springs, NY

"It teaches in such a simplified, straightforward manner."
Richard Boehringer, Miramar, FL

"This book taught me that I'm in control."
Greg Wright, Ashmore, Australia

"...simple, easy to read, and enjoyable. I felt like someone was talking to me."
Jon Marshall, Dover, OH

"The best thing about the book is the readability."
Gerard van Os, The Netherlands

"I appreciate material that assumes me to be lacking in information rather than lacking in intelligence."
Holly Waldrop, Nashville, TN

"I have to say that this is THE book for teaching in this area."
Richard Caladine, University of Wollongong, Australia

"After really close review, I have found it to be superb. The concepts are as clear as I have seen."
Barry Owen, San Juan, CO

"Lest I forget, your bright orange cover and cheat sheet proved to be invaluable amongst a cluttered desk."
Darryl Pang, Honolulu, HI

The Complete Idiot's Guides—For People With Better Things To Do

Who Cares What *YOU* Think?

WE DO!

alpha books

We're not complete idiots. We take our readers' opinions very personally. After all, you're the reason we publish these books! Without you, we'd be pretty bored.

alpha books

So please! Drop us a note or fax us a fax! We'd love to hear what you think about this book or others. A real person—not a computer—reads every letter we get, and makes sure your comments get relayed to the appropriate people.

Not sure what to say? Here's some stuff we'd like to know:

➡ Who are you (age, occupation, hobbies, etc.)?

➡ Which book did you buy and where did you get it?

➡ Why did you pick this book instead of another one?

➡ What do you like best about this book?

➡ What could we have done better?

➡ What's your overall opinion of the book?

➡ What other topics would you like to purchase a book on?

Mail, e-mail, or fax your brilliant opinions to:

Faithe Wempen
Product Development Manager
Alpha Books
201 West 103rd Street
Indianapolis, IN 46290
FAX: (317) 581-4669

CompuServe: 75430,174
Internet: 75430.174@compuserve.com